POSTCARD HISTORY SERIES

Route 7
The Road North

NORWALK TO CANAAN

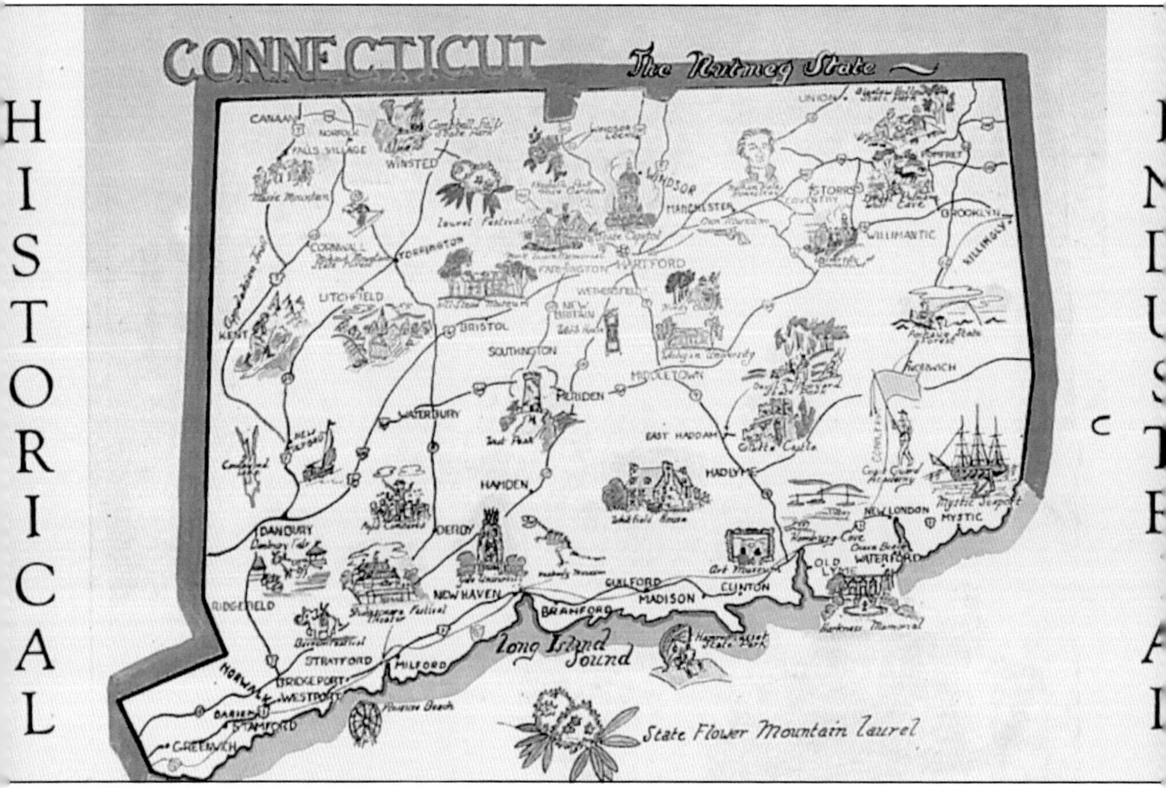

Shown here is a map of Connecticut.

POSTCARD HISTORY SERIES

Route 7
The Road North

NORWALK TO CANAAN

Laurie J. Bepler and Virginia B. Bepler

ARCADIA
PUBLISHING

ISBN 978-0-7385-0256-4

Published by Arcadia Publishing
Charleston, South Carolina

Printed in the United States of America

Library of Congress Catalog Card Number: Applied for

For all general information contact Arcadia Publishing at:
Telephone 843-853-2070
Fax 843-853-0044
E-mail sales@arcadiapublishing.com
For customer service and orders:
Toll-Free 1-888-313-2665

Visit us on the Internet at www.arcadiapublishing.com

Dedicated to Katharine D. Bepler and Bernadette B. Bepler
and their future memories.

Contents

ACKNOWLEDGMENTS

Harry Abbott
Elizabeth Bader
Brigid Devlin Bepler
Joan Bepler
Mary Devlin
Terry Falk
Sue Luzzi
Jack Sanders
Daniel Sturges
Danbury Museum and Historical Society
New Milford Historical Society, Delores Dunn
Gaylordsville Historical Society, Barbara Thorland
Kent Historical Society, Emily Hopson
Wilton Historical Society, Carol Russell

Introduction

Route 7 is an ancient path. Area histories state that the Woodland Indians moved down to the seashore in the summer to clam and fish. My family, like others, also traveled south to the Norwalk shore to clam, fish, swim, and boat from the 1930s through the 1960s. The two groups used approximately the same route. This route has been called "The Great Road" by Danbury settlers. Its varying sections have had other names: Norwalk-Danbury Turnpike, Schaghticoke Trail, and the Ethan Allan Highway. The road extends in Connecticut between Norwalk and Canaan, through Massachusetts and Vermont, to the Canadian border.

In 1921, the federal government passed a highway bill. Route 7 was christened in 1926. Over the years, changes have been made; a hill was lowered, a curve was straightened, an old bridge was replaced, and dirt was covered by pavement. Some of these changes have left old portions of the road, allowing continued access to homes and businesses. At one point, the state designated landscaped rest areas for the convenience of travelers. In 1999, pressure from increasing development and traffic, particularly at the southern section of the road, is continuing to change the landscape. Old vistas are disappearing rapidly.

This book is a visual record of the rich history of this important "road north."

—Virginia B. Bepler

Like many families in the 1950s and 1960s, we went for a Sunday drive every week. Most often, those drives took us north on Route 7. I remember Val's 15¢ Hamburger Stand in Brookfield, picnics at Macedonia State Park in Kent, and the excitement of arriving as a camper at The Girl's Friendly Society Holiday House Camp in Canaan. Virginia's memories go back even further. She remembers driving through the Schaghticoke Indian Reservation as a child, canoeing on the Housatonic River as a teenager in the 1930s, and trips to her grandparents' farm on Treasure Hill in Kent.

This book is for all those who have pleasant memories of Route 7 and for everyone to use as a guide for exploring and creating new memories.

—Laurie J. Bepler

One

Norwalk Including Winnipauk

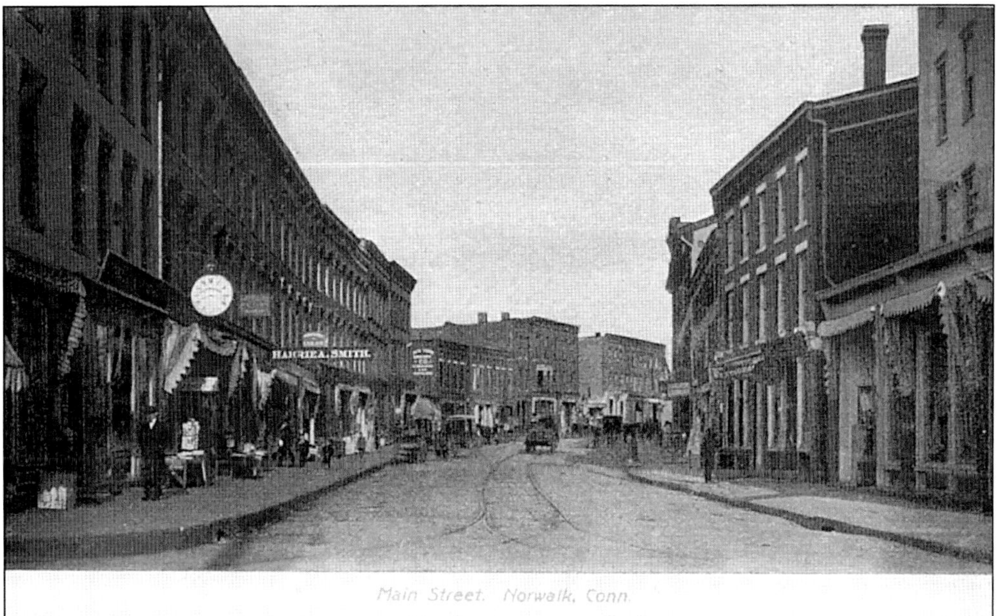

Settled in 1640 by immigrants from the Massachusetts colony, Norwalk developed industries that produced hats, tires, corsets, and hardware. In the 1990s, it is a thriving city of multiethnic population.

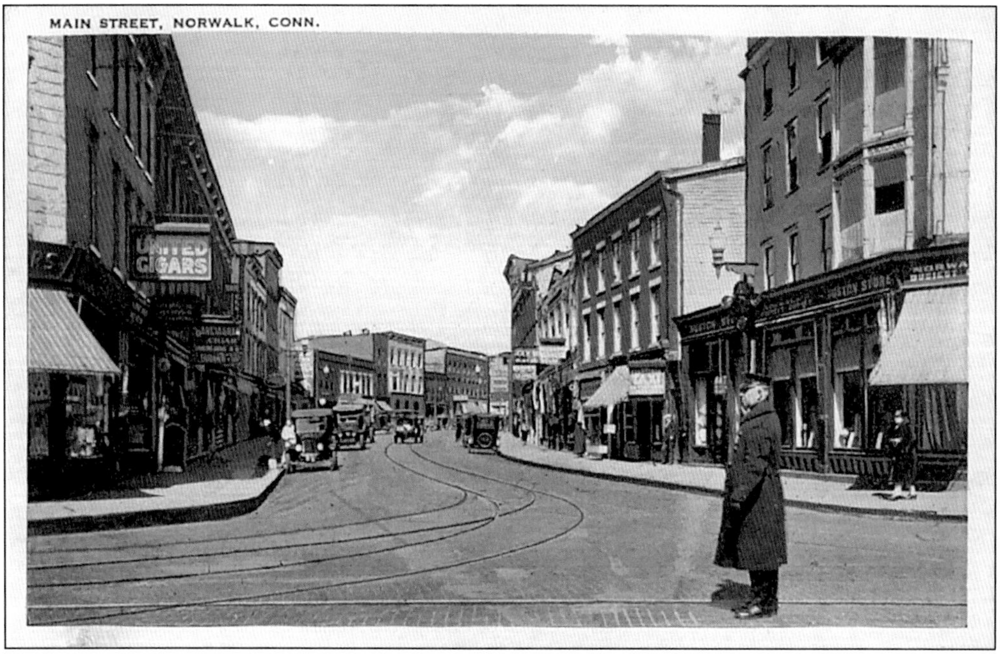

Main Street, later Route 7, started near the bridge at Wall Street. In the vicinity were the Trolley Barn, the Boston Store, and Schultz's Meat Market, as well as the below street-level railroad stop. In this later view, Officer Murphy is patrolling a street little changed since "horse and buggy" days.

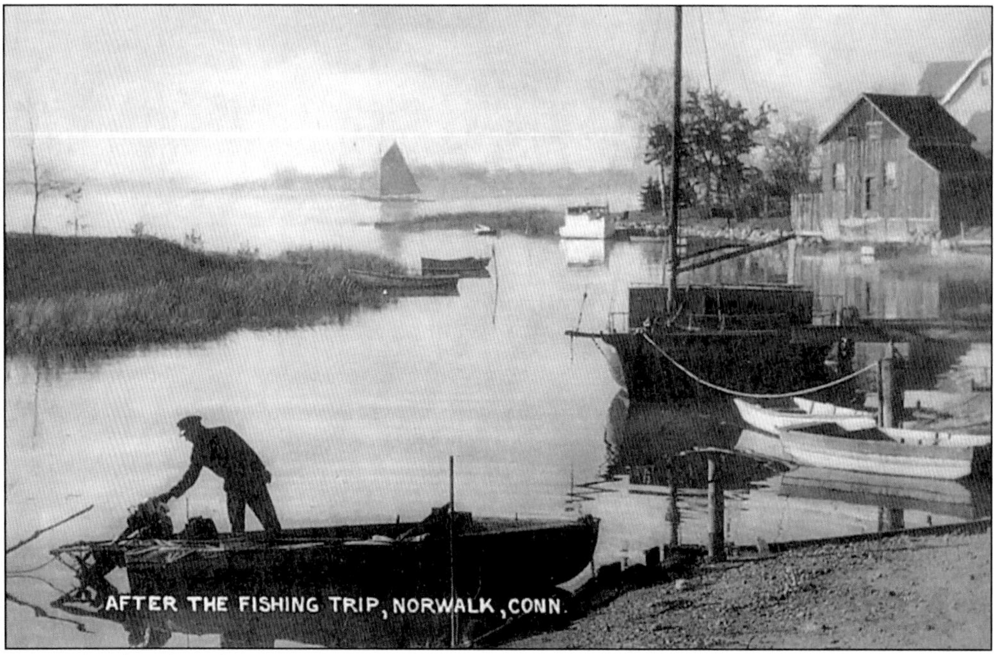

Norwalk's shoreline has encouraged utilization, both for commerce and for pleasure. Beaches, marinas, oystering, and seaside homes are among the city's pluses.

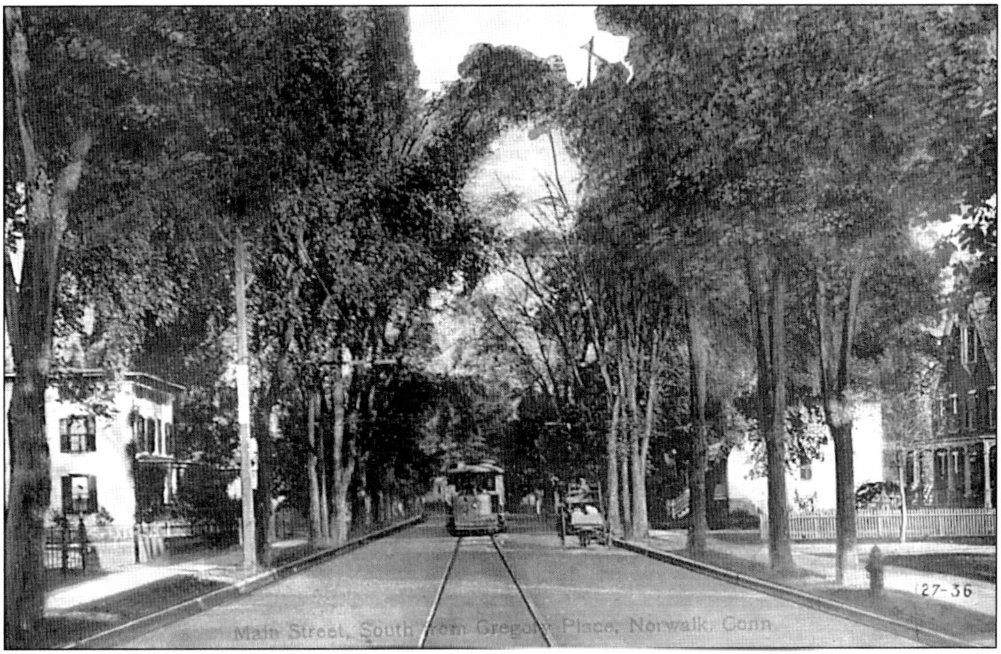

This scene from Gregory Place looks very much like the views of East Avenue.

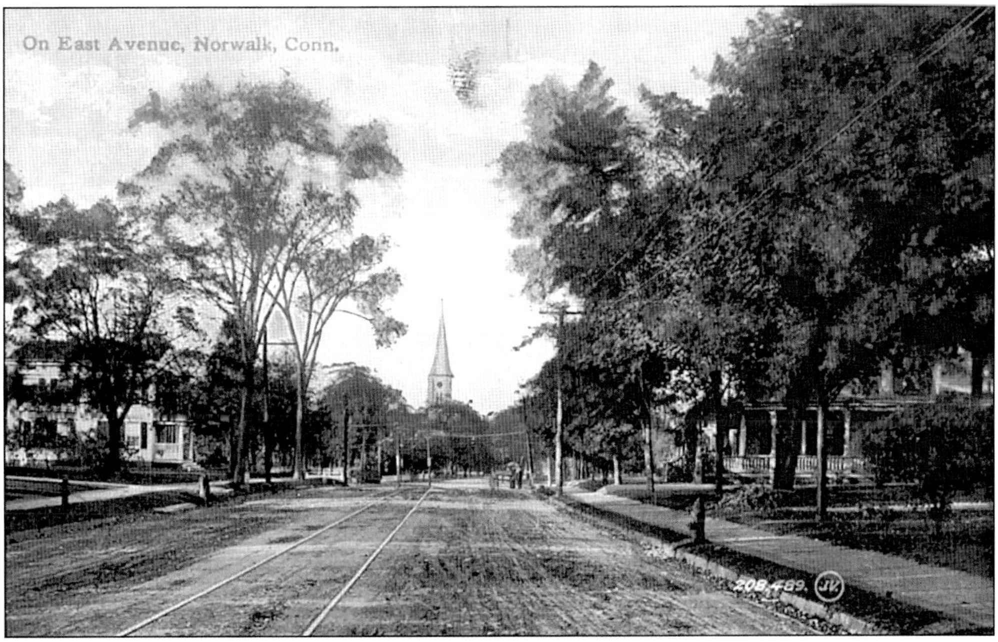

Just up the hill from Main and Wall was a broad street of stately Victorian homes. Many of these homes have been converted to offices and medical facilities.

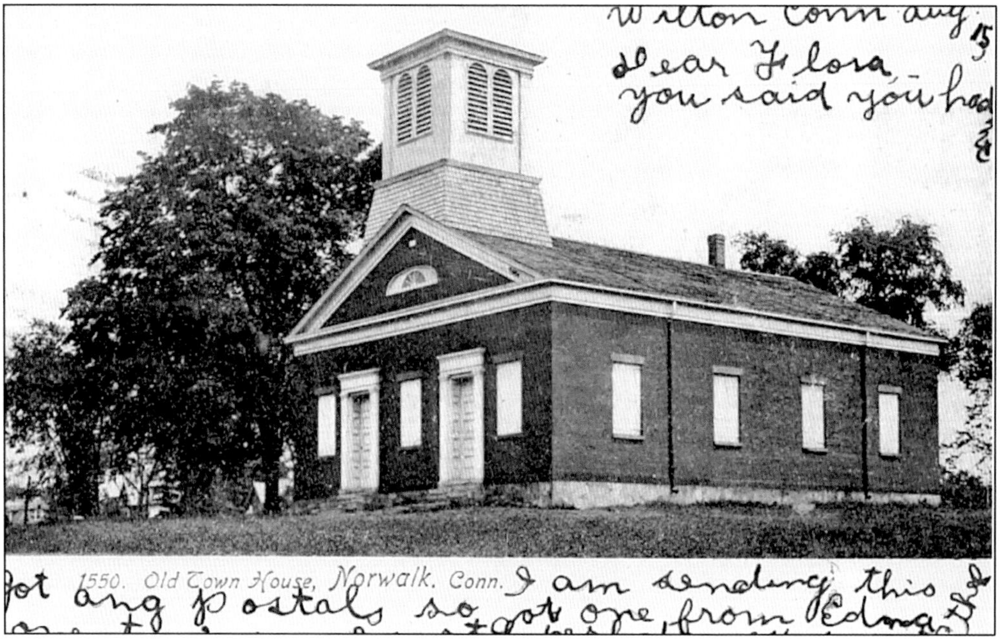

The Old Town House on East Wall Street, built in 1835, has been preserved and stands as the center of a historic complex, the Mill Hill Historical Park. This card was sent to Aunt Flora Bradley in 1906.

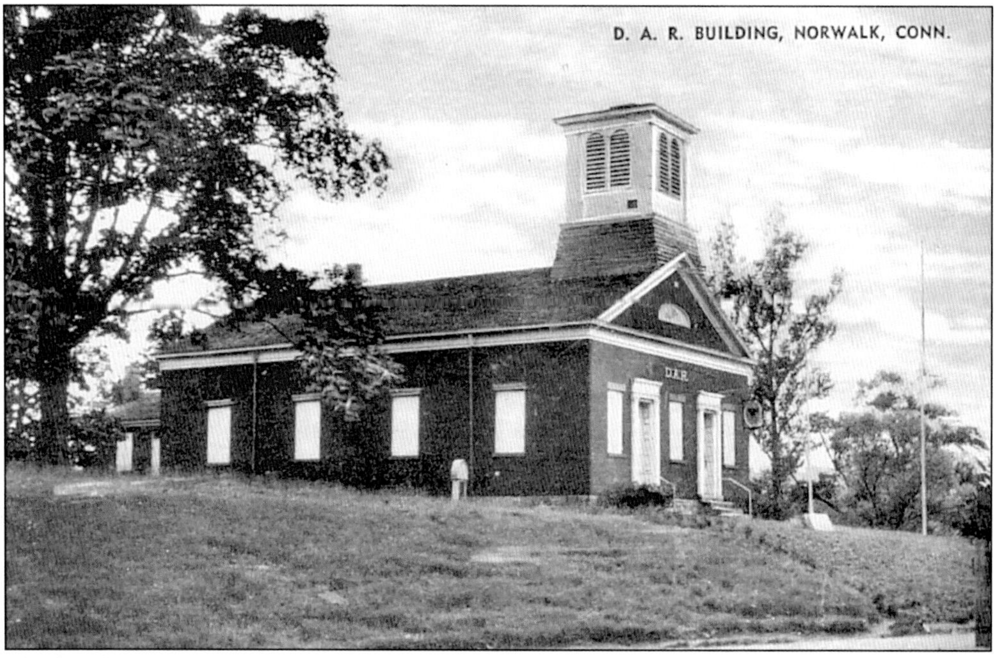

The local DAR (Daughters of the American Revolution) chapter has been instrumental in maintaining this building as its meeting house. It served as the Town House until 1913.

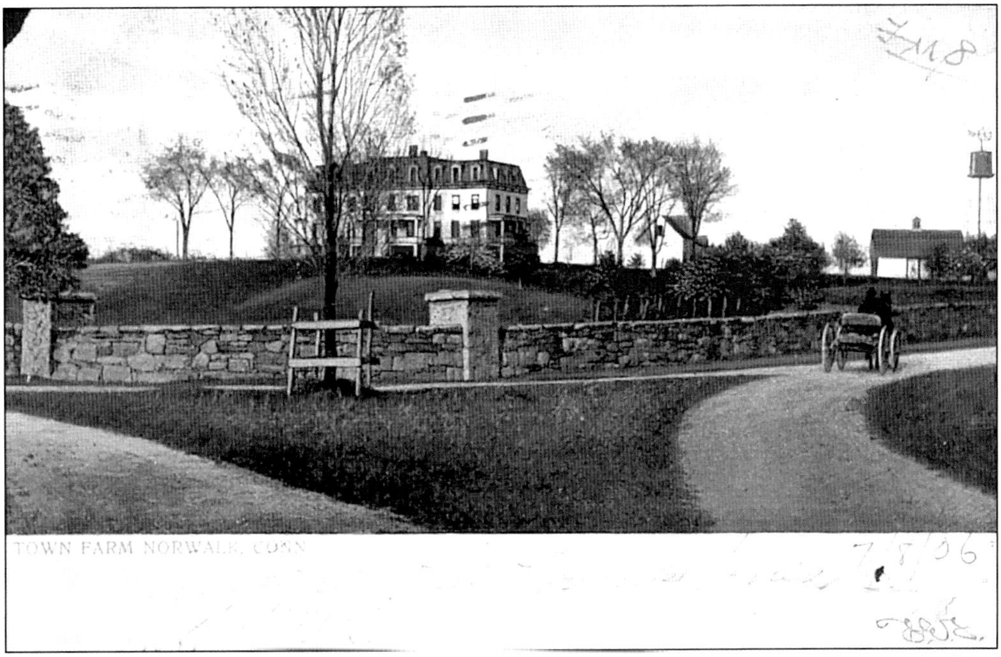

The Town Farm, pictured here in 1906, was run by the city. At this time, many towns had so-called "poor farms" to care for those unable to care for themselves. It was located on Westport Avenue, not far from Route 7.

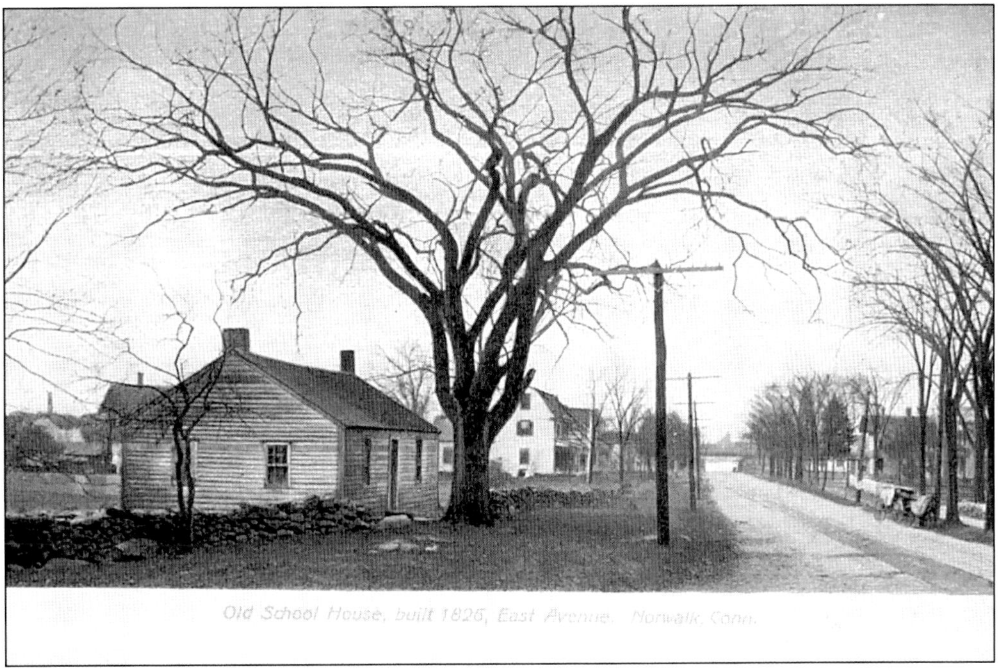

This one-room school was formerly located on East Avenue near Strawberry Hill but is now preserved at the Mill Hill Historical site.

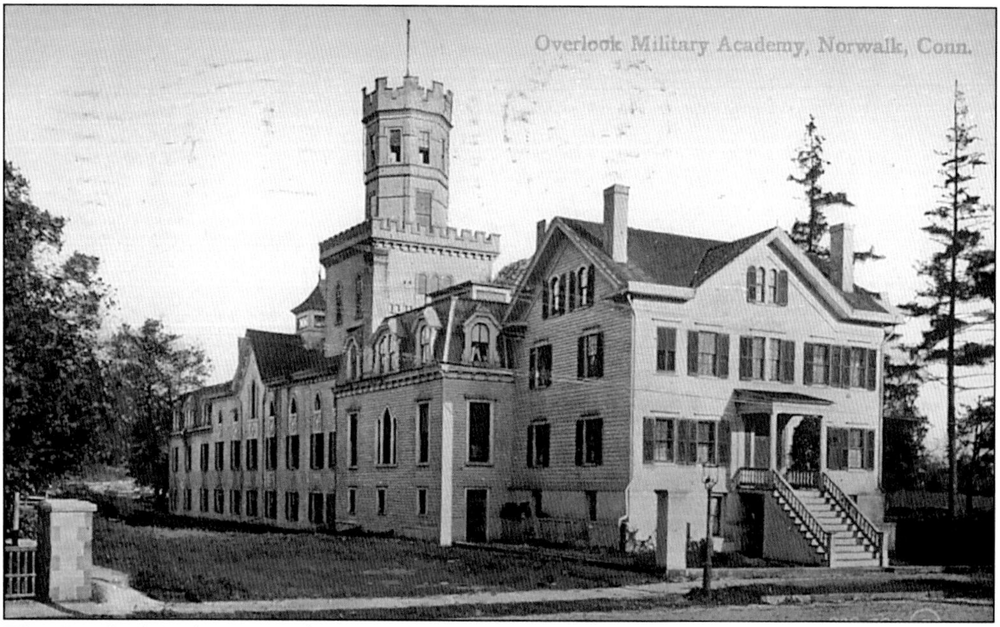

The Overlook Military Academy taught military precision as well as academic subjects when this card was sent in 1909. Postcards from 1905 and 1908 call it Selleck's school. Before this, in 1898, it was called the military school of Colonel Frank Roberts, on East Avenue.

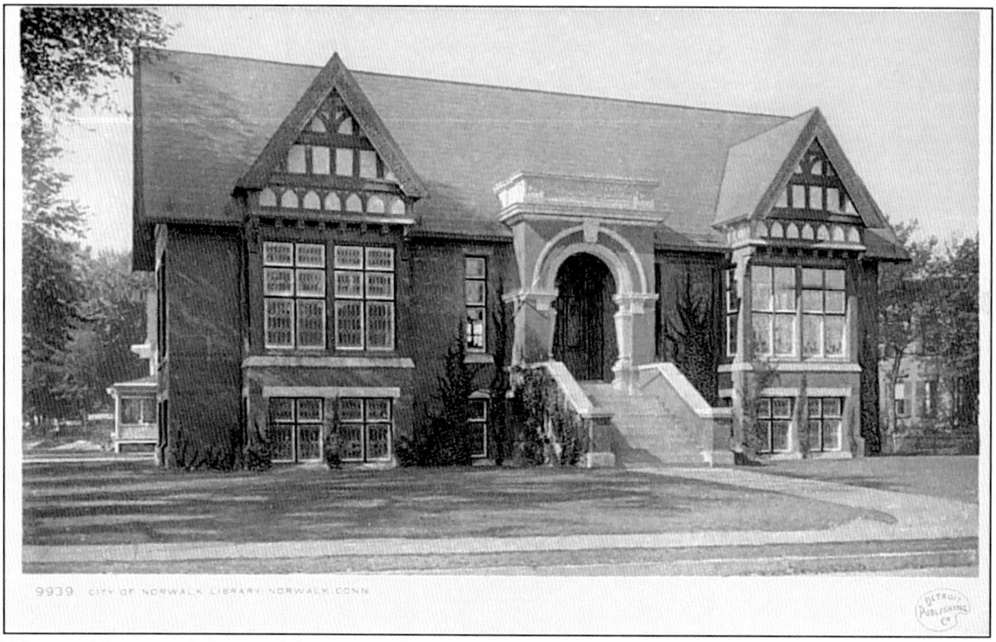

This building, with later additions, still serves as a library. It is located on the corner of Belden Avenue and Mott Avenue.

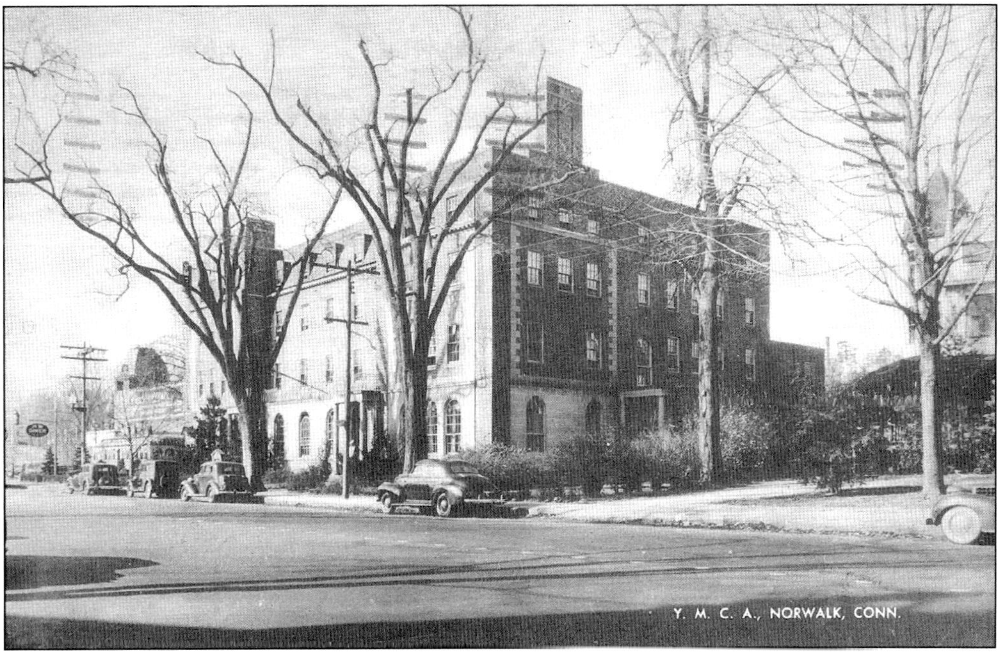

Main Street and Wall Street led to West Avenue. The YMCA pictured in this 1944 postcard is still located on West Avenue and continues to serve the Norwalk community. The sender wrote, "We're very tanned and go to the beach every day."

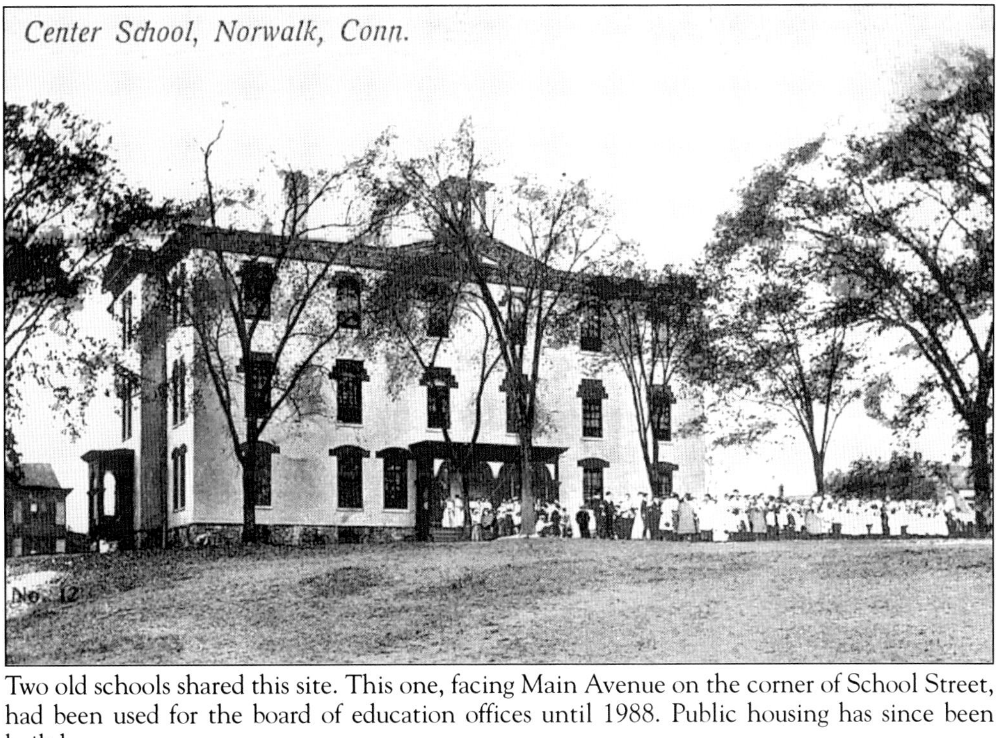

Two old schools shared this site. This one, facing Main Avenue on the corner of School Street, had been used for the board of education offices until 1988. Public housing has since been built here.

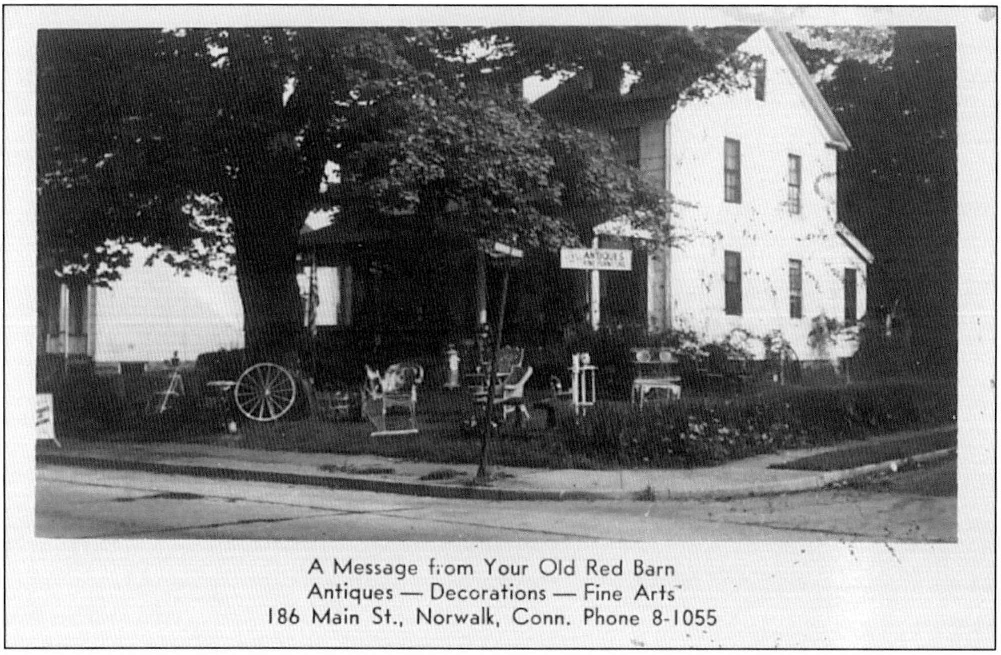

Main Street as well and East and West Avenues had many large homes. This house on the northeast side of Main Avenue and Ohio Street became an outdoor flea market, according to this 1952 postcard.

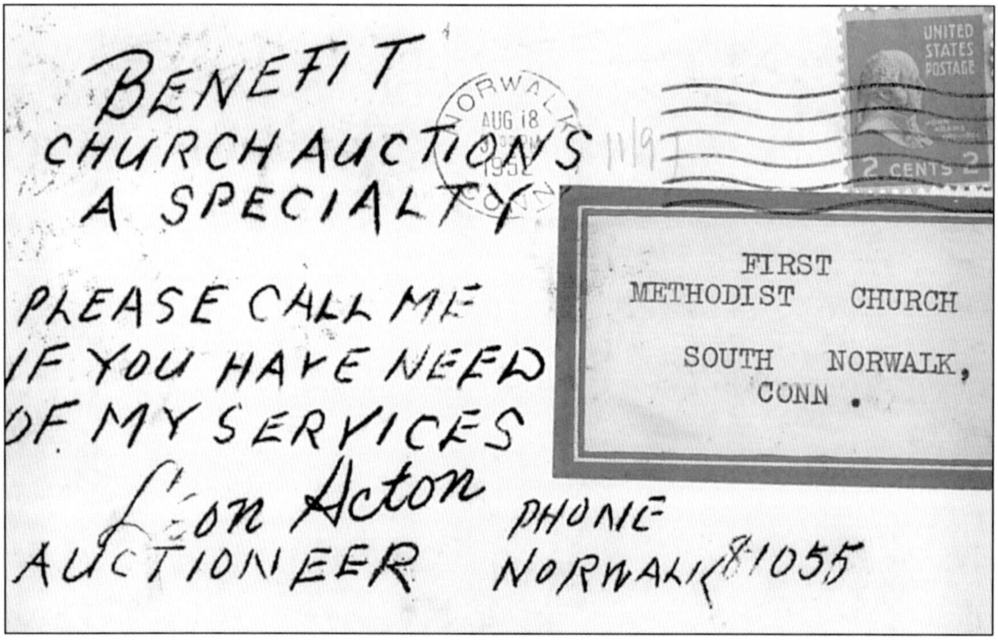

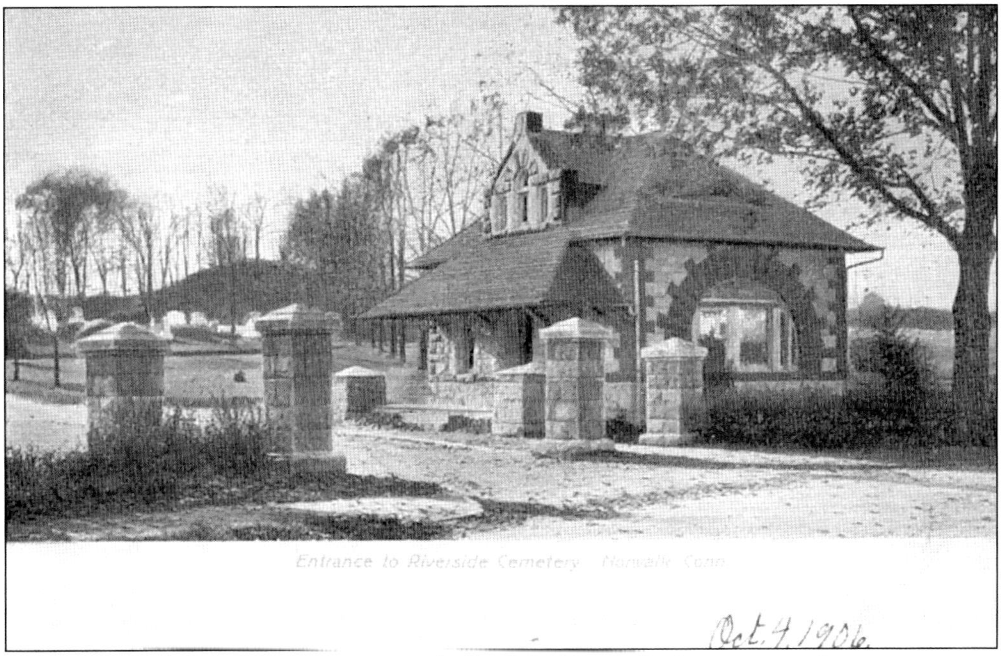

Off Main Avenue, New Canaan Avenue leads to the Riverside Cemetery gatehouse.

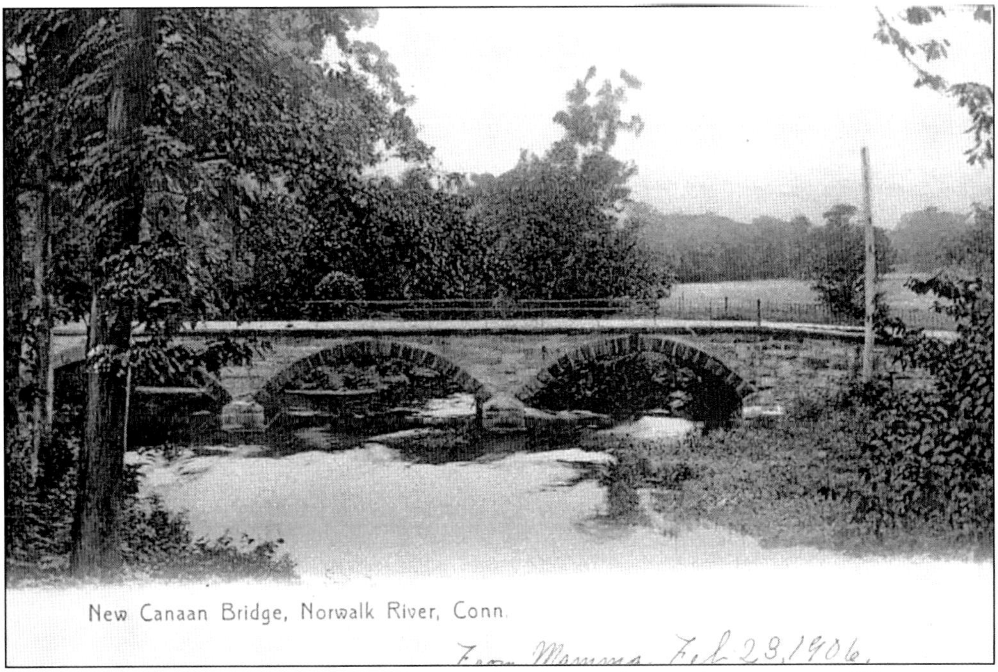

The New Canaan Avenue Bridge has been replaced since this card was sent in 1906.

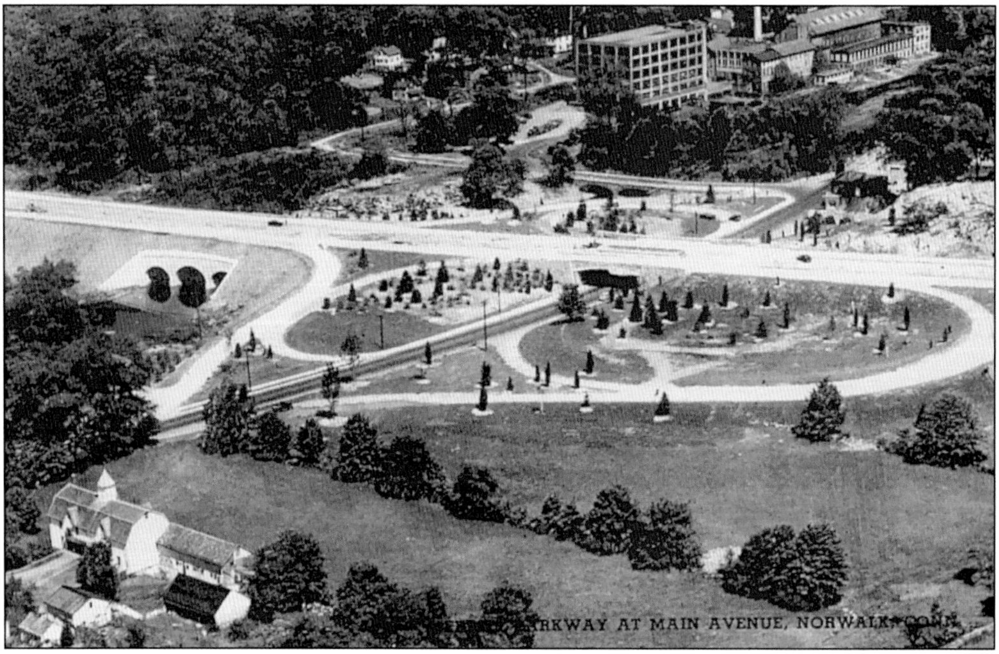

With increased traffic, new roads like Route 95 and the Merritt Parkway were built. The interchange of the parkway and Route 7 changed the face of the section affectionately known as "downtown Winnipauk."

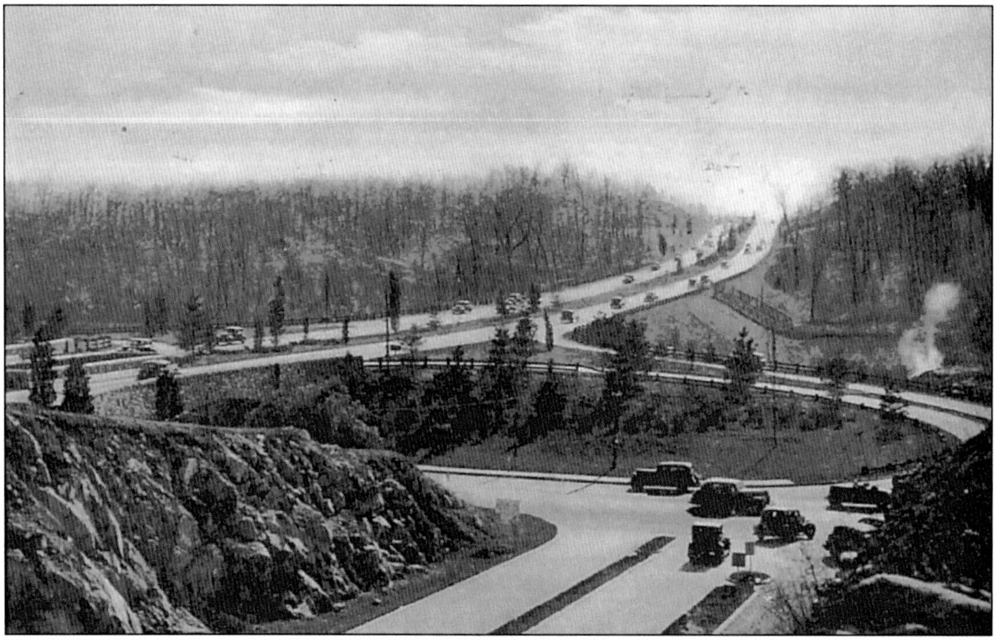

Another view of the interchange shows the ledge on which the old Winnipauk School stood. This was removed to lay the exit and entrance ramps to the parkway.

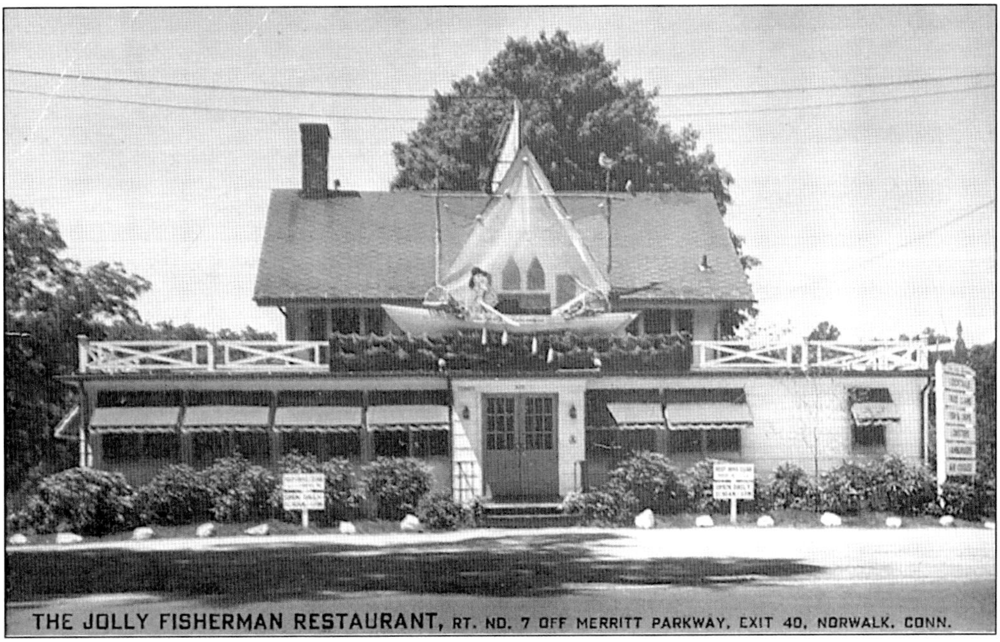

Jolly Fisherman Restaurant was located at the junction of Main Avenue and the Merritt Parkway at exit 40. According to the back of the postcard, it had "inviting sea food with many good things to eat at popular prices, cocktails…" and was air-cooled and open daily year round.

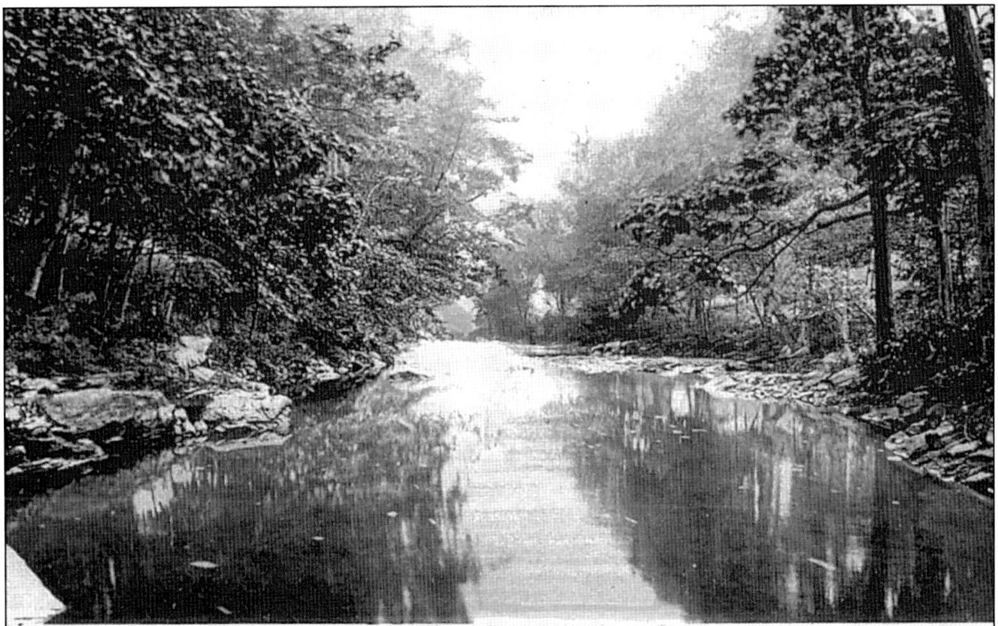

"Looking Downstream, Winnipauk" was sent in 1908.

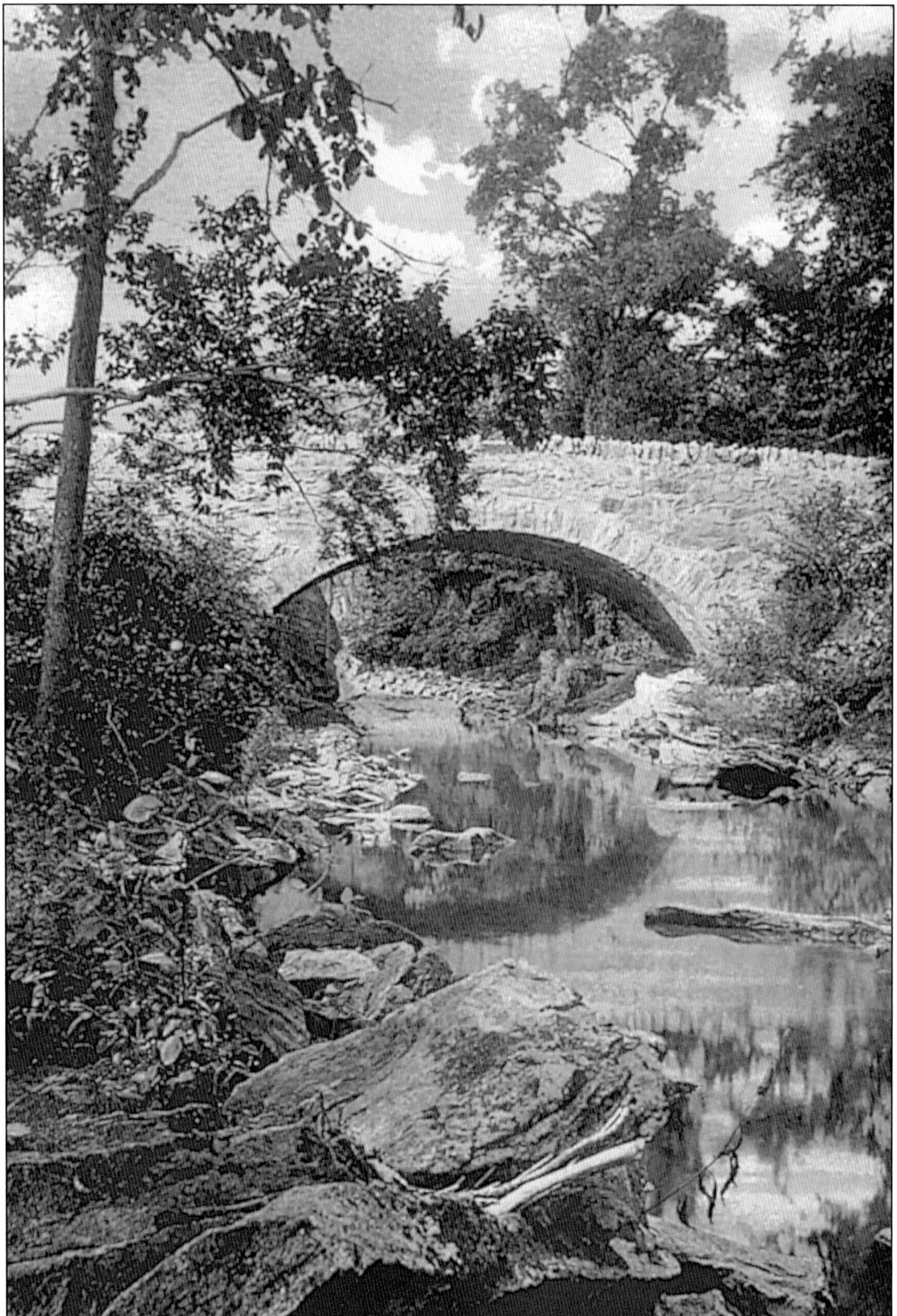

This bridge was located at the terminus of the new Route 7 connector, formerly Grist Mill Road. The Norwalk River was long a source of water power for mills.

Two

WILTON

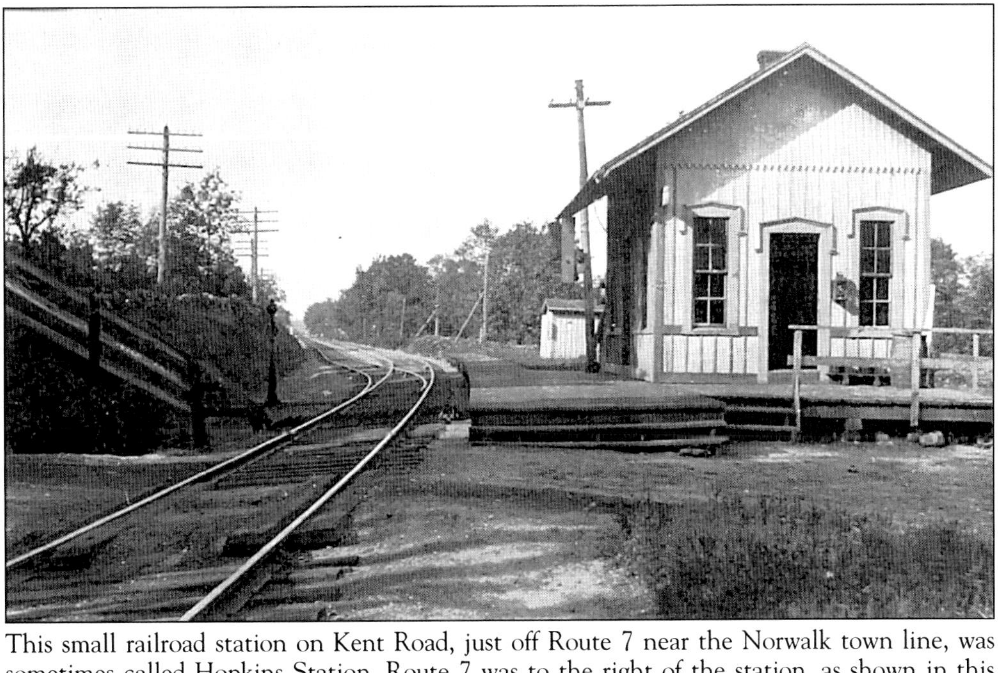

This small railroad station on Kent Road, just off Route 7 near the Norwalk town line, was sometimes called Hopkins Station. Route 7 was to the right of the station, as shown in this picture.

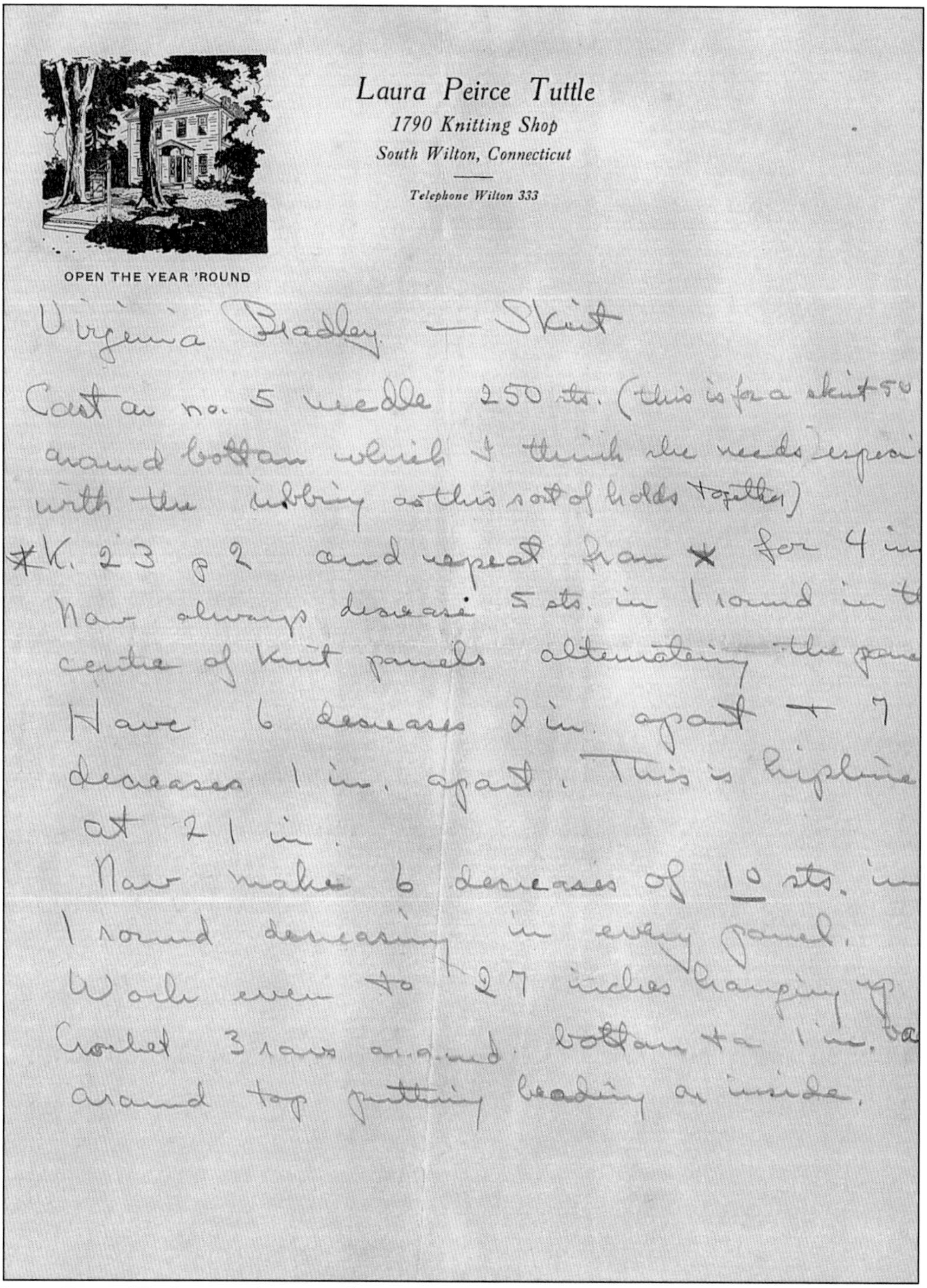

Laura Pierce Tuttle
1790 Knitting Shop
South Wilton, Connecticut

Telephone Wilton 333

OPEN THE YEAR 'ROUND

Virginia Bradley — Skirt
Cast on no. 5 needle 250 sts. (this is for a skirt 50
around bottom which I think she needs especi
with the ribbing as this sort of holds together)
*K. 23 p 2 and repeat from * for 4 in
Now always decrease 5 sts. in 1 round in the
centre of knit panels alternating the pan
Have 6 decreases 2 in. apart + 7
decreases 1 in. apart. This is hipline
at 21 in.
Now make 6 decreases of <u>10</u> sts. in
1 round decreasing in every panel.
Work even to 27 inches hanging up
Crochet 3 rows around bottom + a 1 in. ba
around top putting beading on inside.

Laura Pierce Tuttle ran a knitting shop in one of Wilton's old houses in the southern part of town. She worked out the pattern, then hired expert knitters to complete the garment. The Tuttle's property is now the site of the Hitchcock Furniture store at 22 Danbury Road.

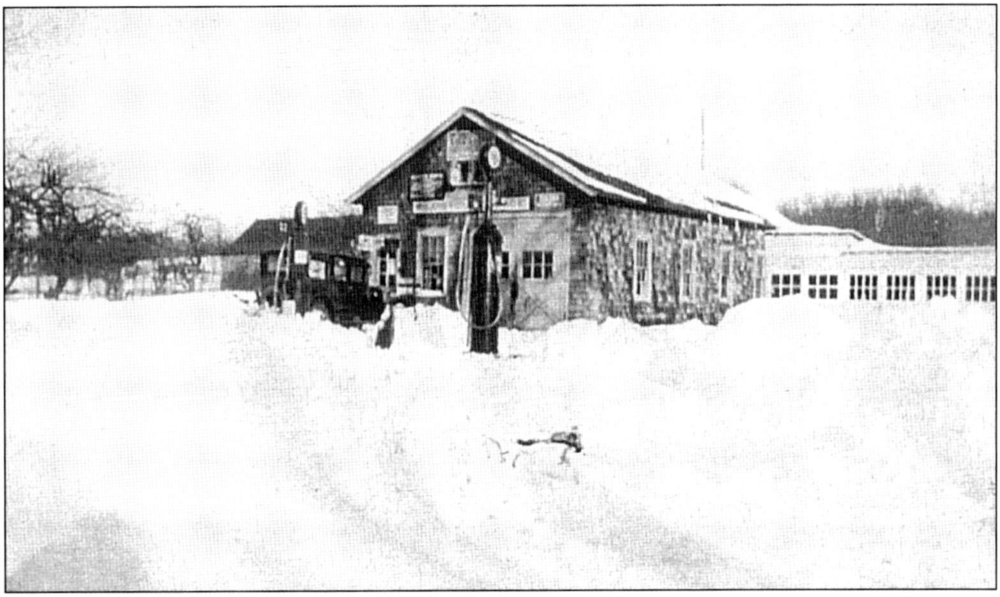

Disbrow's Garage, run by John and Marcella Disbrow, offered many services, including auto repair, taxi service, gasoline, and school bus transportation. Employees Leonard Bradley, Frank Eberhard, and Stanley Hawks divided their day between working in the garage and driving.

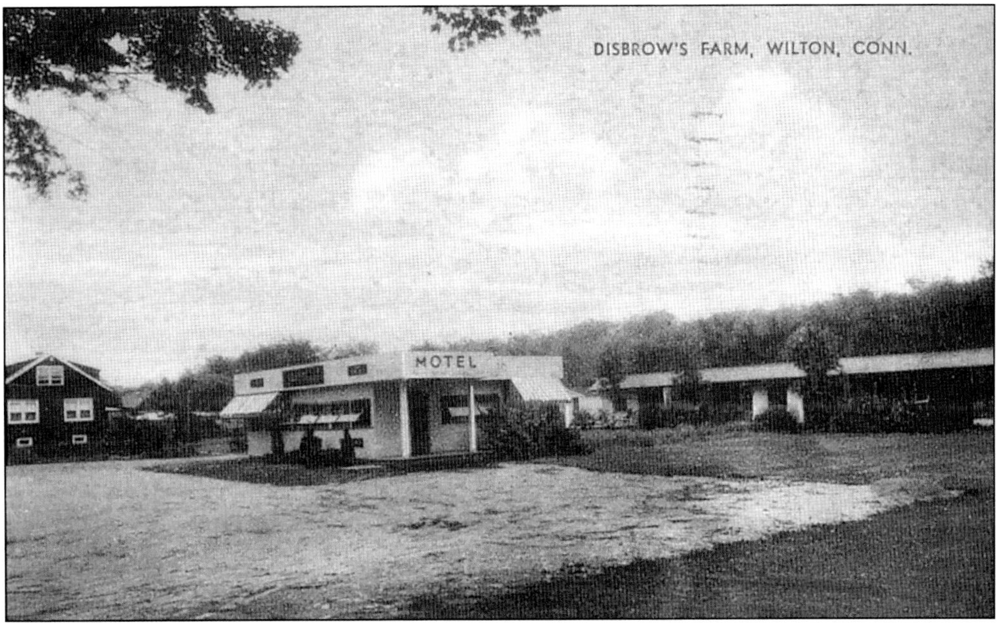

The Disbrows also built cabins and a restaurant, under the name of Disbrow's Farm Cabins and the Pepperpot Restaurant. This card was sent in 1941.

WILTON SOD FARM

MERION Blue Grass: also SUN and SHADY mixtures

Wholesale & Retail

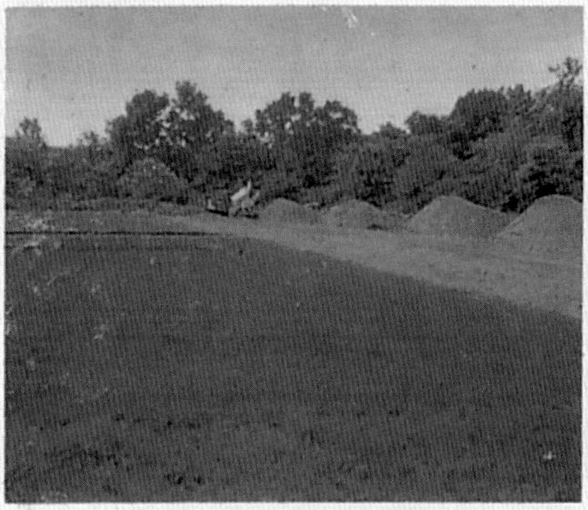

Turf in the Field

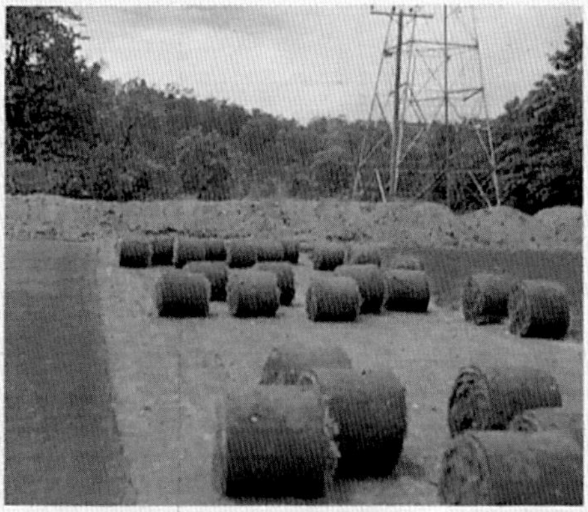

Cut, rolled, ready to lay

The Sod Farm was on the west side of Route 7, just south of the Wilton Supply Company. It was run by William Spencer. The property later became the site of the Holson Company, a producer of photo albums, and now houses a storage center.

Avoid disappointment of delayed starts, washouts.

SELECT YOUR LAWN HERE . .

for immediate and certain results . . Best selections. Start ENJOYING Your Lawn Today ! !

Partial (or total) use of SOD can save you money. It costs you nothing to pay us a visit.

WILTON SOD FARM
Rt. #7, 2½ mi. No. of Pkwy.
Wilton, Conn.
POrter 2-7530

19305-B

Pub. by Edward Wells, Dumont, New Jersey

DEXTER

PLACE STAMP HERE

POST CARD

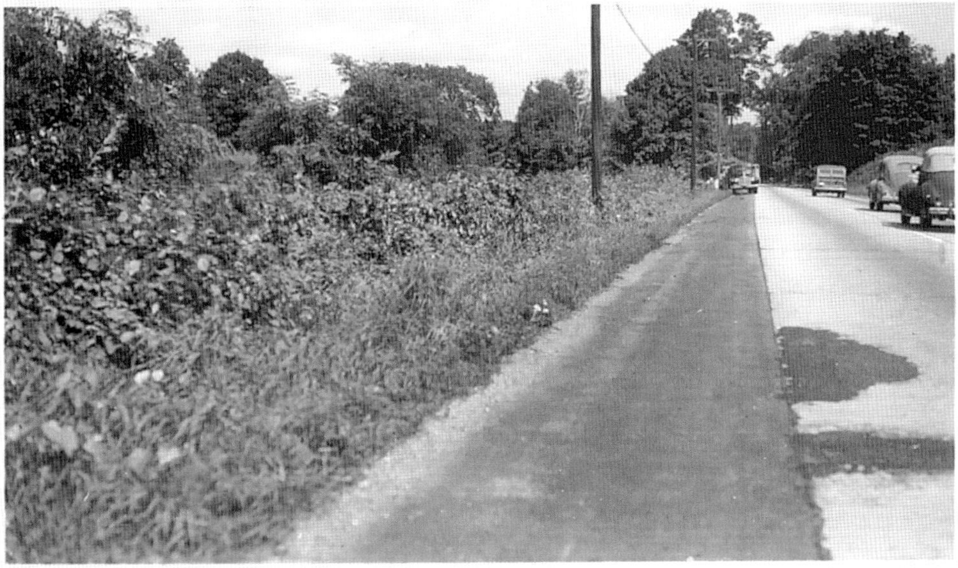

This was the view on Route 7 in 1946, just before the Wilton Supply Company (now Yankee Lumber) was built. When ground was broken to build the Wilton Supply Company, it began to change the face of that stretch of the road.

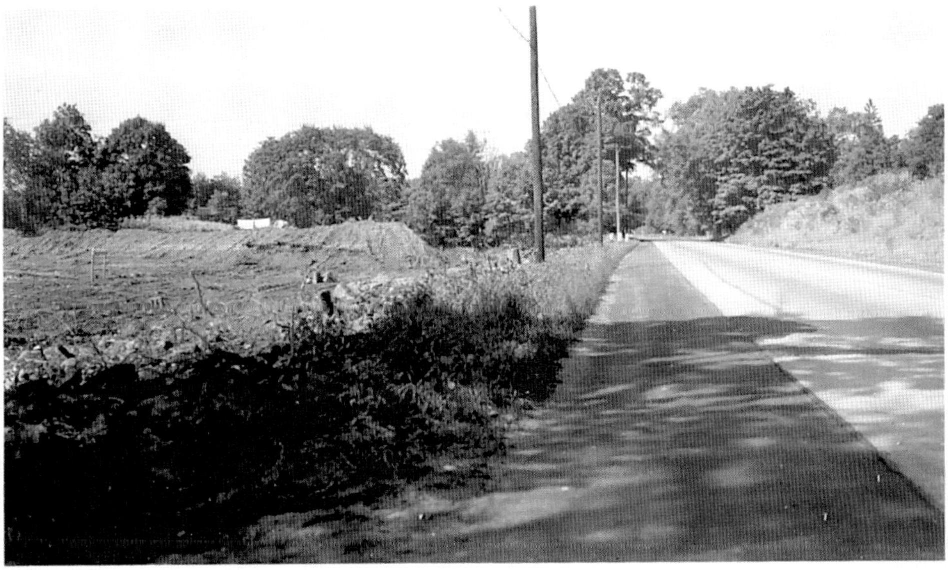

ANNOUNCEMENT

We are pleased to announce that we are now open for business under the name of

WILTON SUPPLY COMPANY, Inc.,

yard and office located opposite the Hollyhock Inn, Wilton. We cordially invite you to call on us for your requirements in Coal and all Building Supplies.

Monroe W. Tuttle and "Bill" Bepler who are associated together in the Wilton Supply Company, Inc., hope you will feel at liberty to come in at any time to discuss your Coal and Building requirements.

WILTON SUPPLY COMPANY, Inc.

TELEPHONE 330

These announcements were sent in 1947 when the Wilton Supply was located across from Grumman Hill Road at what is now 71 Danbury Road.

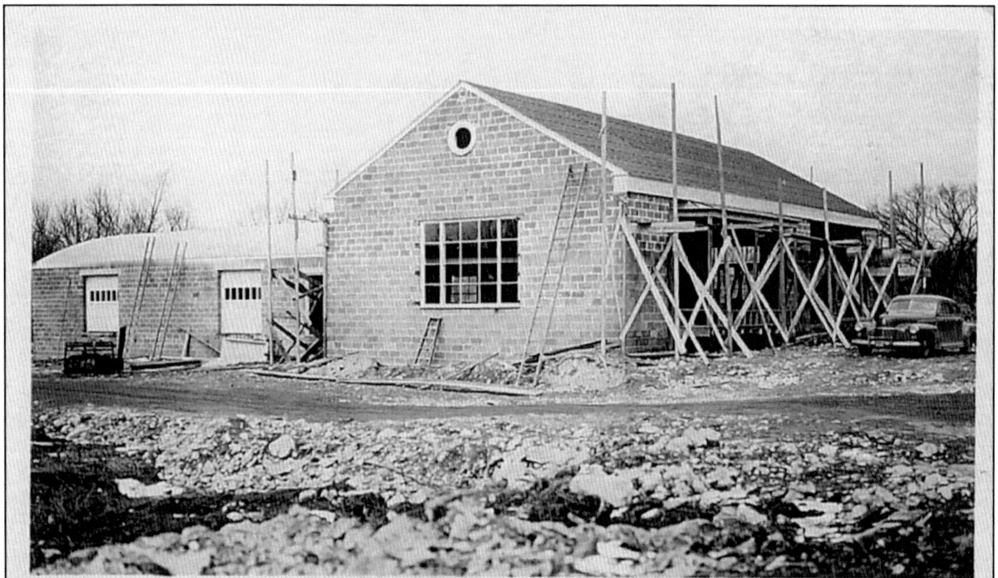

The photo below shows the early stages of construction of the "new" Wilton Supply building at 129 Danbury Road.

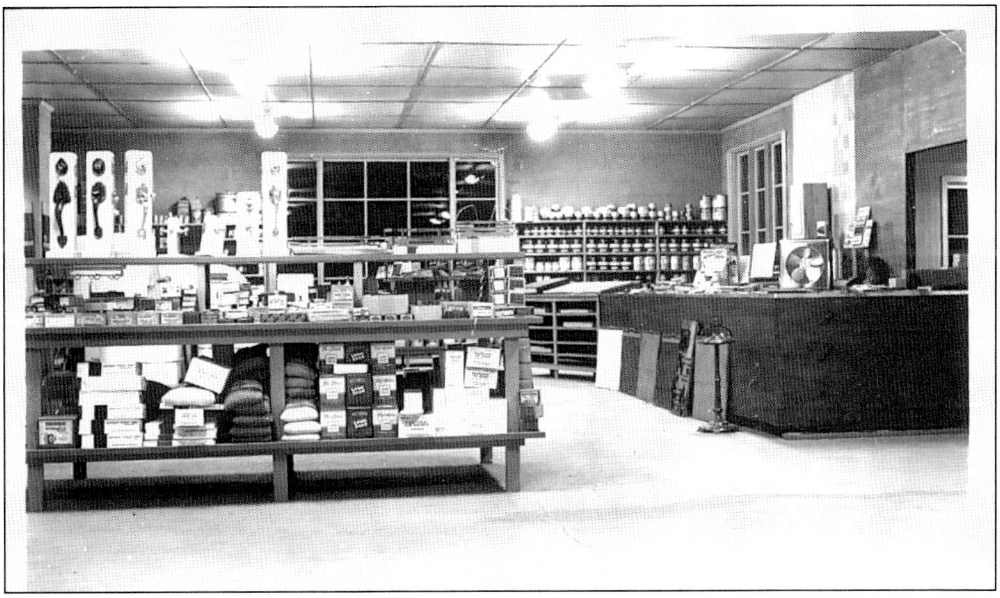

Here is an early interior view of the sales area at the Wilton Supply Lumber Company.

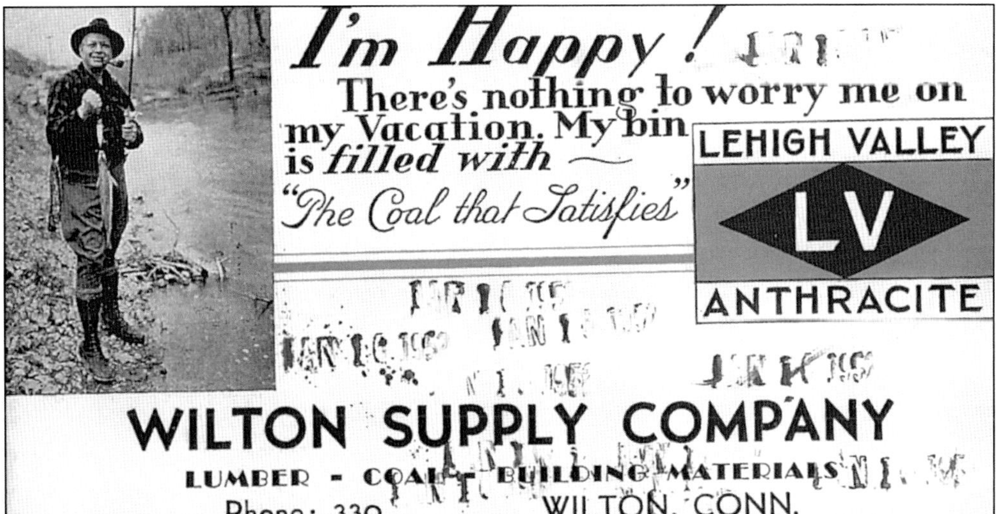

This advertising card features friend and local executive Bill Edwards. Bill and Grace Edwards developed what we now know as Crossways at the intersection of Routes 7 and 33.

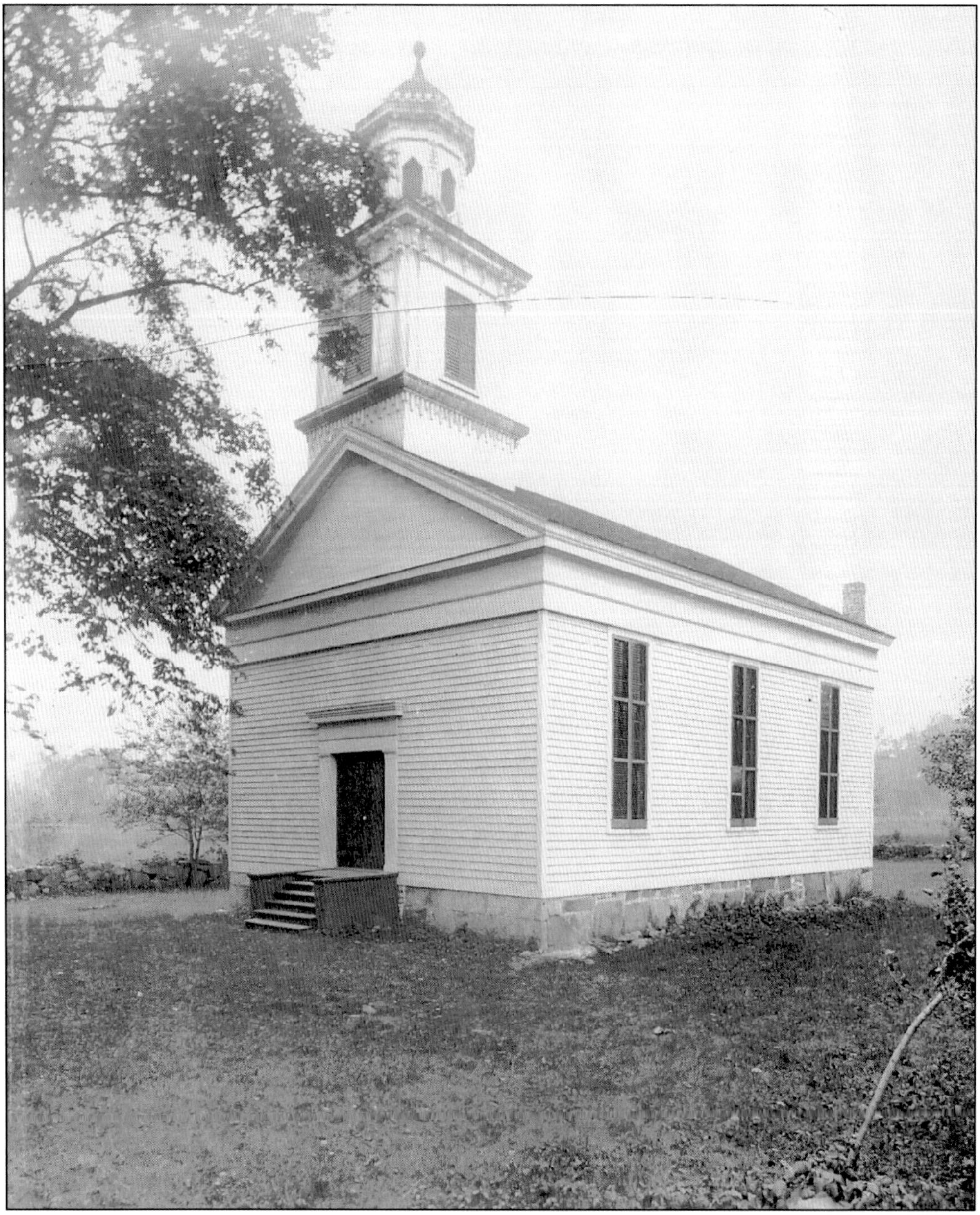

The South Wilton Methodist Church was on the west side of Route 7 below Westport Road. It had a domed ceiling and wide floorboards. By the mid-1930s, it had been abandoned, and local boys played basketball in it when no homeless men were sleeping there.

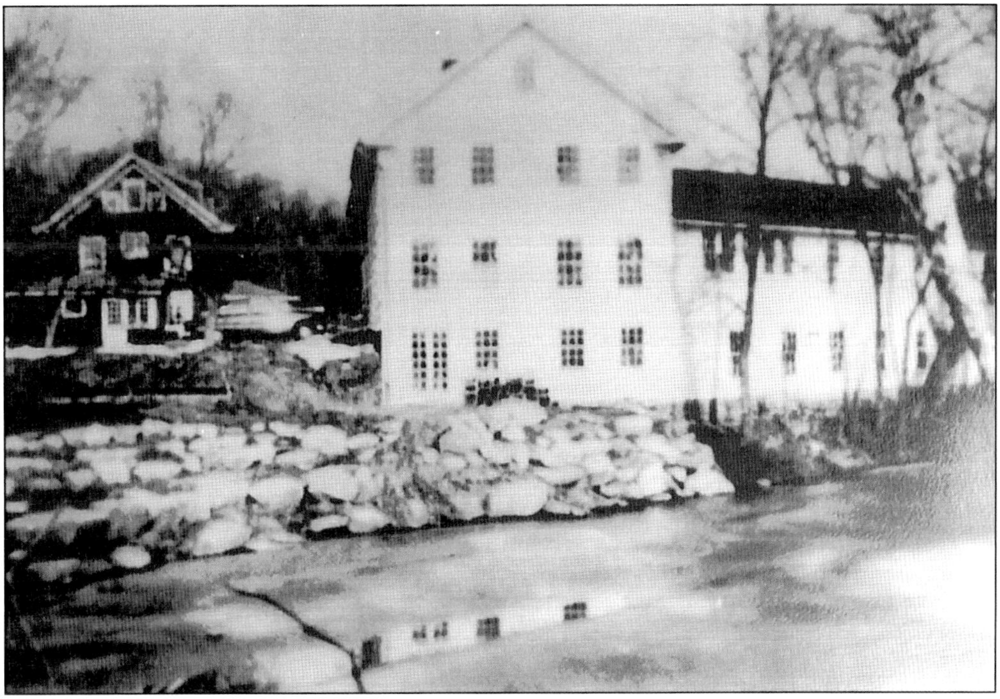

Meyer Brothers ran a building firm at the corner of Wolfpit Road and Route 7. Fritz Meyer lived on the south corner, and Charles Meyer lived on the north corner of Wolfpit Road. The picture is of the mill where machines and lumber were stored. The rear of the house held the company office.

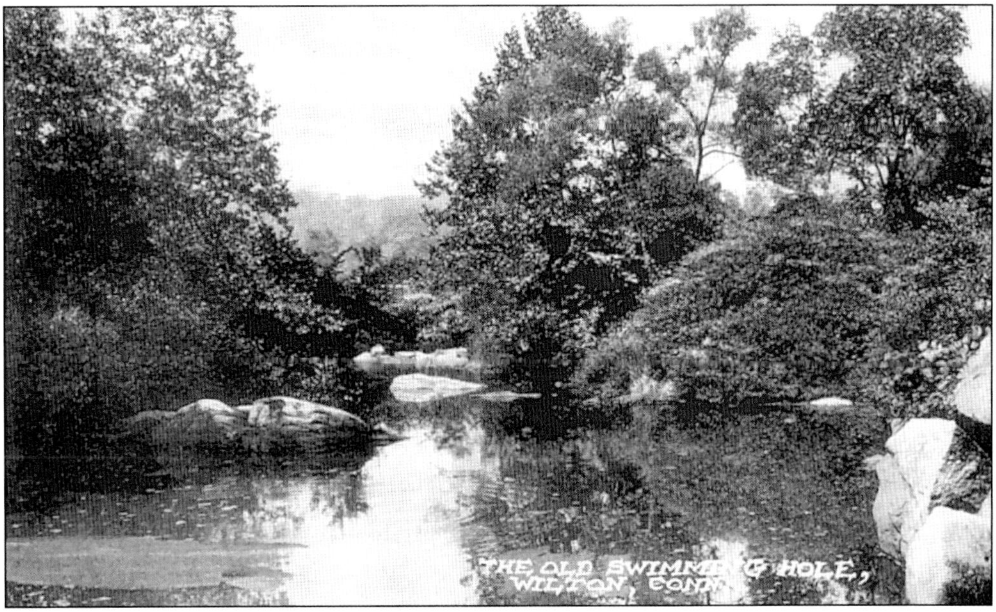

Depicted here is another popular swimming hole behind "Orem's Diner."

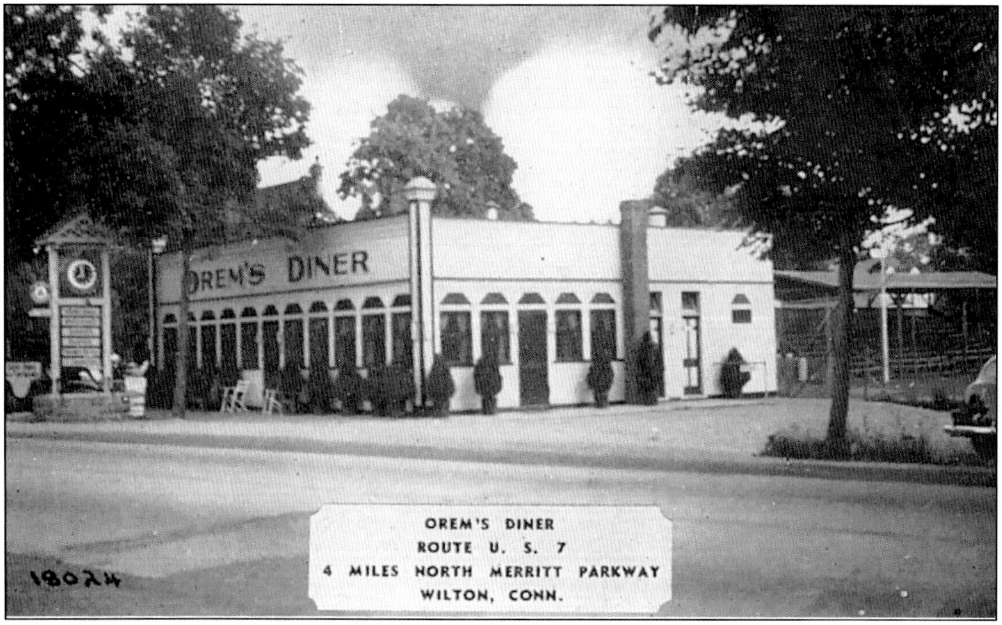

In the early 1920s, Charles Orem started a dairy with his own herd of cows, opened a small refreshment store, and built a ball field. The store became Orem's Diner and continues in business today. This view was taken in the 1930s. Potential widening of Route 7 may take this historic structure.

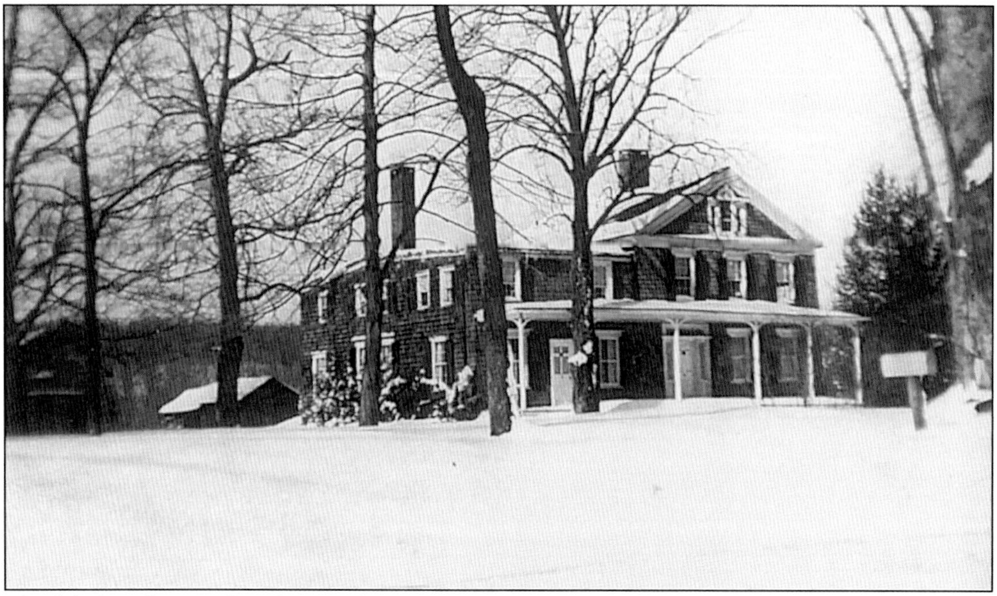

The life-long home of F. Clerc Ogden and his parents was sold to Our Lady of Fatima parish for their church and school. The house was moved to the back of the property, where it remains.

CROSSWAYS

TURN AT WILTON CONNECTICUT

ROUTE 7 • **WILTON 31**

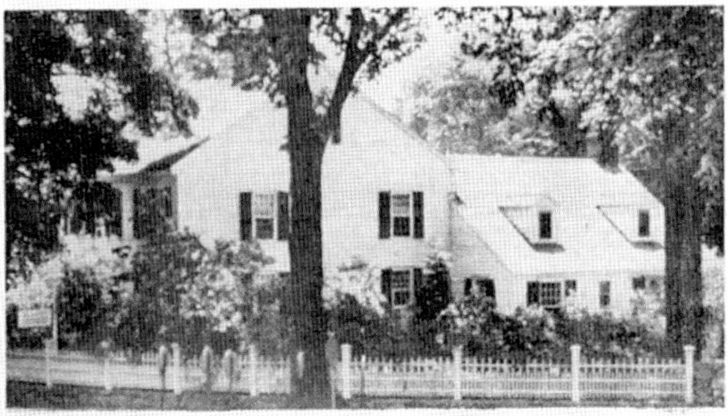

A Delightful Place of Many Interests

People came to Crossways for dining or antique shopping. Crossways was located in the Raymond-Fitch House, built in 1732, which is now the headquarters of the Wilton Historical Society. When the tea room moved to Routes 7 and 33, that location came to be known as Crossways.

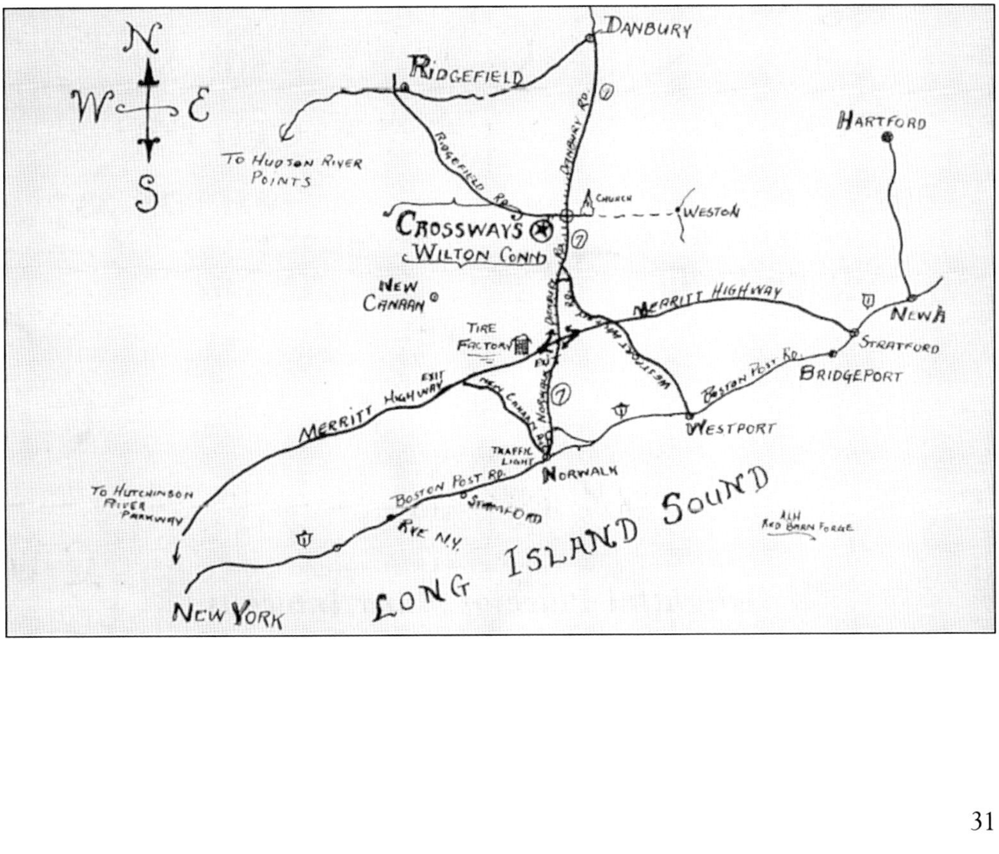

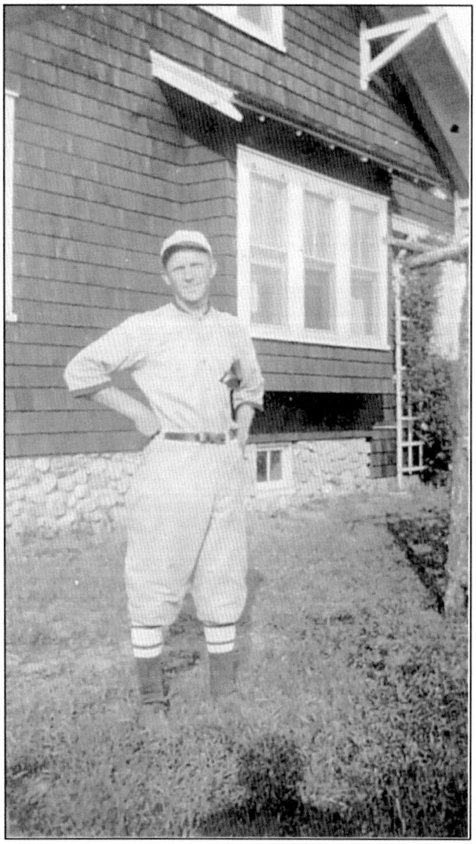

Grover Howard Bradley stands as a young man in front of one of the houses he built on Sharp Hill, just off Route 7.

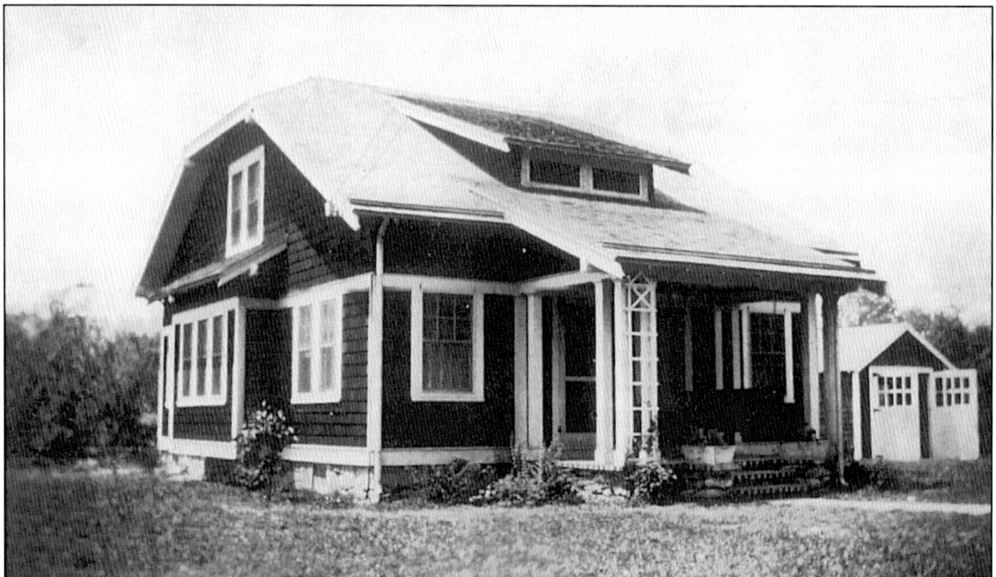

Known in the family as the Little Brown House, Grover H. Bradley built two houses and a shed here. This house, located at 261 Danbury Road, is currently the office of lawyers George Olexo and Edward Hyde.

Three

RIDGEFIELD

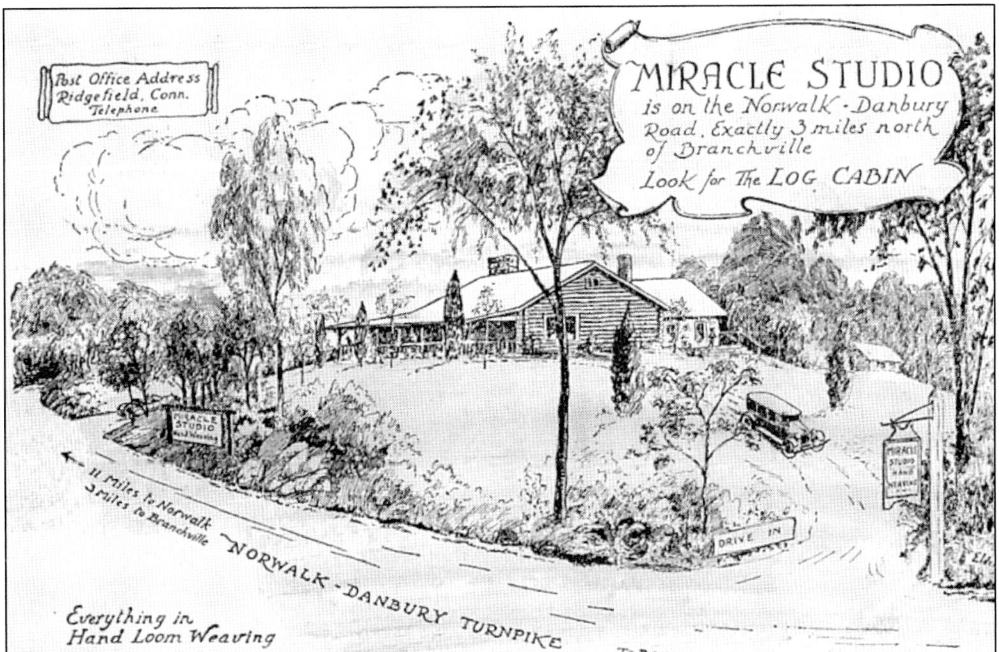

The Miracle Studio was a needlework shop on the west side of Route 7, near New Road. The location is shown on a 1935 map from the *Fairfield County Atlas*.

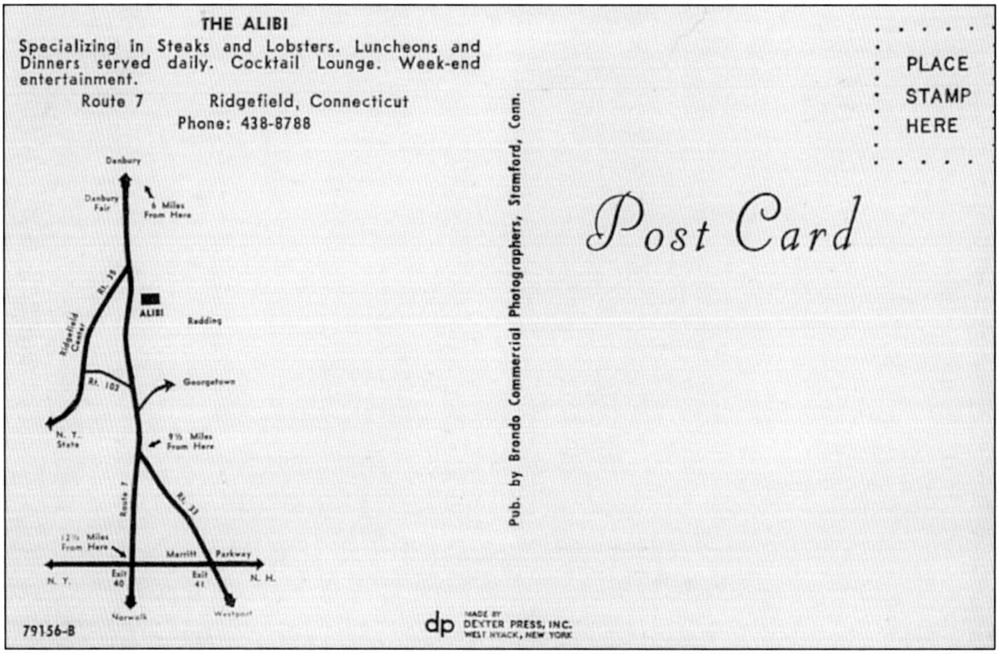

This is the back of an advertising card for the Alibi. The Alibi burned down in the mid 1970s. It was in a pull-off north of Topstone Road across from the Golf Art Shop, formerly Black Pond Mall. Before the Alibi, Mr. Mugavero ran a roadhouse there. There were once cabins behind it along the Norwalk River.

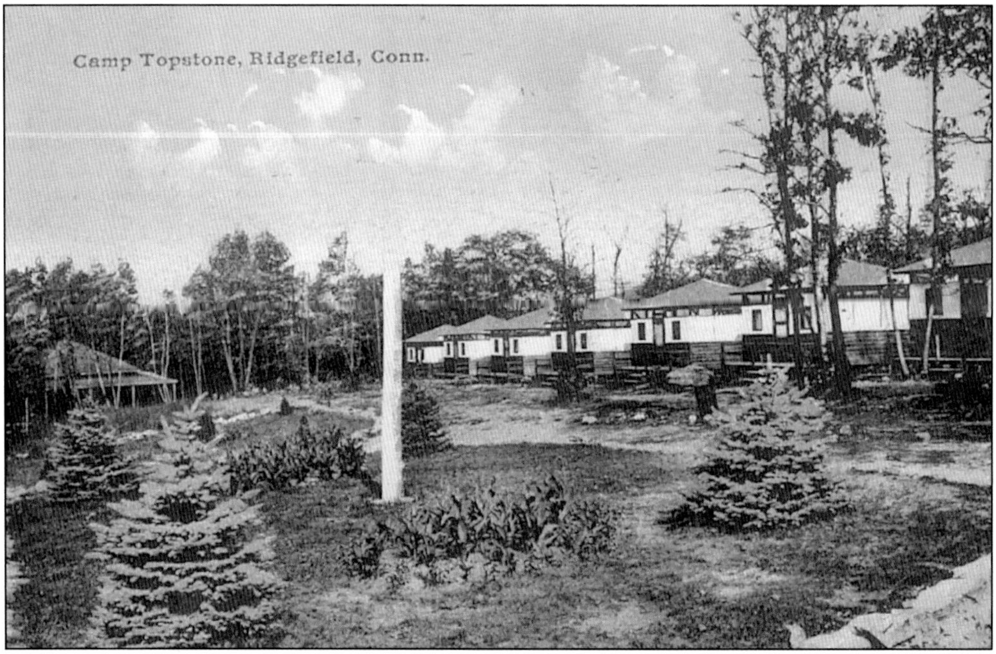

This postcard is dated 1930. Judging from the layout of the cabins, this was later Camp Adventure.

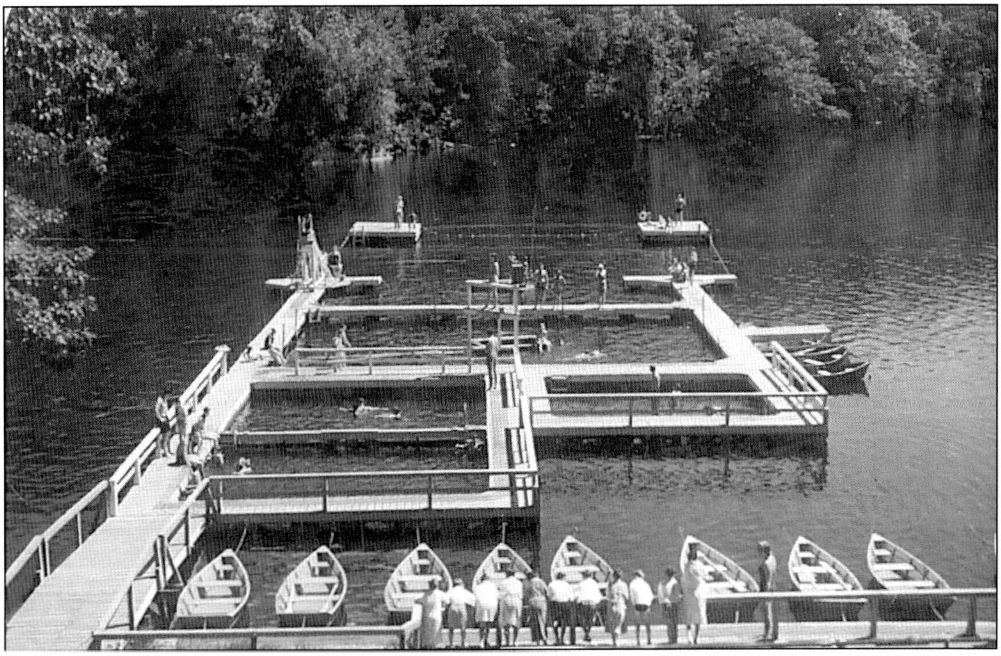

Camp Adventure was founded in 1931 and located on 11 acres, with 700 feet on Great Pond. Much of the land now belongs to the town of Ridgefield and is designated as open space.

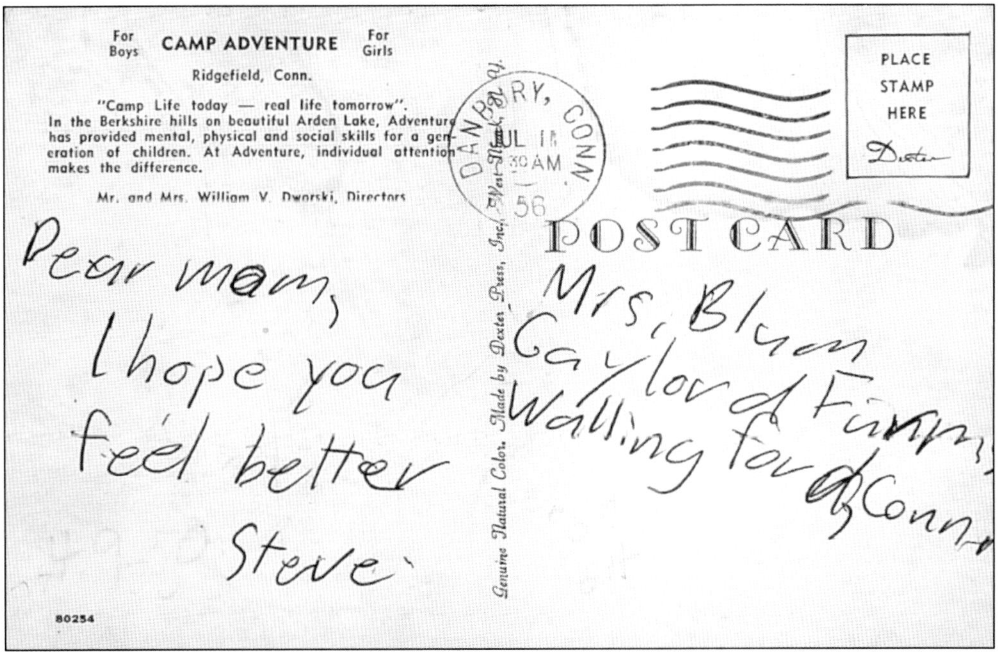

In the 1960s, the Volunteers of America purchased Camp Adventure and named it Camp Arden Lake, where underprivileged children were charged $15 a week to attend camp.

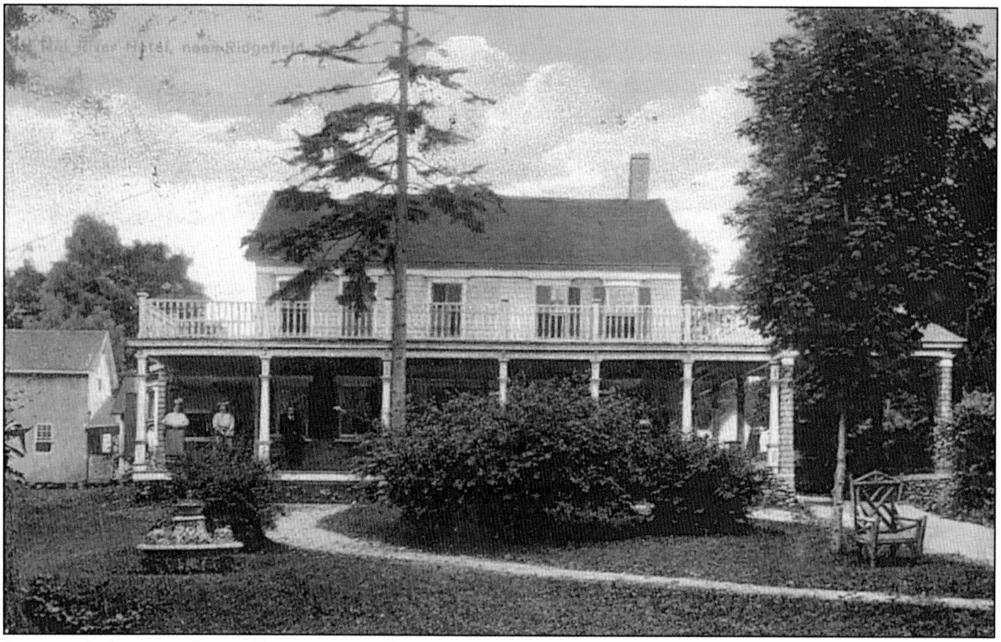

Pictured above is the Mill River Hotel, which is believed to be the forerunner of the Stonehenge Inn. The 1908 picture of the pond at Mill River was published by H.B. Bissell of Ridgefield.

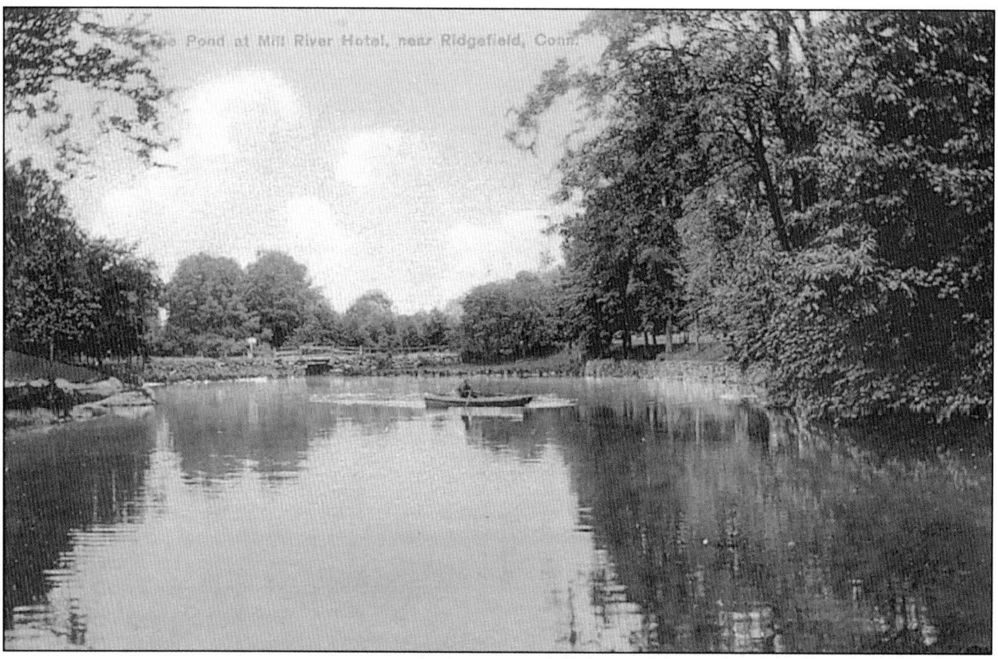

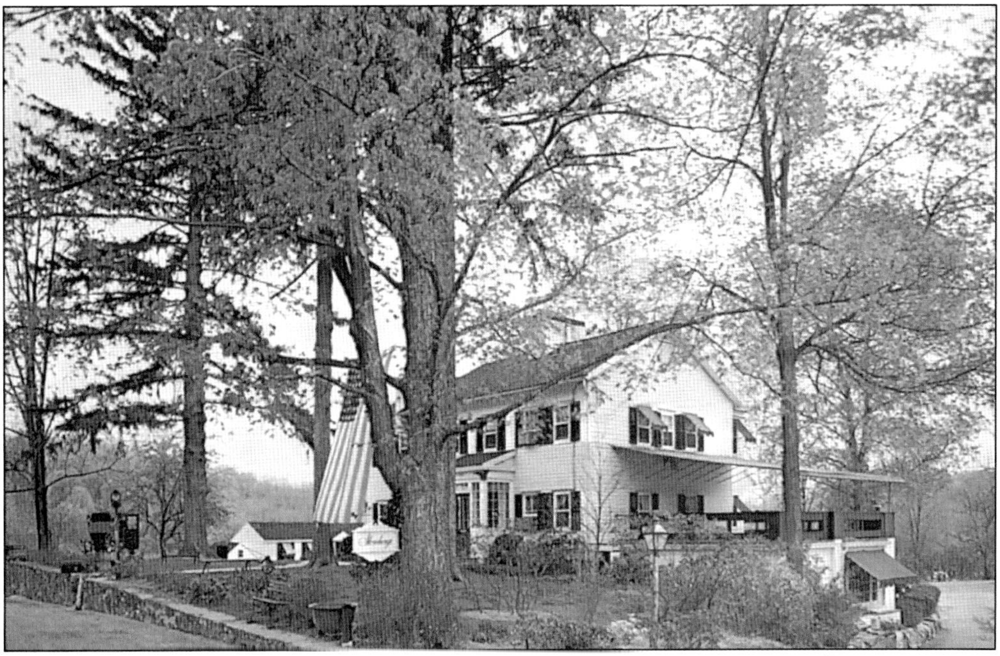

Stonehenge was started by innkeeper Victor Gilbert in 1948. This was "One of America's great country inns," according to the back of the card.

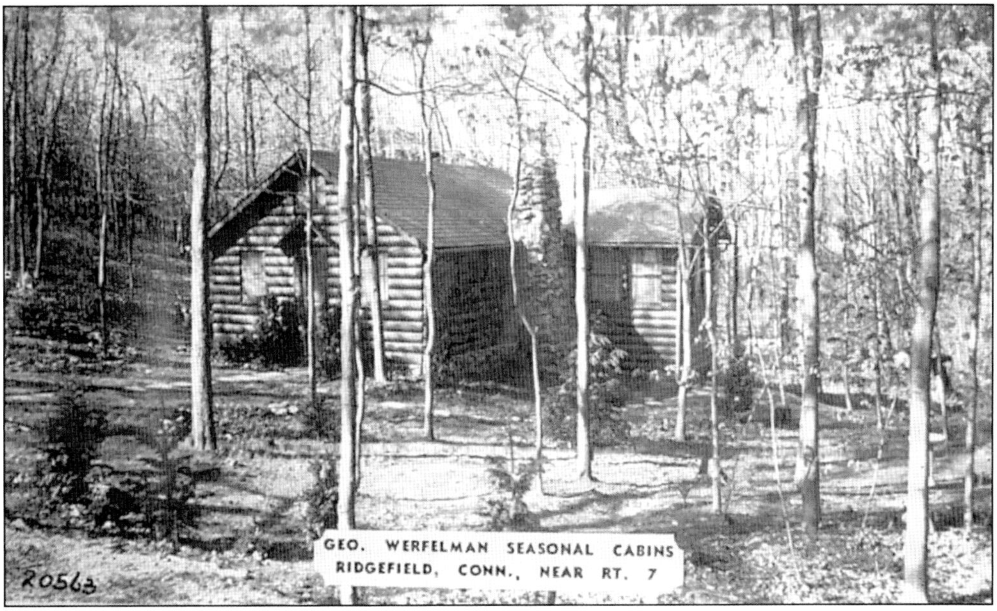

These rustic cabins were in Redding on Picketts Ridge Road. According to the back of the card, they were "fourteen miles west of the Merritt Parkway and one mile north of Route 7." Today these cabins have been converted to year-round homes. This one, however, remains close to the original look of the cabins and is actually located on Starrs Ridge Road.

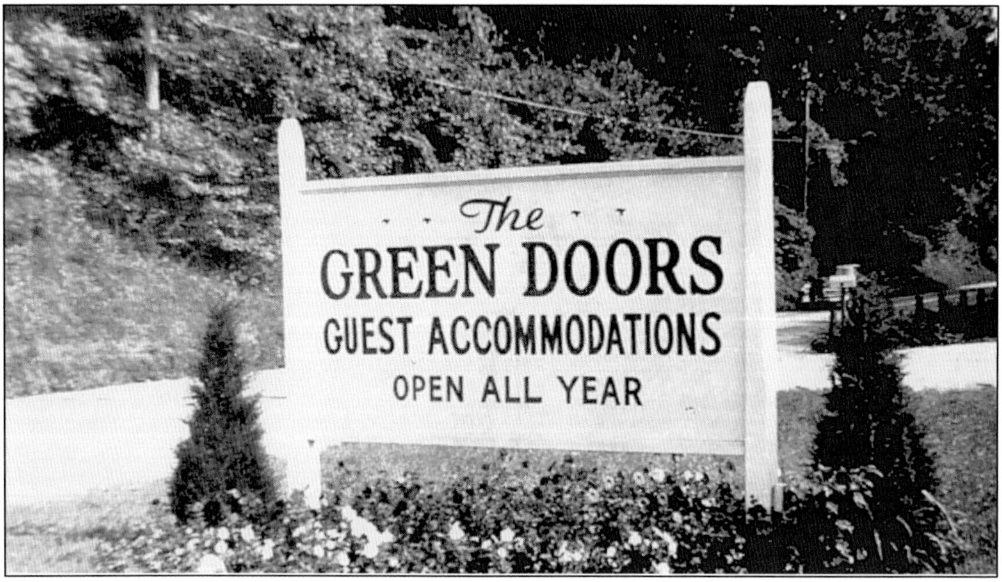

The Green Doors was just south of the intersection of Routes 35 and 7.

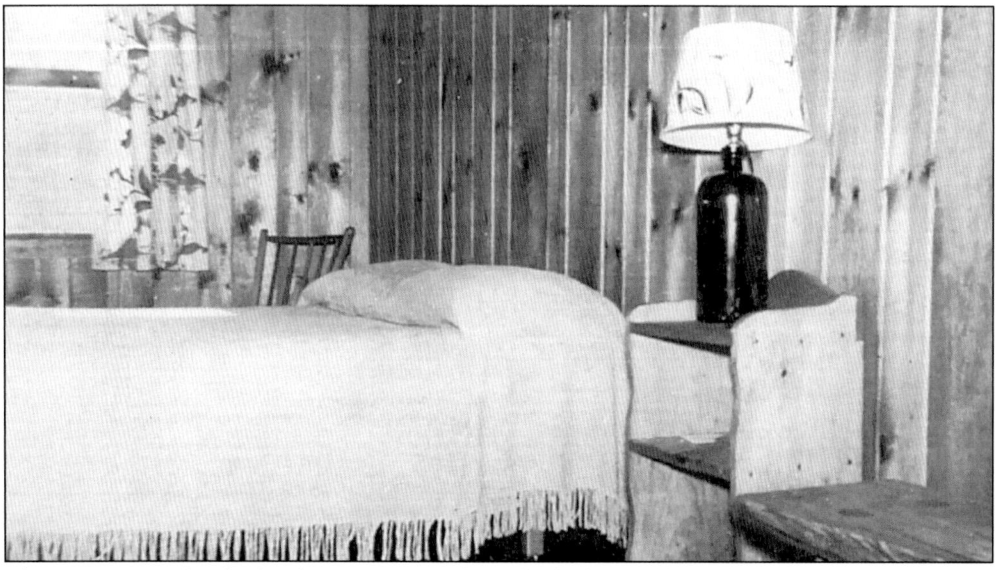
The rooms were finished in knotty pine and overlooked a small pond. In its place today is the Ridgefield Pizza restaurant.

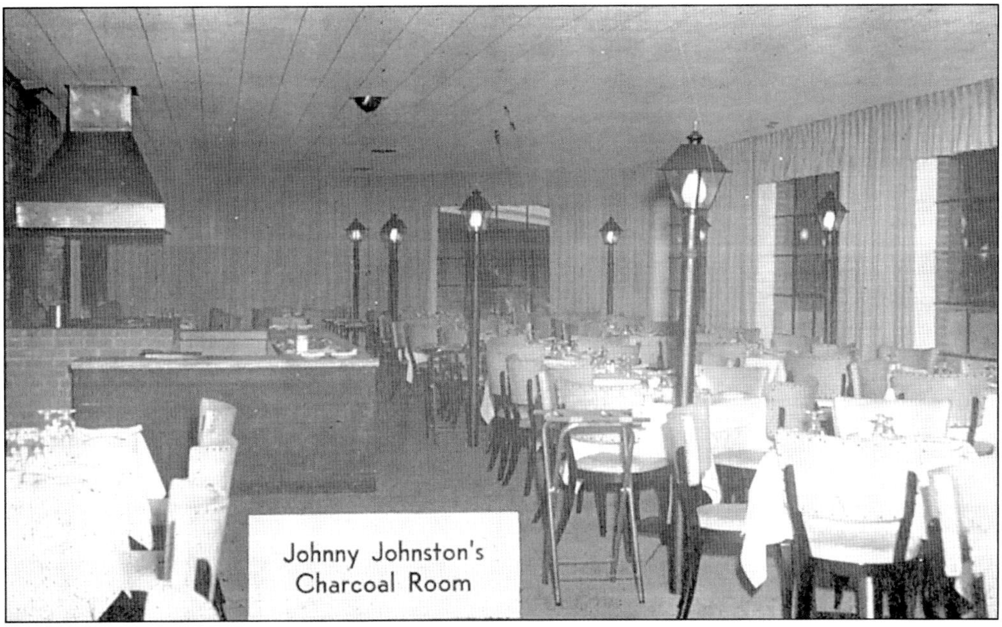

Johnny Johnston's served "the best of broiled foods prepared over the open charcoal pit" on the Danbury-Norwalk Road in 1957.

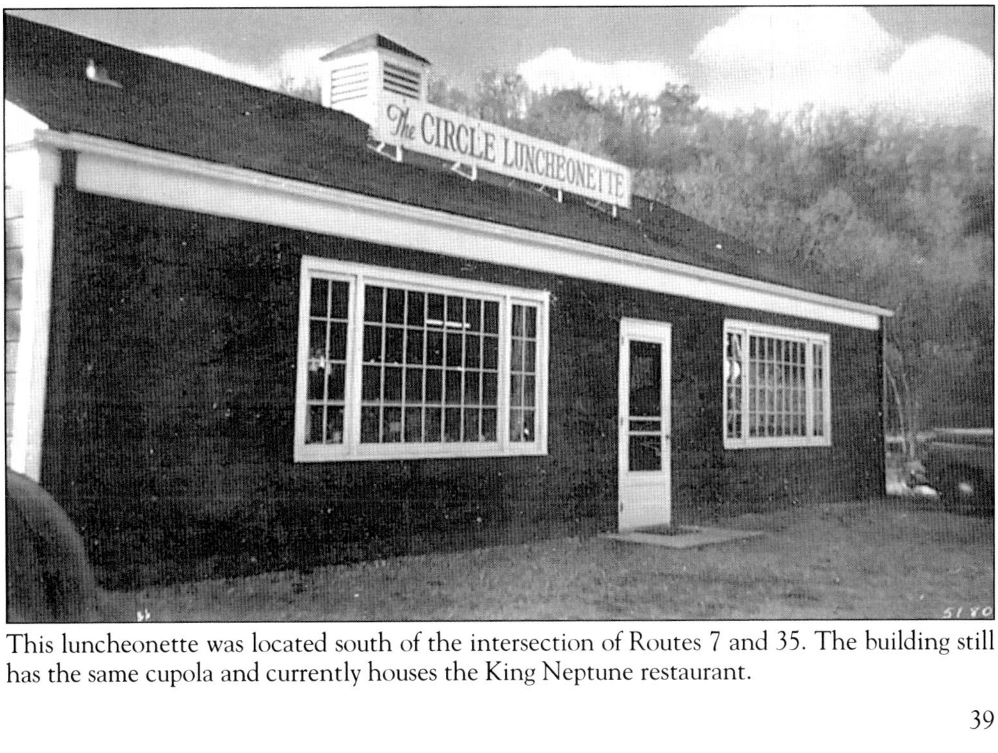

This luncheonette was located south of the intersection of Routes 7 and 35. The building still has the same cupola and currently houses the King Neptune restaurant.

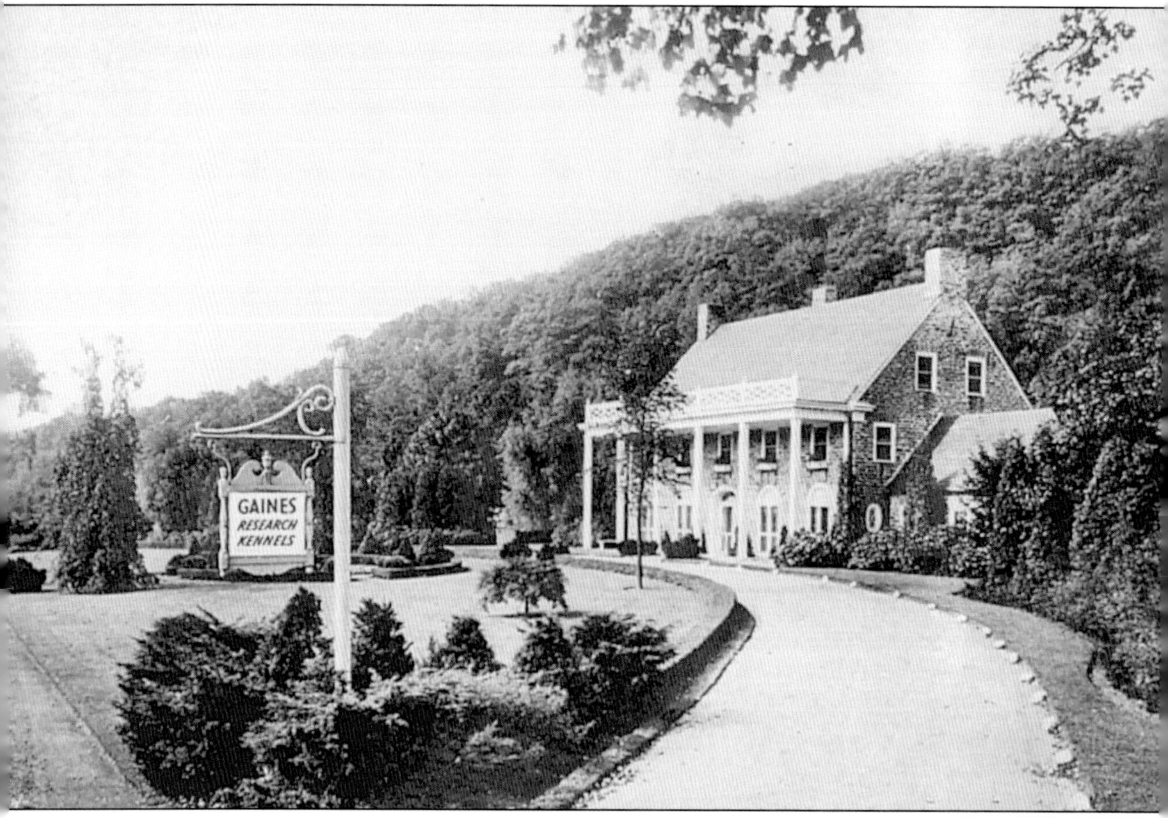

The main building was formerly the Gaines Dog Food Company's research headquarters. It was built by Colonel Connolly. It is now part of Stone House Commons, a condominium complex.

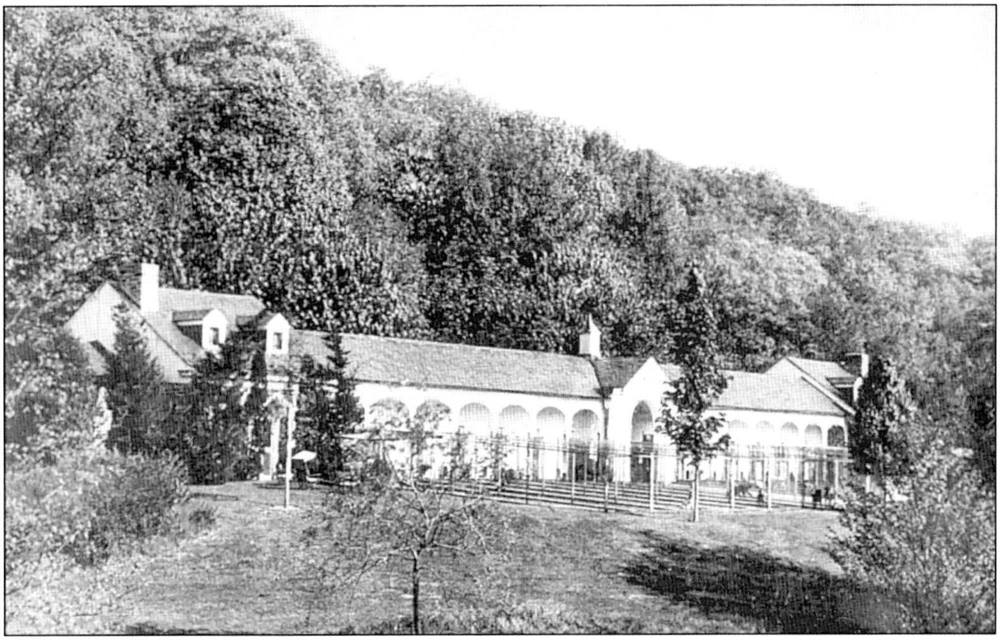

These were the research kennels. The stone structures on each end of the building housed employees. It was formerly the Red Lion Restaurant and has been the Belzoni Grill for several years.

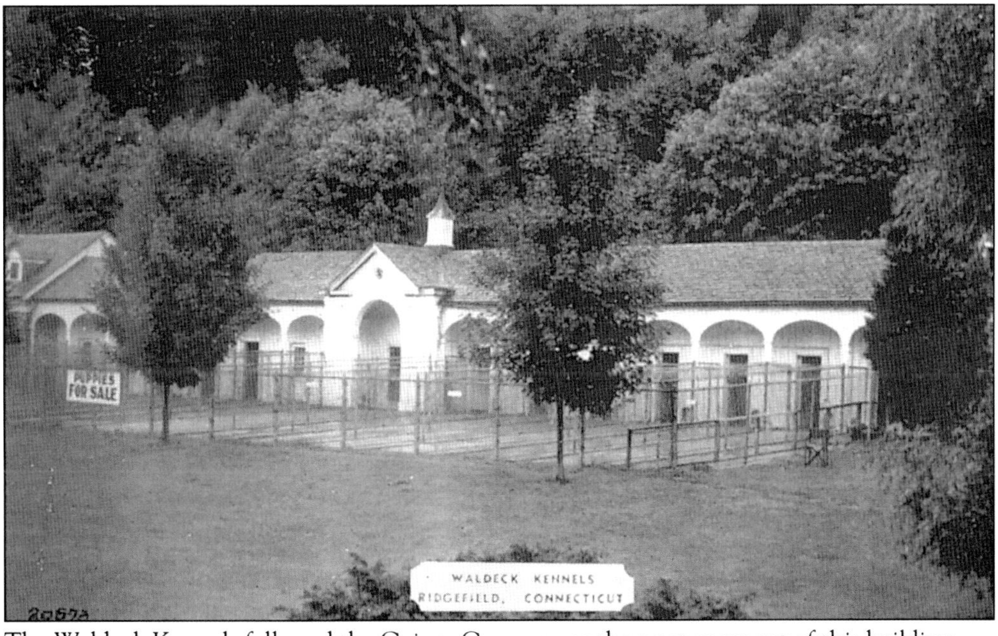

The Waldeck Kennels followed the Gaines Company as the next occupant of this building.

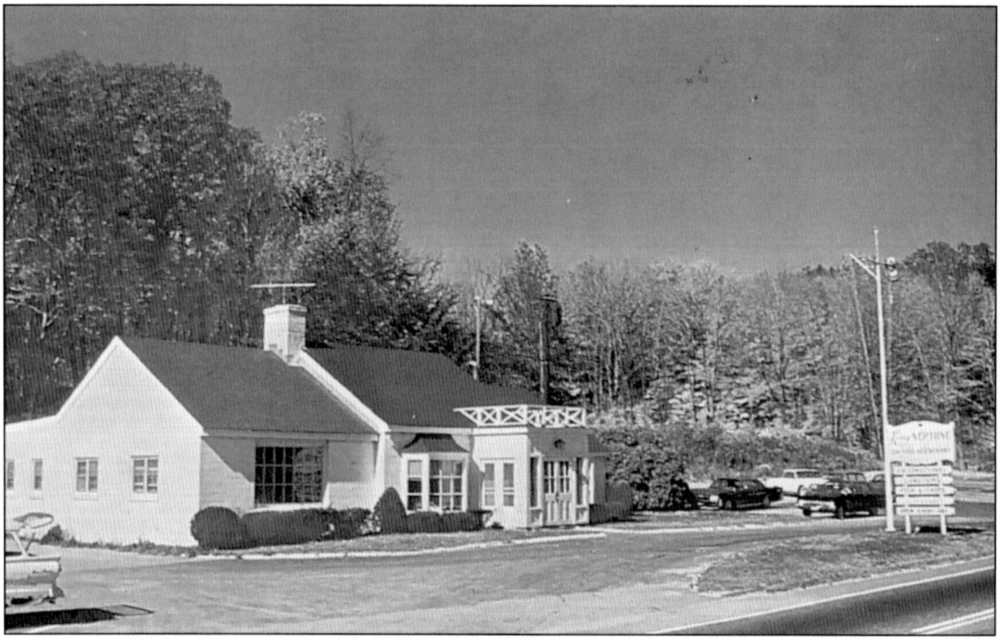

This is the original location of the King Neptune restaurant. The property at 665 Ethan Allen Highway (Route 7) is now occupied by Pamby Lincoln-Mercury-Dodge Motors.

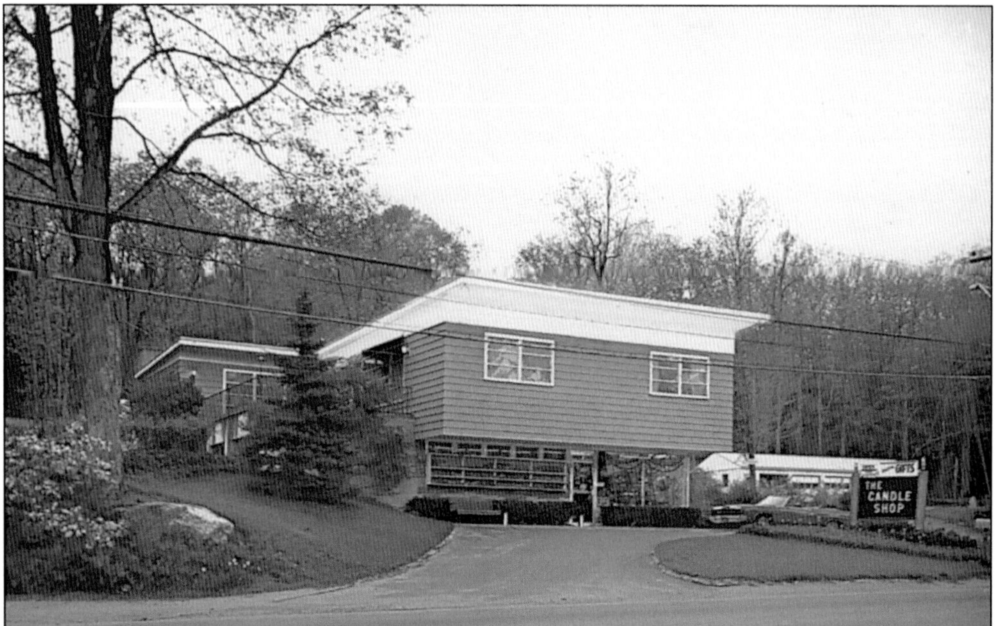

The Candle Shop on Route 7 sold gifts and candles for many years.

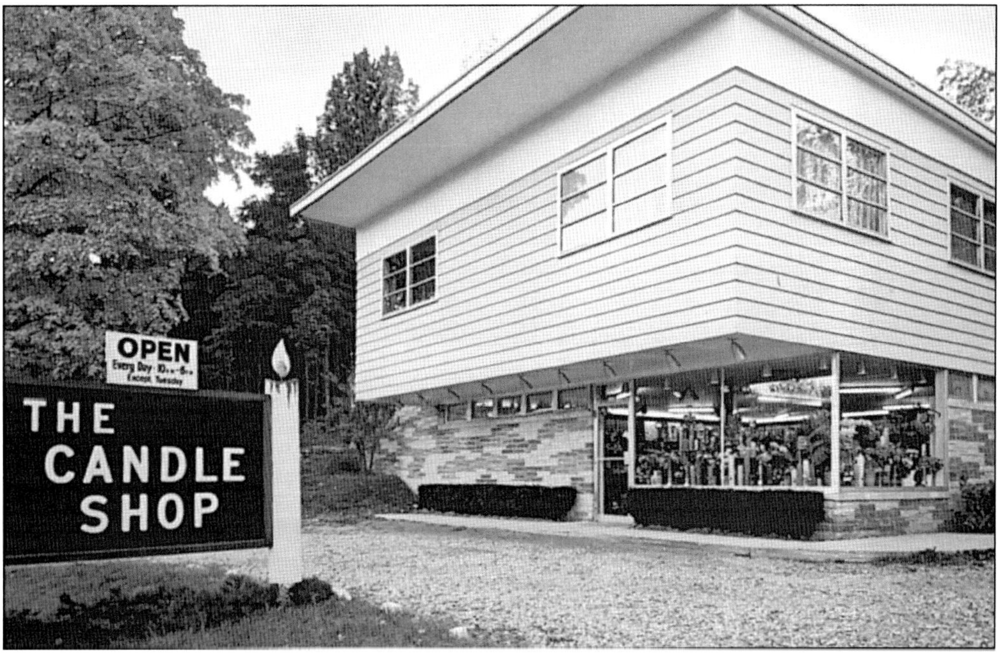

The Candle Shop has housed many businesses since and is now a mobile telephone store.

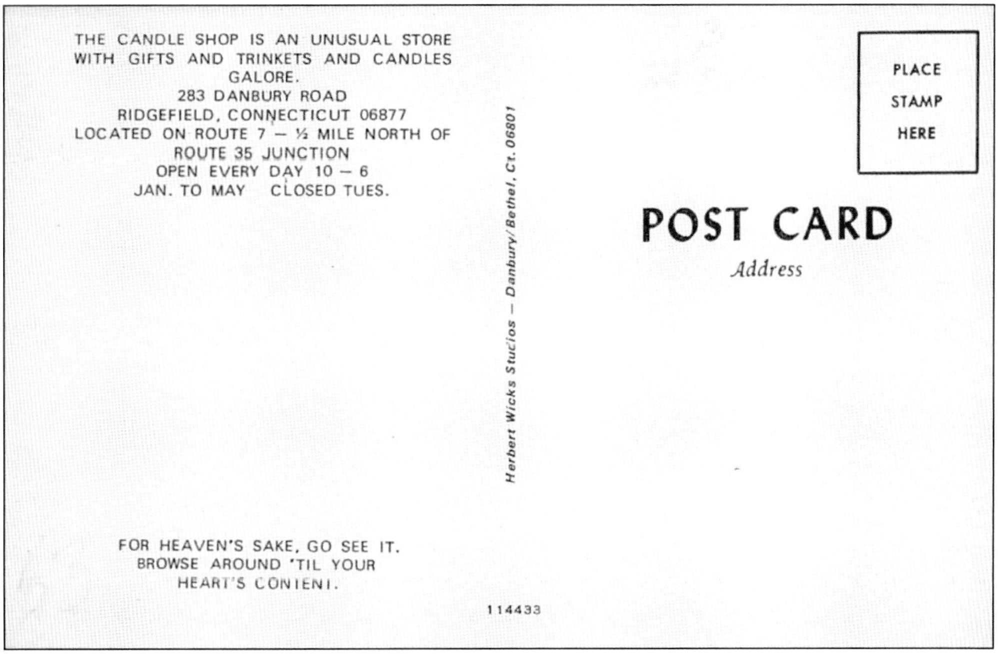

THE CANDLE SHOP IS AN UNUSUAL STORE
WITH GIFTS AND TRINKETS AND CANDLES
GALORE.
283 DANBURY ROAD
RIDGEFIELD, CONNECTICUT 06877
LOCATED ON ROUTE 7 – ½ MILE NORTH OF
ROUTE 35 JUNCTION
OPEN EVERY DAY 10 – 6
JAN. TO MAY CLOSED TUES.

Herbert Wicks Studios – Danbury/Bethel, Ct. 06801

PLACE
STAMP
HERE

POST CARD

Address

FOR HEAVEN'S SAKE, GO SEE IT.
BROWSE AROUND 'TIL YOUR
HEART'S CONTENT.

114433

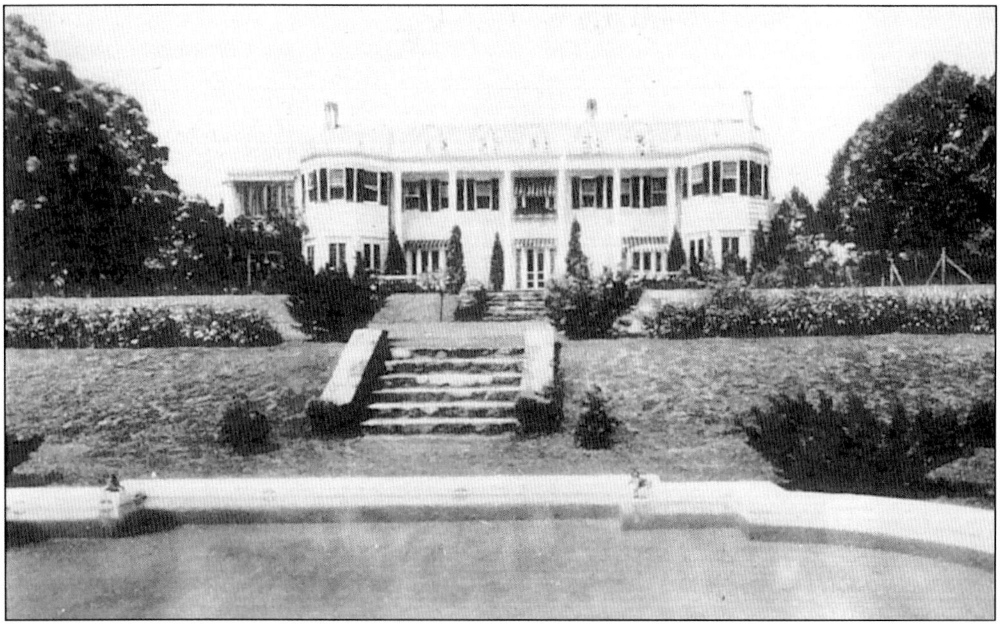

Colonel Louis Connolly built this house in the early 1900s and called it Outpost Farm. After World War II, the property was sold and used as the Fox Hill Inn until the early 1970s. It was torn down in the early 1980s by then owners IBM. The lower card was sent in 1951. Although identified on the card as being on Route 7, it is actually on Bennett's Farm Road, near Route 7.

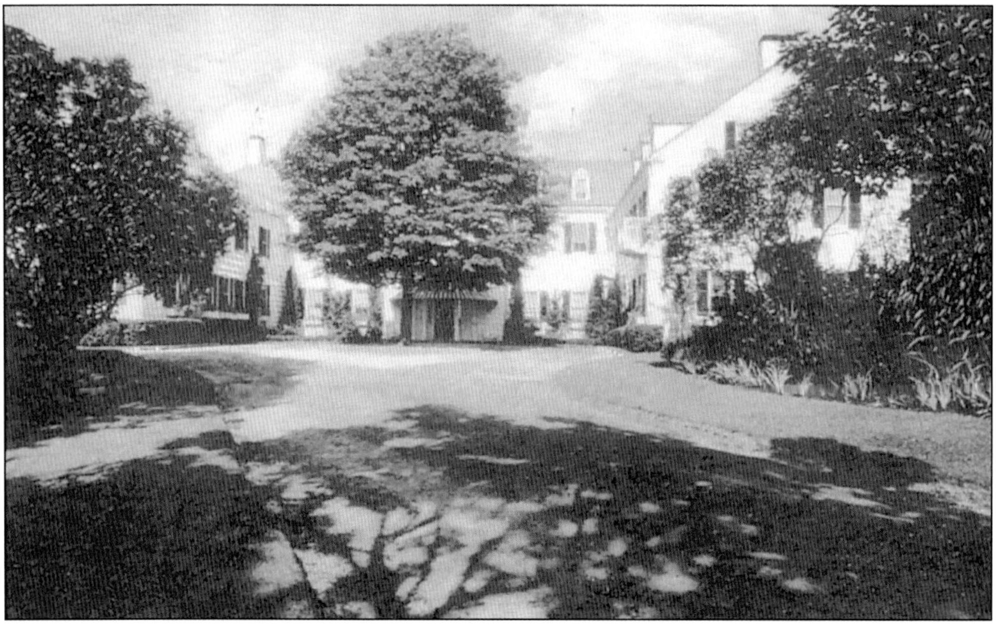

Four

Danbury Including Sugar Hollow

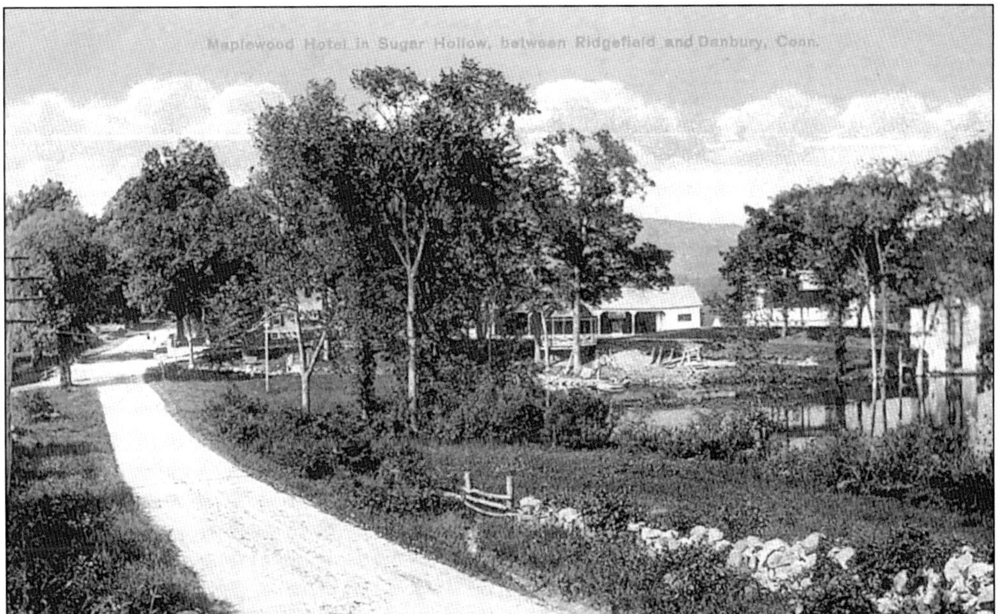

This view shows the Maplewood Hotel in the early 1900s, when Route 7 (then Danbury Road) was still a dirt road.

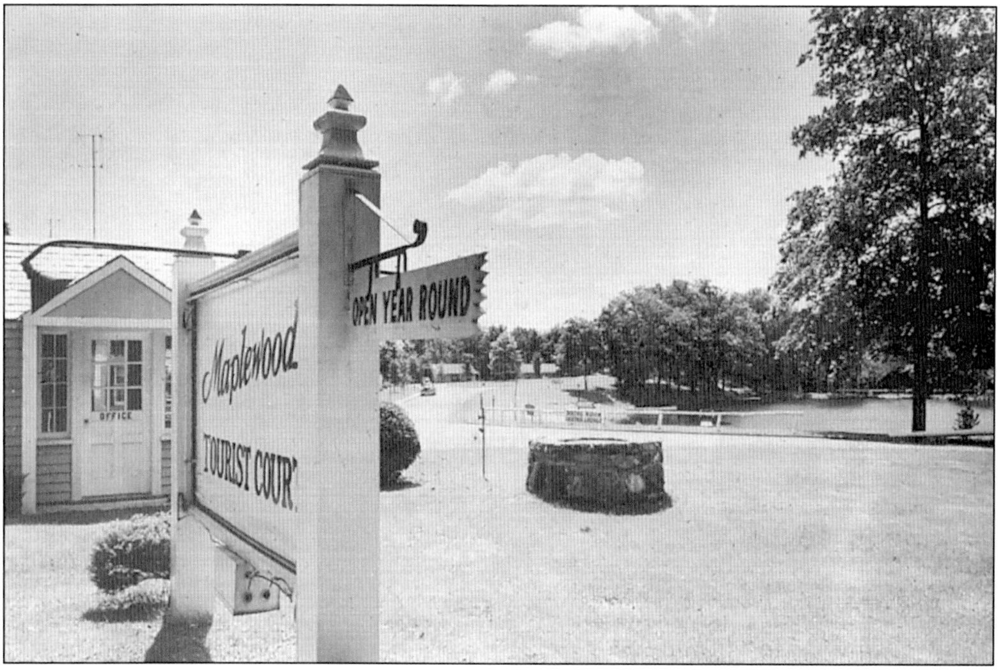

The Maplewood Tourist Court in Sugar Hollow was a "year-round tourist court in the foothills of the Berkshires," which offered a private lake with boating and fishing, a dining room, and a cocktail lounge.

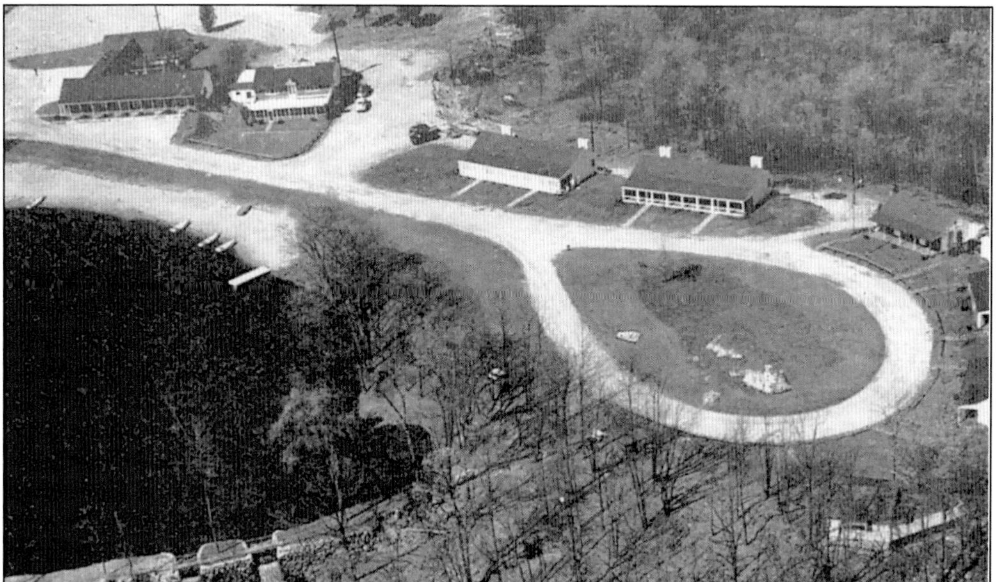
In the 1980s, cabins from the former Maplewood Tourist Court were rented on a long term basis. In 1999, the cottages have been demolished, and Amish Outdoor Furniture surrounds the lawn next to the pond. This property is across from Bennett's Farm Road.

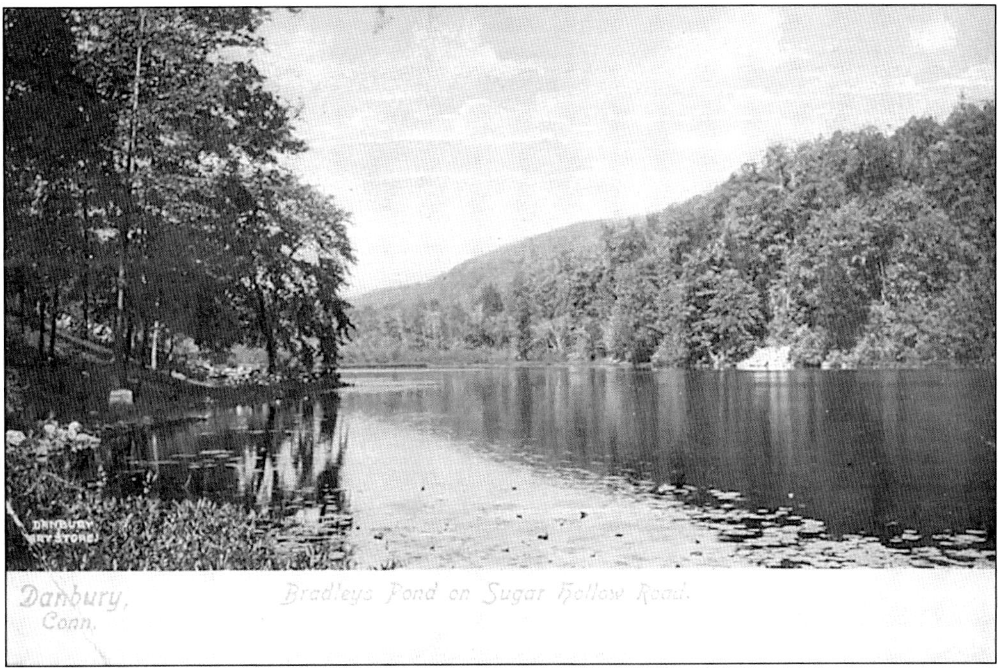

Bradley Pond, just beyond Starrs Plain Road, is the backdrop for the Indian Trading Post. The shop remains an intriguing place to browse and buy moccasins and toys. At one time, the Trading Post also rented cabins.

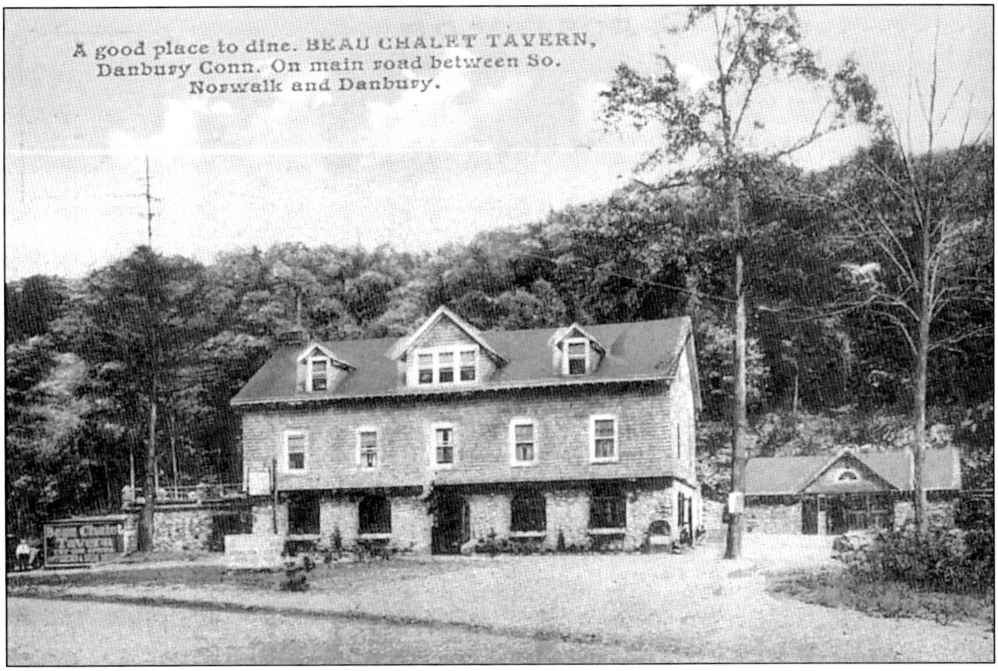

Only a raised rectangle of dirt and a generous roadside pull-off remain where this tavern once stood. It was located on the east side of Route 7, just north of Bradley Pond.

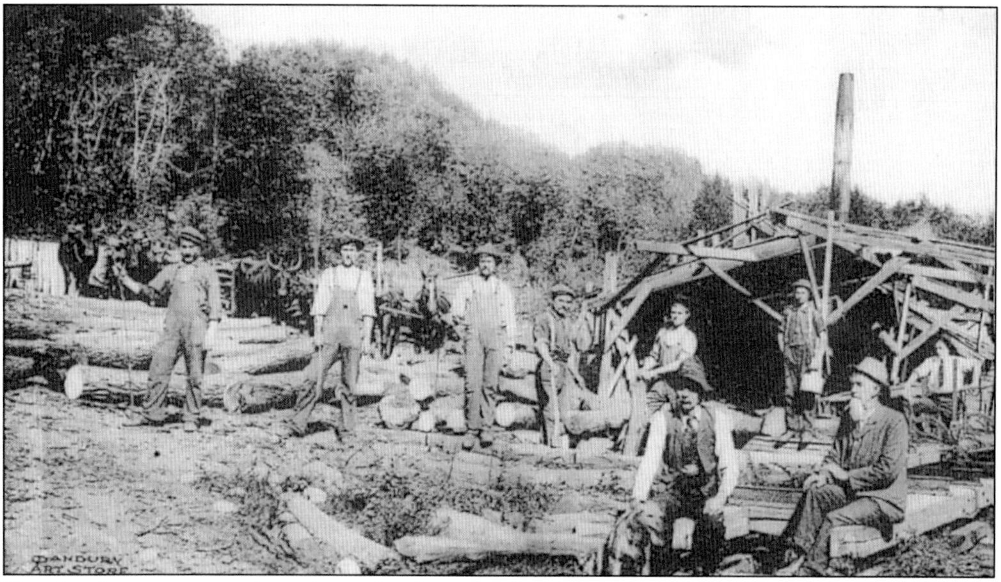

This lumber camp may have been for the crew that was laying out or widening the stretch of Route 7 known as Sugar Hollow.

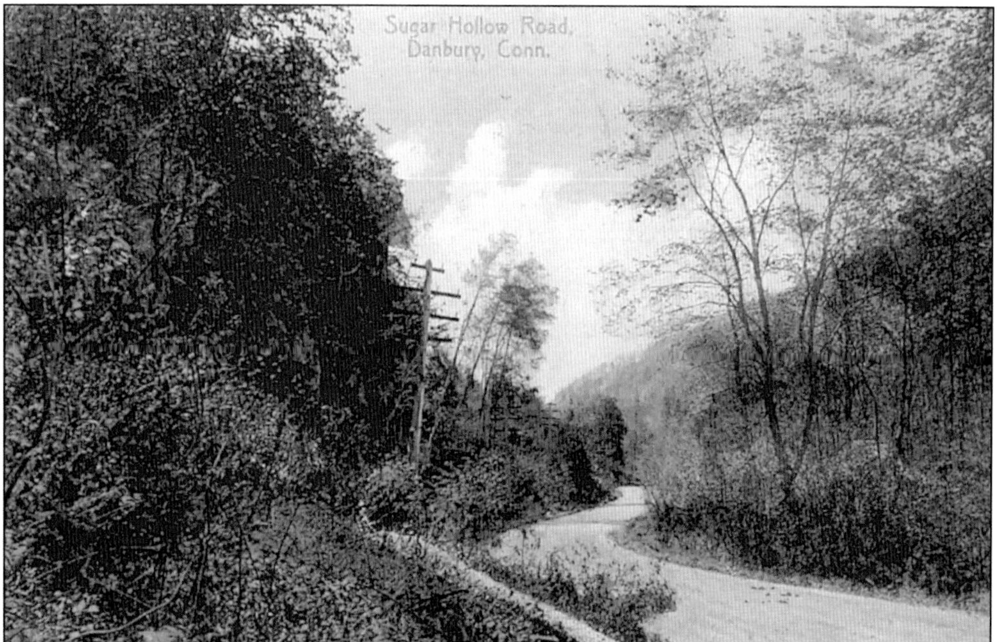

Horses were still the method of travel in 1908 when this card was sent. One legend about the name Sugar Hollow says that a group of teamsters, transporting barrels of molasses, had their wagons mired along this stretch and had to leave the molasses in order to get the wagons out.

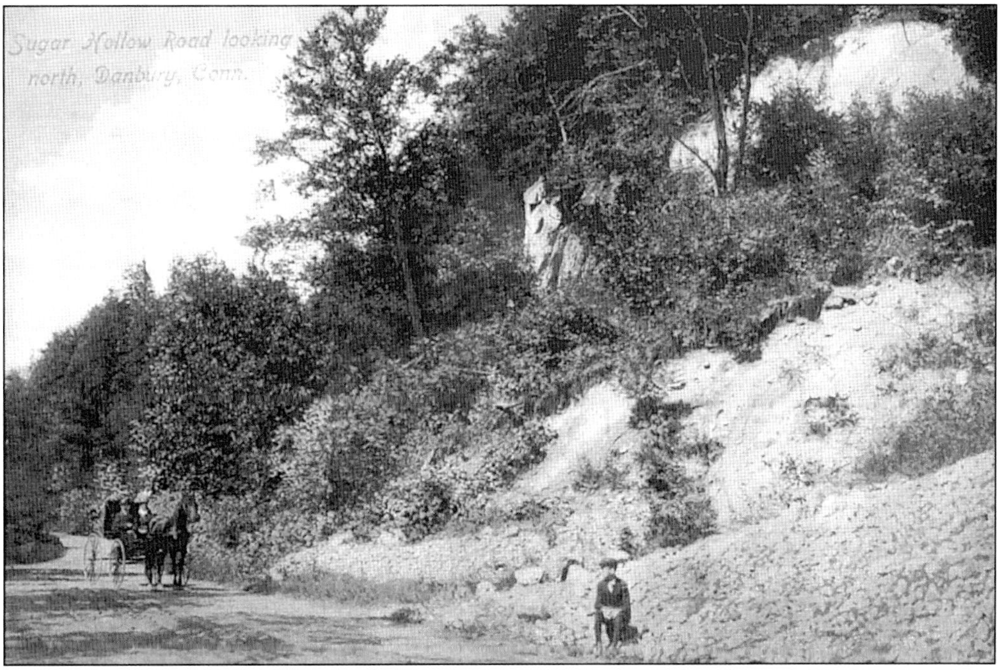

Another legend about the origin of the name says that early settlers had to collect honey from wild bees in the early days. This view of the area is from 1909.

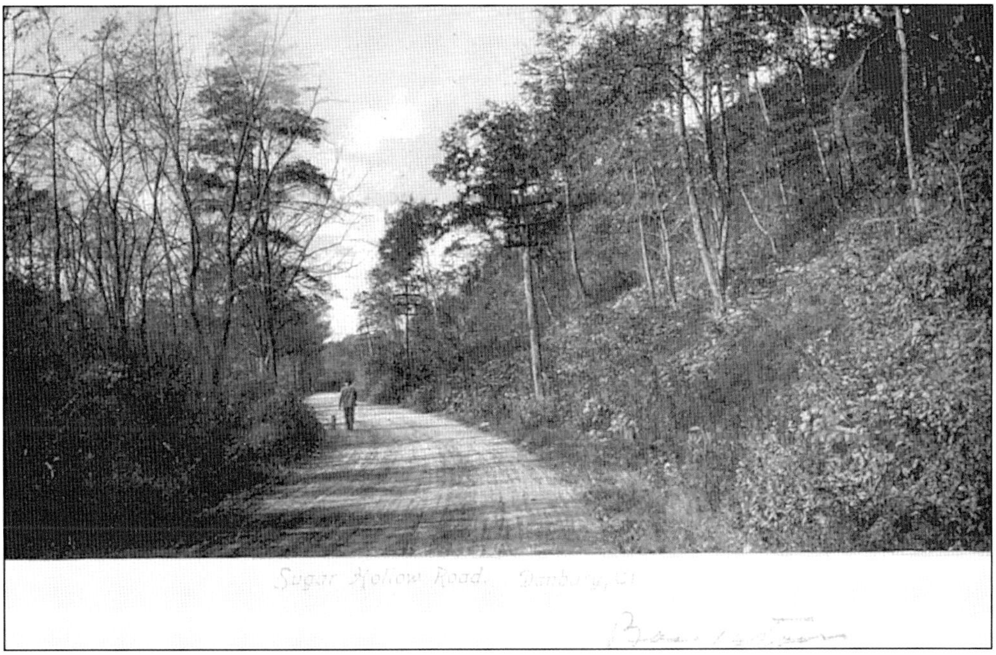

This stretch of road, now just south of Route 84 and the Danbury Fair Mall, appears very isolated in 1912.

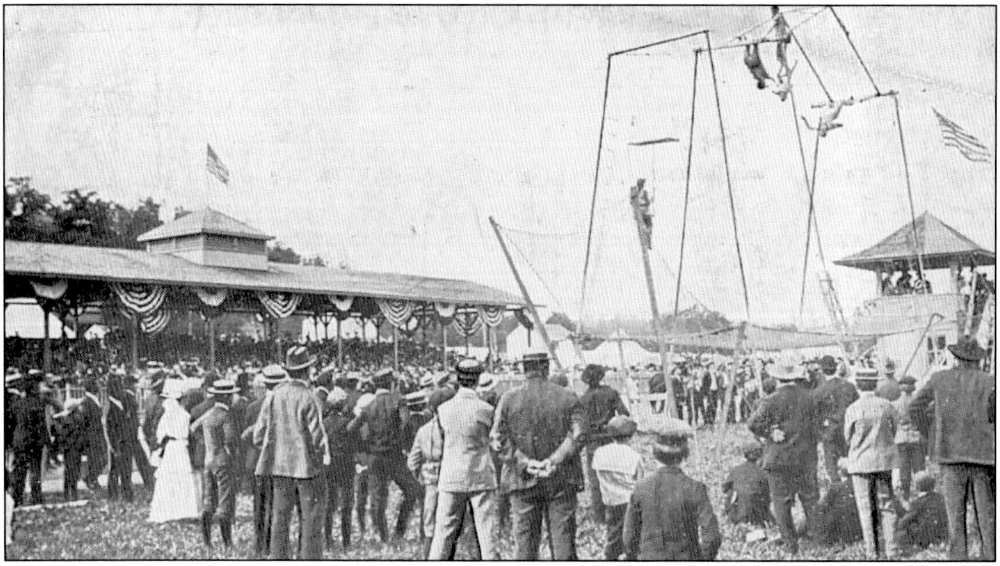

The Danbury Fair brought throngs every autumn to see farm products, watch horse racing, enjoy carnival rides, and experience the food. Later, stock car racing was an added attraction.

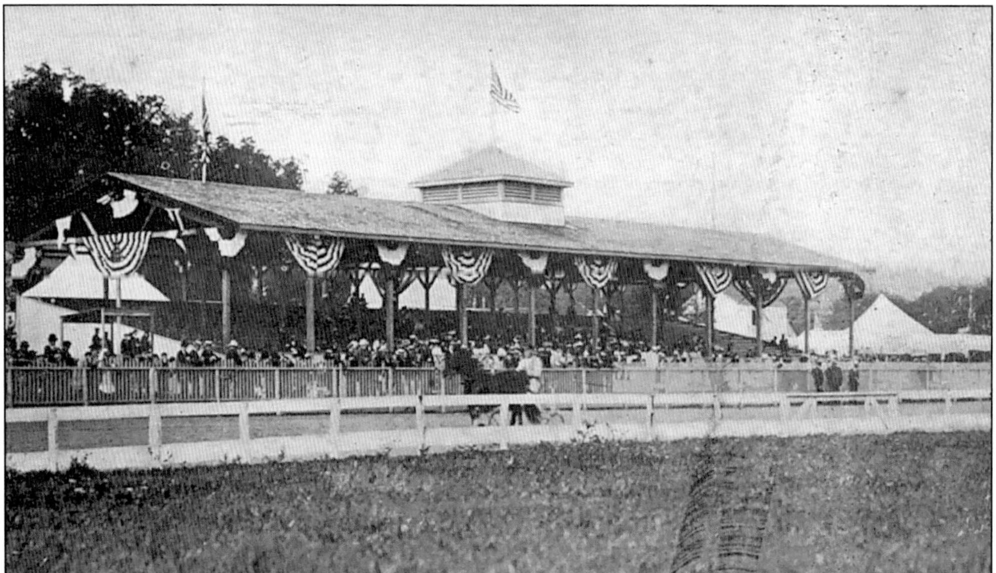

Grand Stand, Danbury Fair.

The grandstand at the fair overlooked many races, exhibits, and happy crowds before John Leahy's death brought it all to a close in 1981.

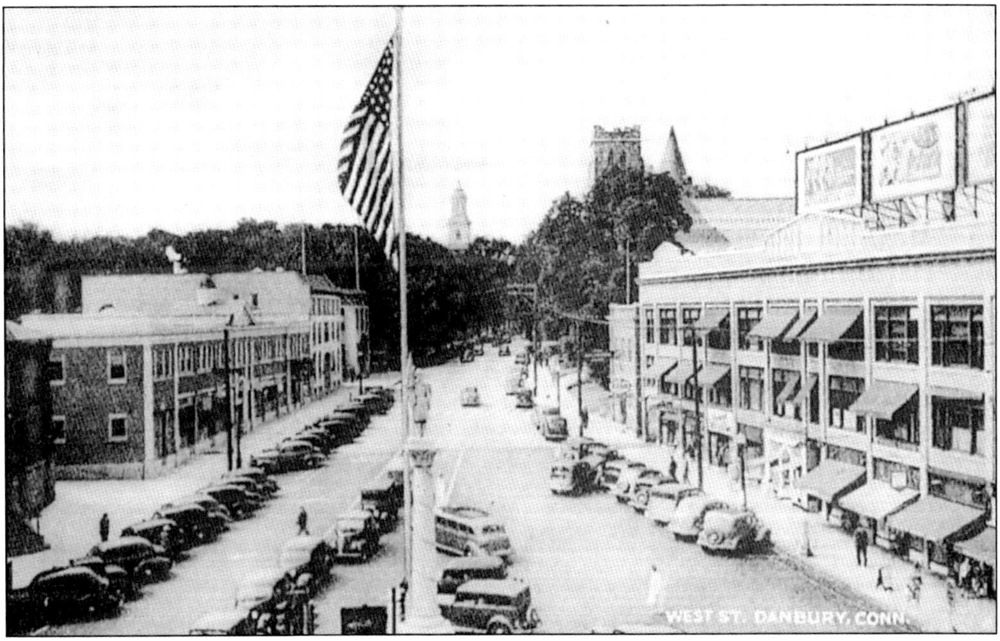

West Street in early days was referred to as "up the lane" from "Towne Street" or Main. Route 7 originally followed West Street and then turned onto Main.

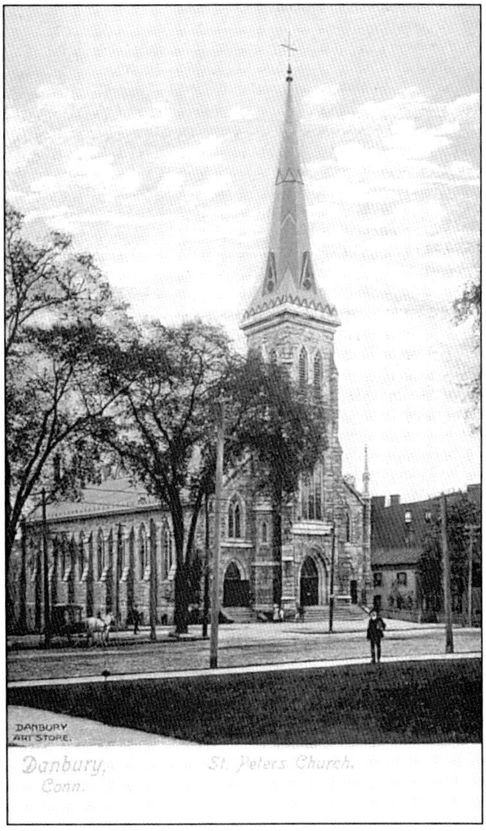

St. Peter's Church, built between 1869 and 1875 on Elmwood Park, served as the focal point of the Irish community in Danbury.

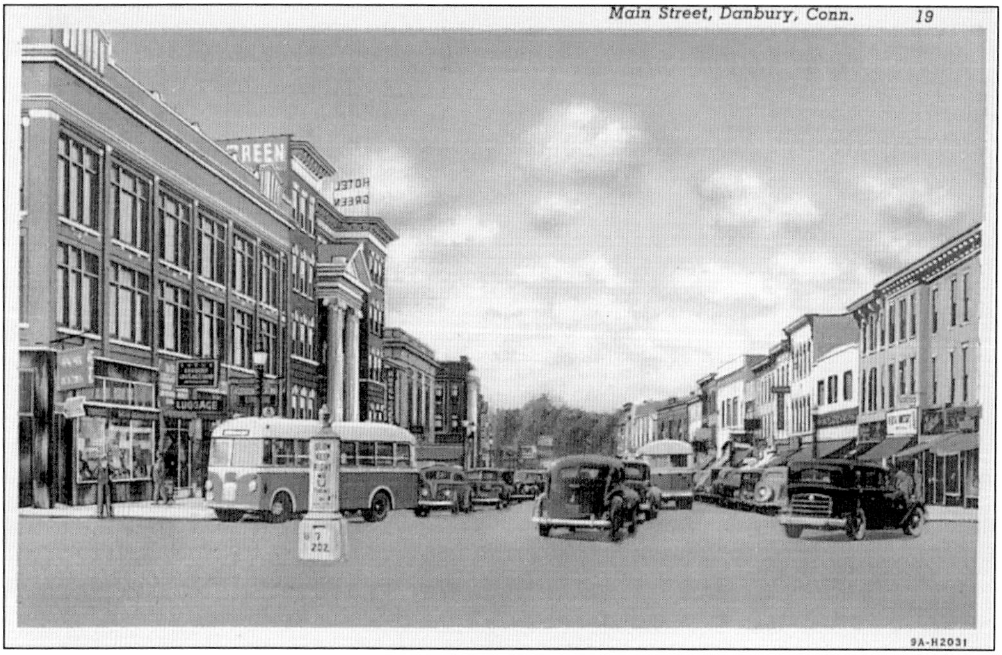

Virginia sent this card of Main Street in Danbury to her folks on a bike trip from Wilton to Bridgewater in 1943. Notice the Route 7 and Route 202 designation on the monument.

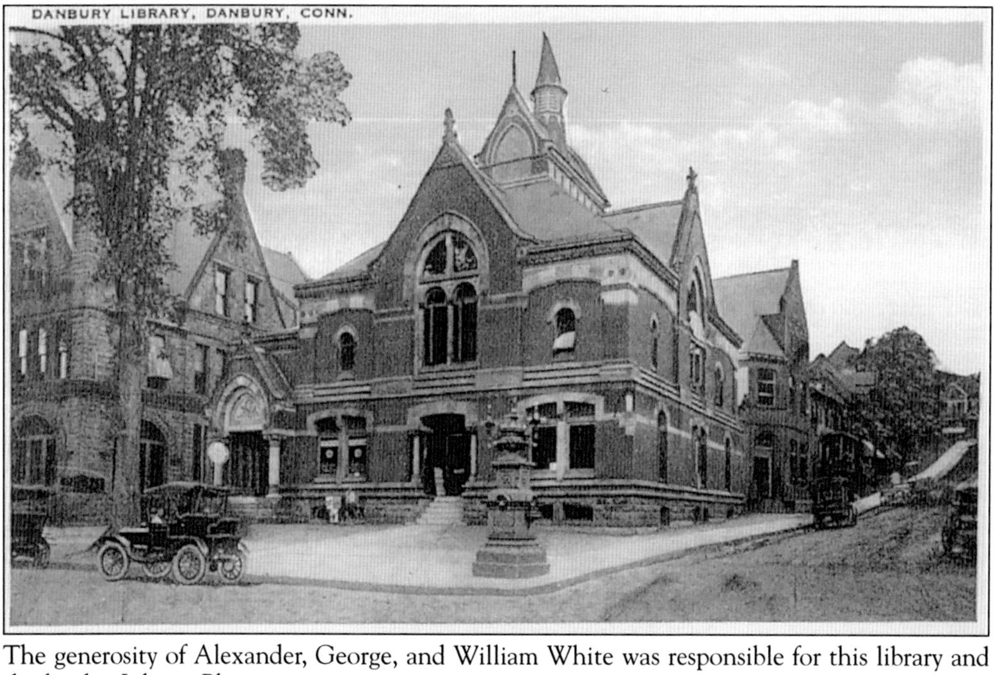

The generosity of Alexander, George, and William White was responsible for this library and the land at Library Place.

Originally a two-story building located at 288 Main, this structure had a third story and round tower added. For many years, it was known as the News-Times Building. It is now the office of DaSilva and Sons, a real estate and investment company.

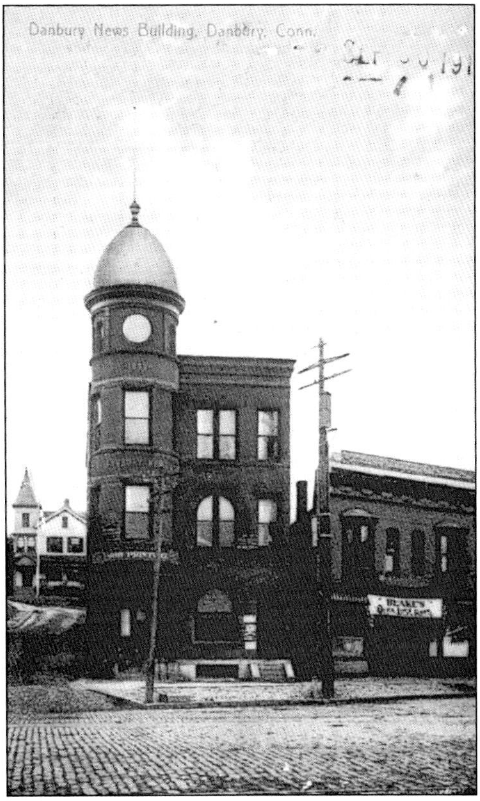

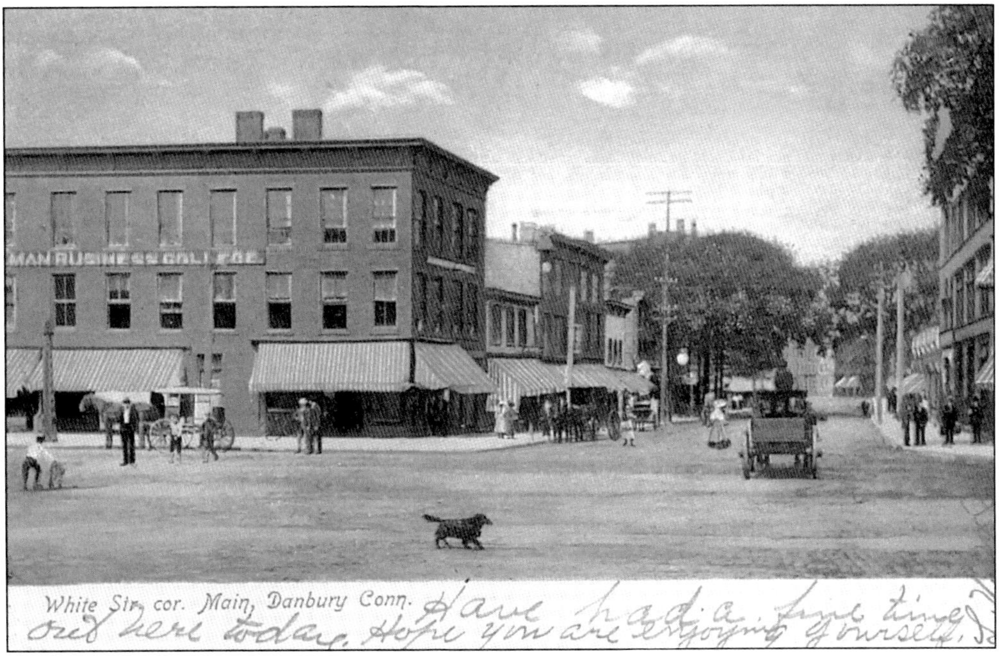

The year 1907 saw an uncrowded Main and White Streets. It appears somewhat like a park, with stores sprouting their summer awnings and Stillman's Business College shaded against the summer heat.

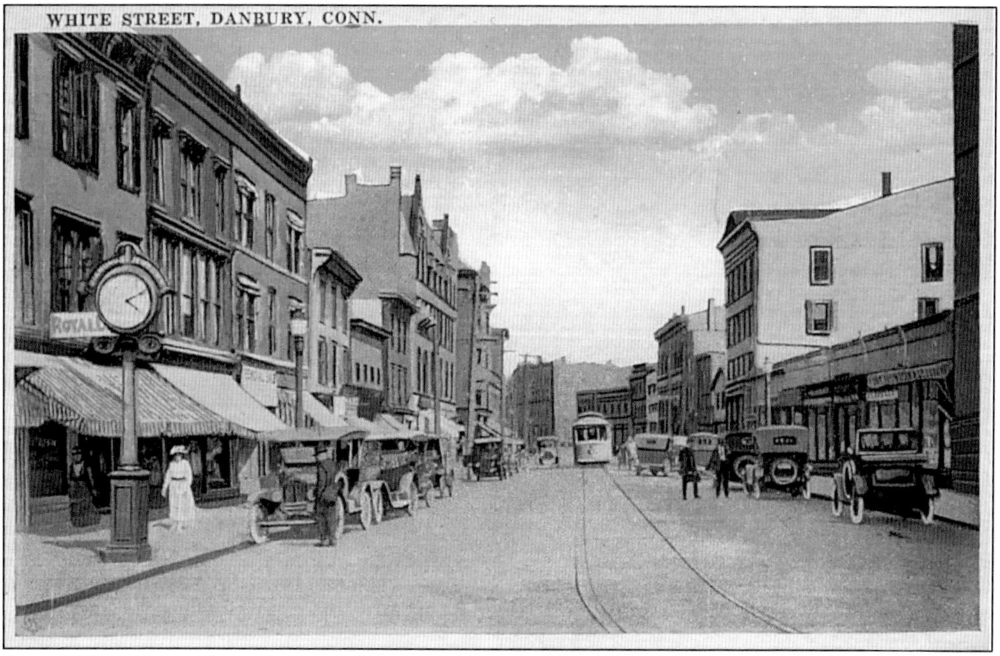

Here White Street, later Route 7, heads north toward Brookfield.

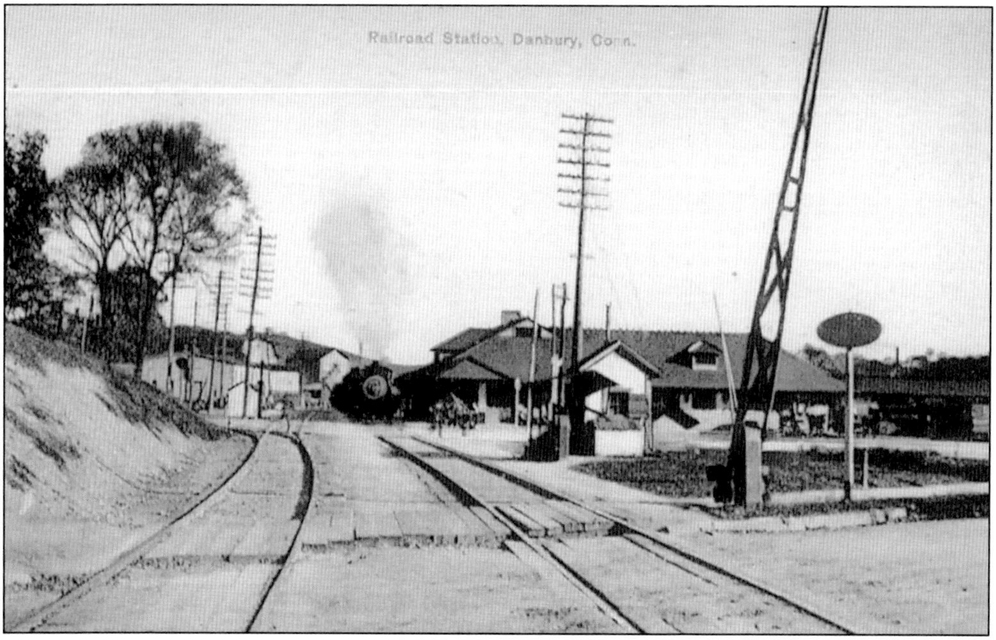

The railroad station is shown here viewed from across White Street.

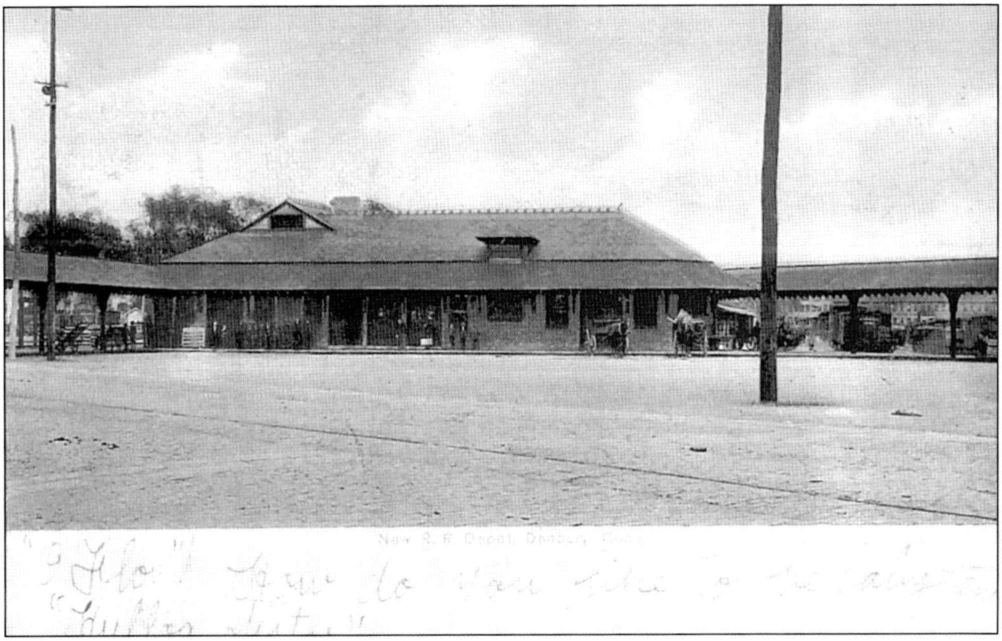

The "new railroad station" on White Street was built about 1901. It is now the Danbury Railway Museum.

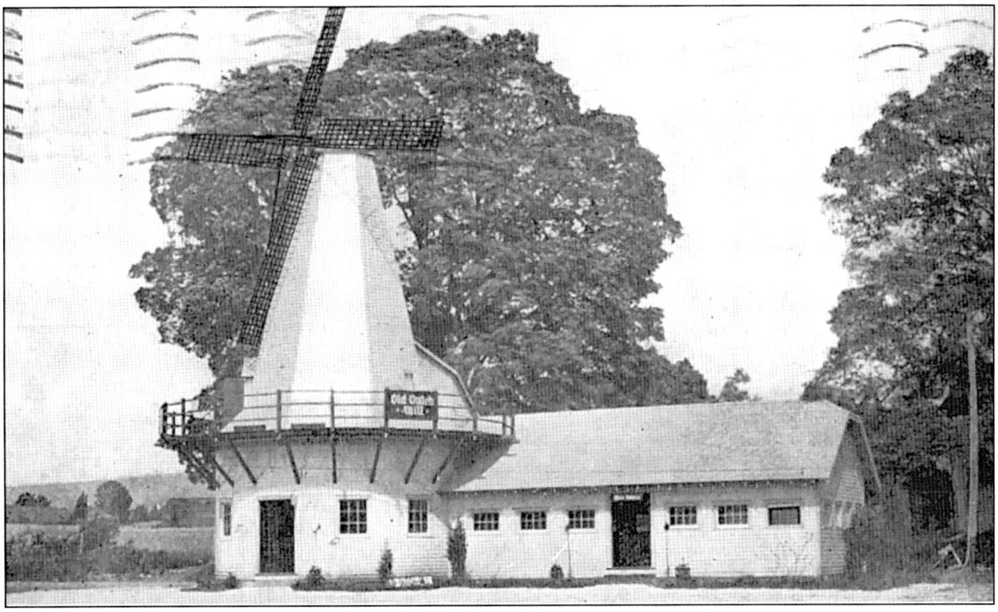

The Old Dutch Mill was a quaint Dutch tea room in 1930. The card says it is on the Housatonic River Highway. Schaghticoke Trail and US. Route 7 are other names for this popular highway.

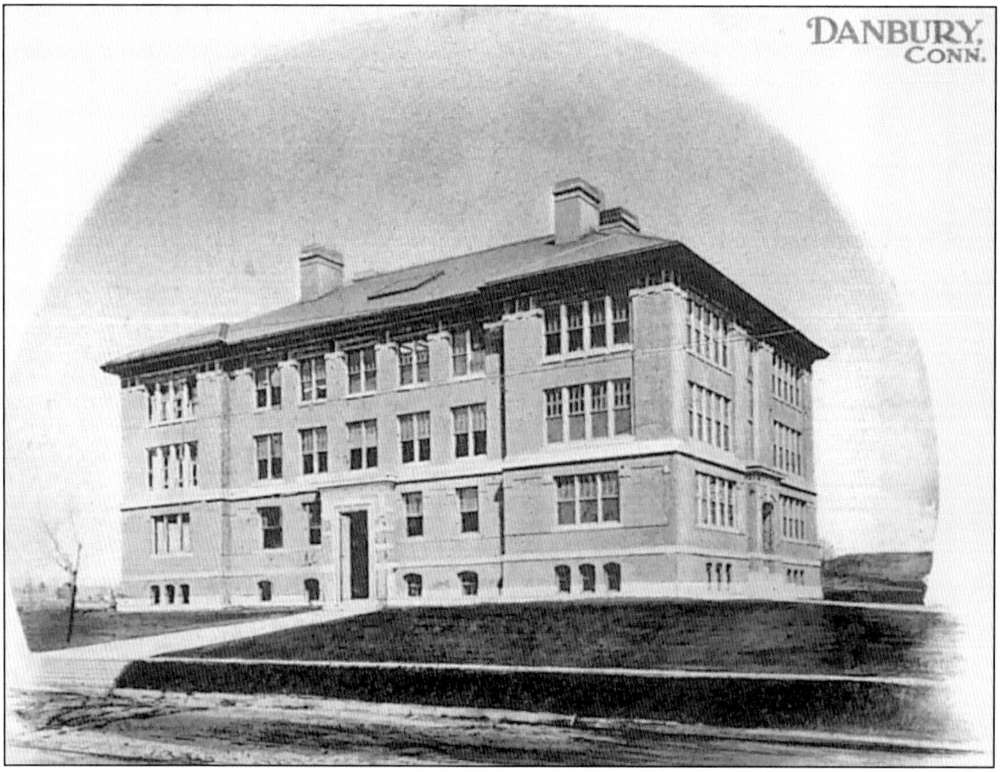

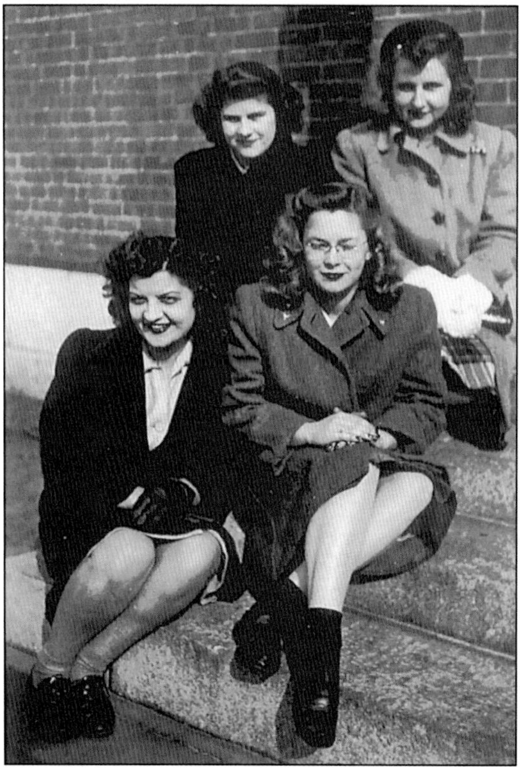

Here is the Old Main Building of the Normal School, which grew through several stages to Western Connecticut University.

These 1940s female students attended the school when it was Danbury State Teachers College. Included are the following, from left to right: Phyliss Ancona (DeStefano), Beverly Tarloff (Nuss), Virginia Bradley (Bepler), and Frances Hollick (Bigham).

Five

BROOKFIELD

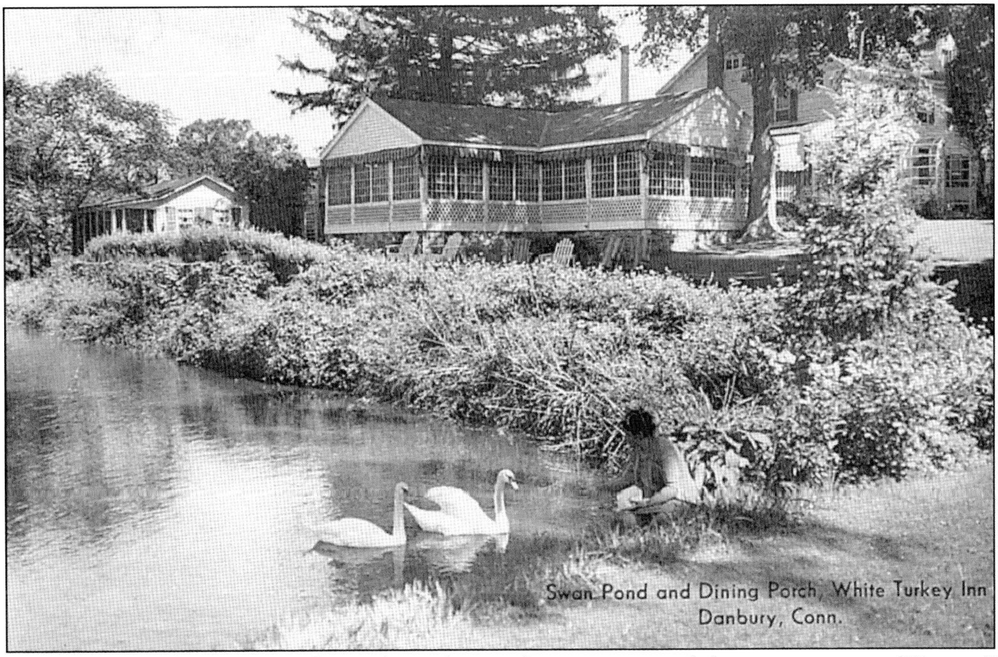

The White Turkey Inn was located on the southwest corner of the intersection of Route 7 and Candlewood Lake Road. It was demolished in 1972. It was replaced by a large block of stores currently called Candlewood Lake Plaza, which houses T.J. Maxx and Office Max, among others.

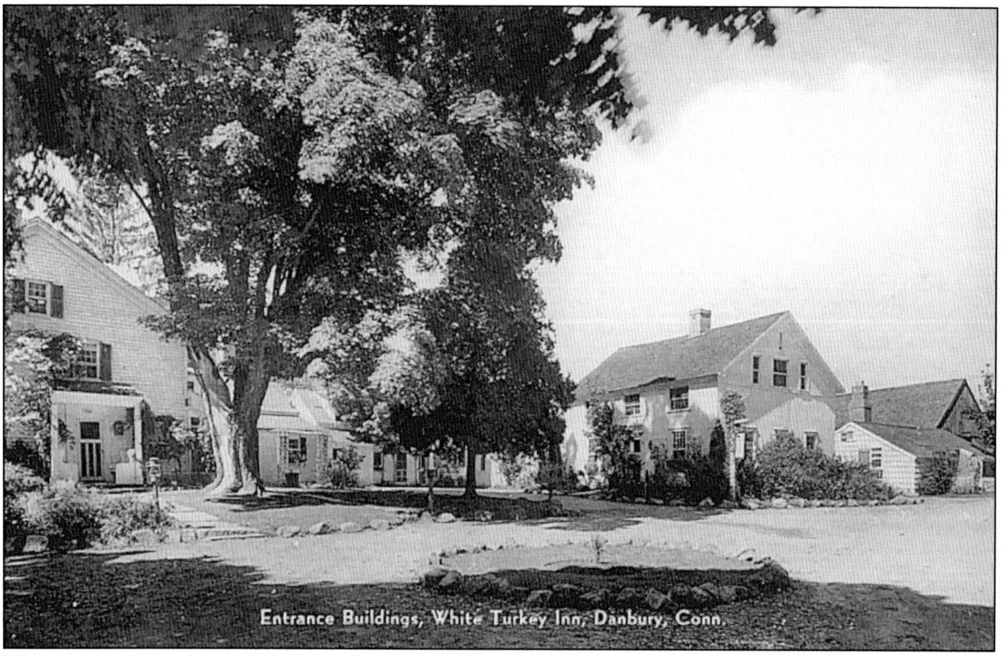

The original farmhouse of the White Turkey was built in 1760 by John Gregory Sr. It became an inn in 1905.

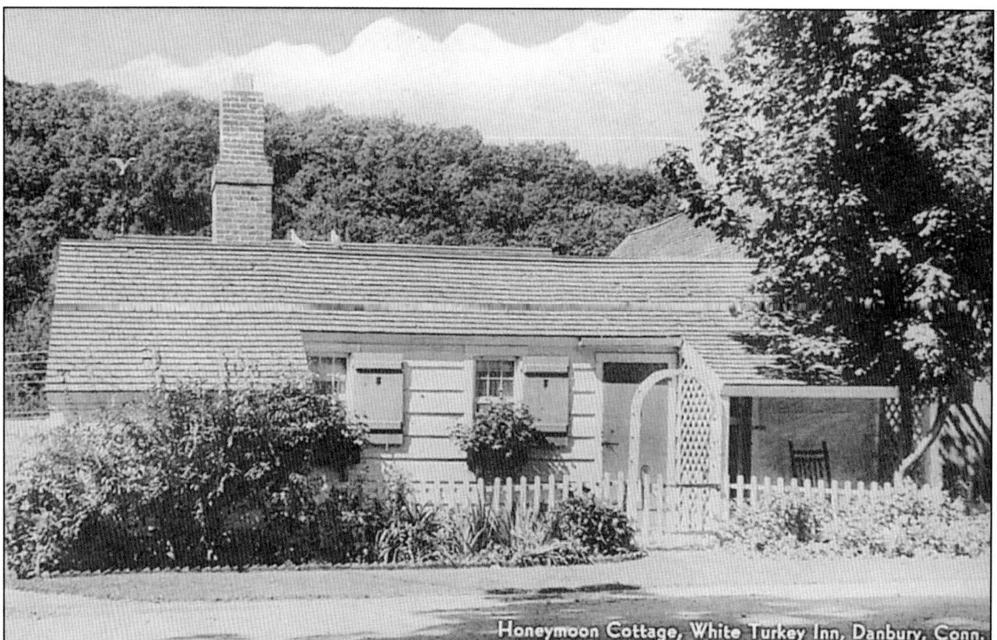

The popular "Honeymoon Cottage" was created from an old woodshed. The entire property included 150 acres.

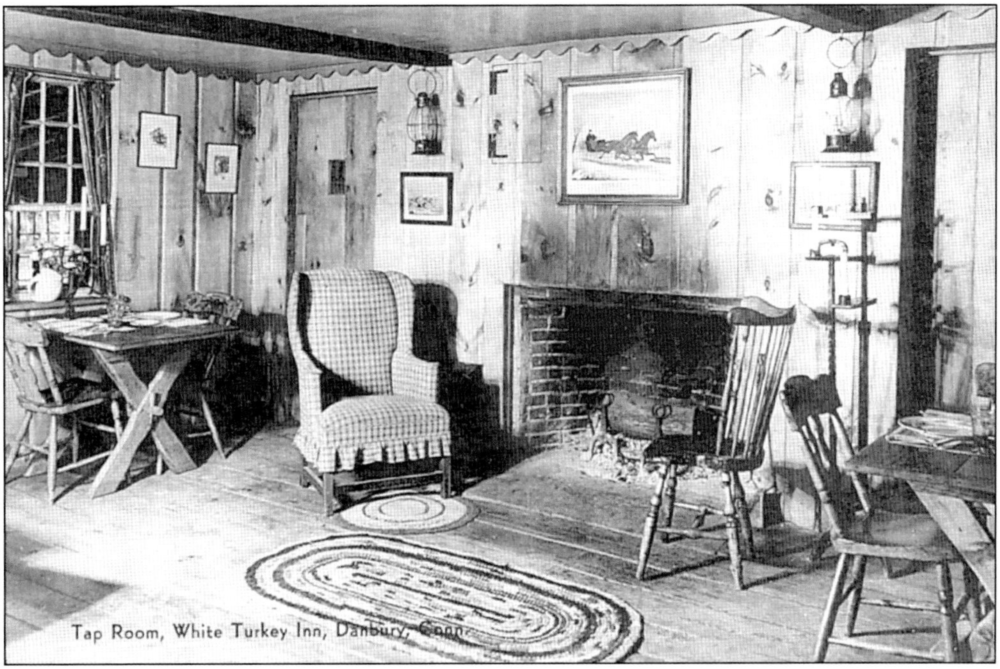

Harry and Dorothy Davegas were the second owners of the White Turkey Inn. They purchased it in 1935 from the Morgan family. The Davegas also operated the White Turkey Townhouses and three White Turkey restaurants, all in New York City.

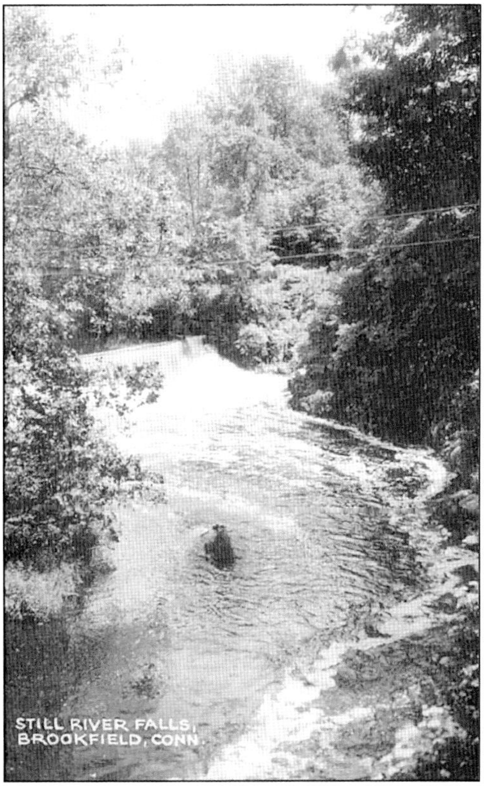

The Still River flows through the entire length of the town and is located between Route 7 and the railroad tracks.

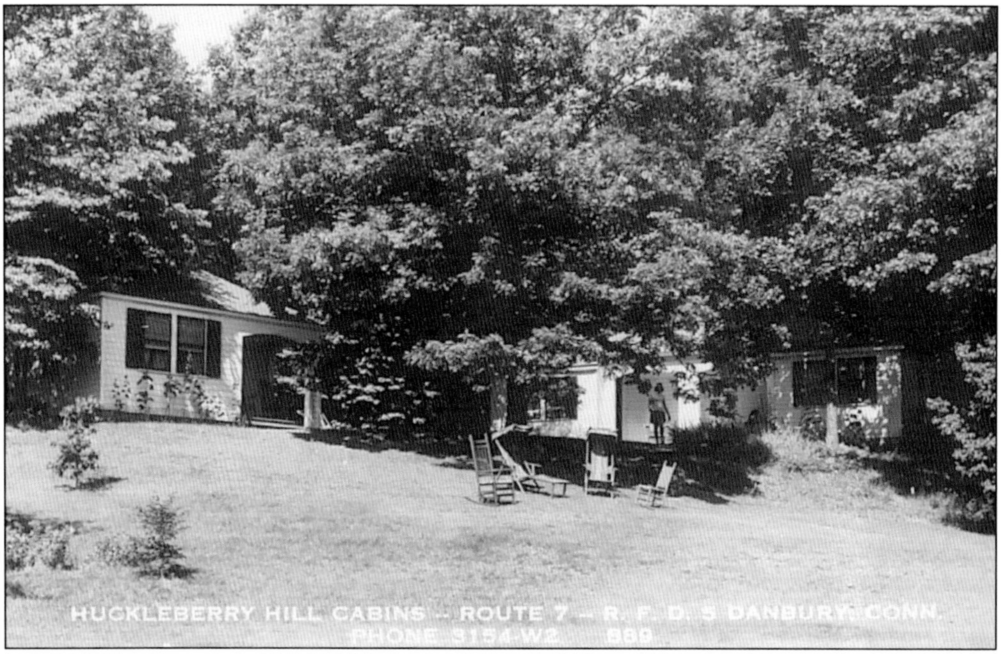

Breakfast was served at the Huckleberry Hill Cabins. They were identified as being "four miles north of Danbury."

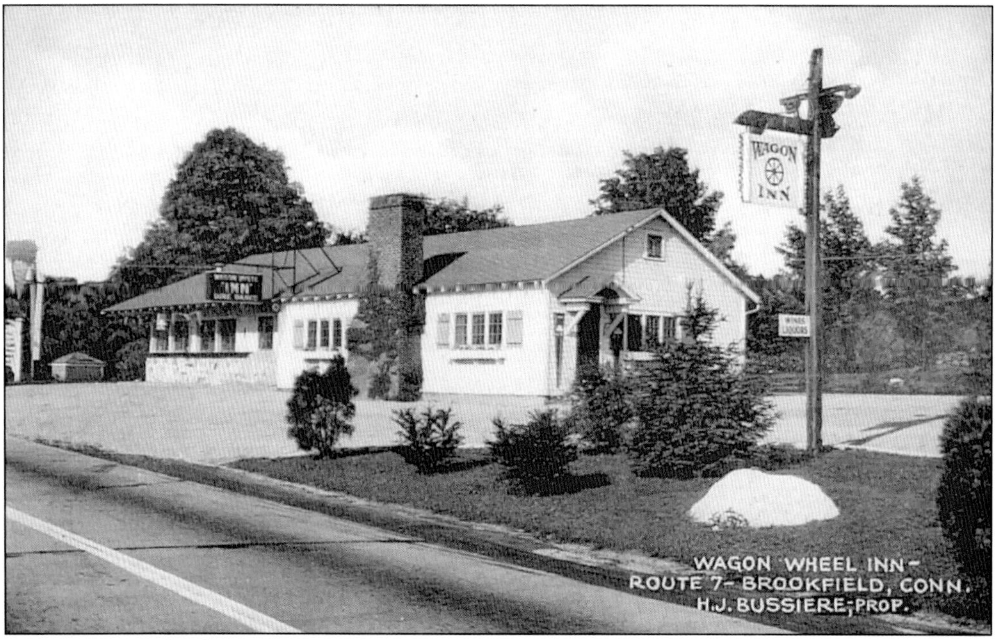

The Wagon Wheel Inn exists today as Rosalia's Ristorante and Pizzeria, on the west side of Route 7. This is at the corner of Old New Milford Road, an older leg of the main road.

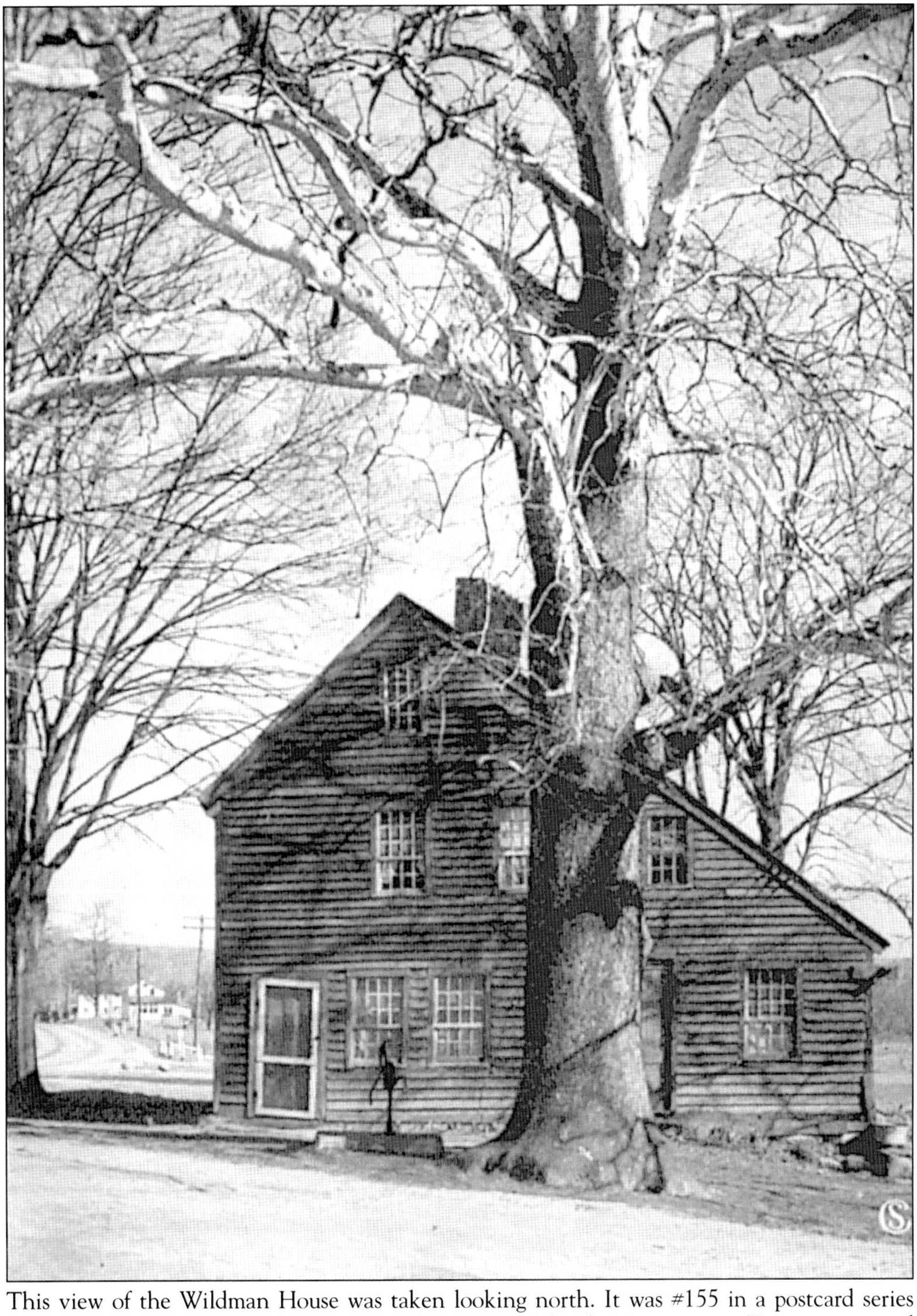

This view of the Wildman House was taken looking north. It was #155 in a postcard series entitled the American Scene, which was done in 1935 for the Connecticut Tercentenary and copyrighted by Samuel Chamberlain. The house, built in 1750, stood on the southeast corner of Junction Road (Route 133) and was replaced by the First Assembly of God Church. The sycamore tree still stands.

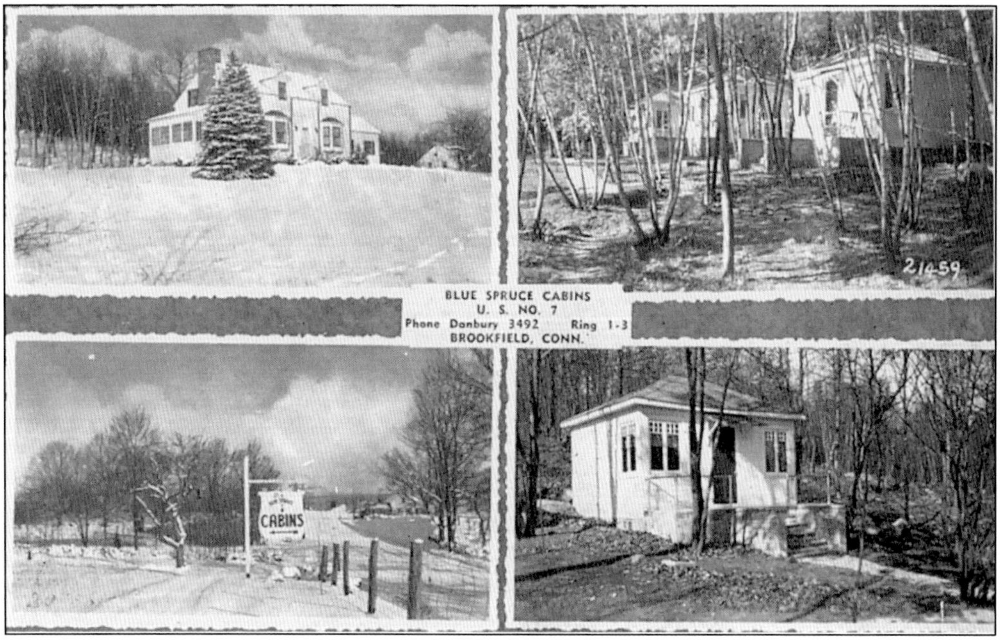

In 1942, the Blue Spruce Cabins, operated by W.C. Mulrein, offered "all modern improvements" and "a six minute drive to Candlewood Lake." The back of this postcard included directions to the cabins from New York City and Long Island.

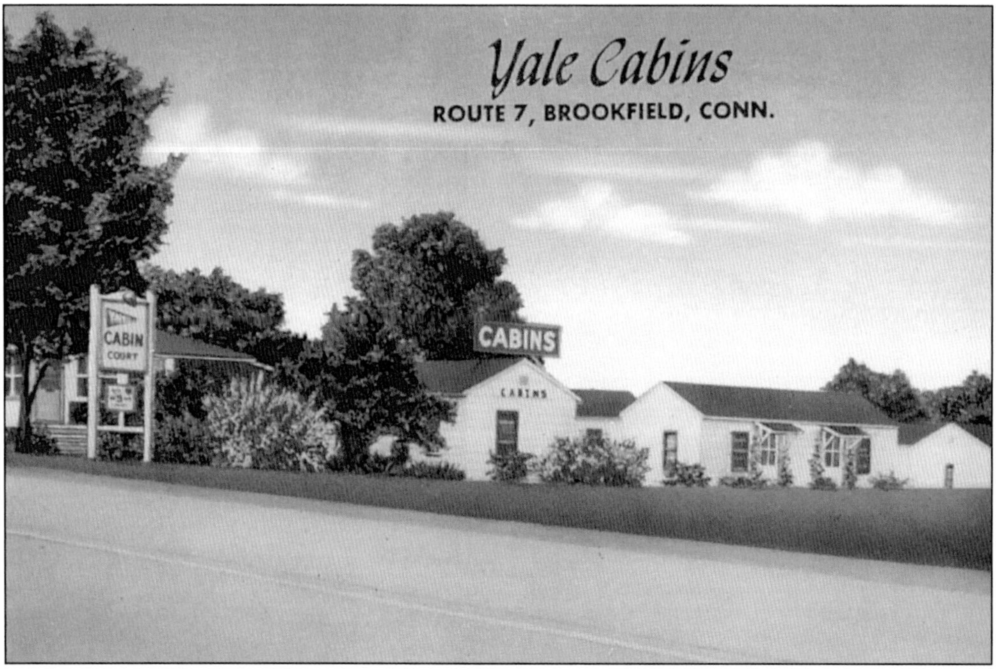

The Yale Cabins were located "five miles north of Danbury" and also "near Candlewood Lake." They had spacious lawns and were available by the night, week, or month.

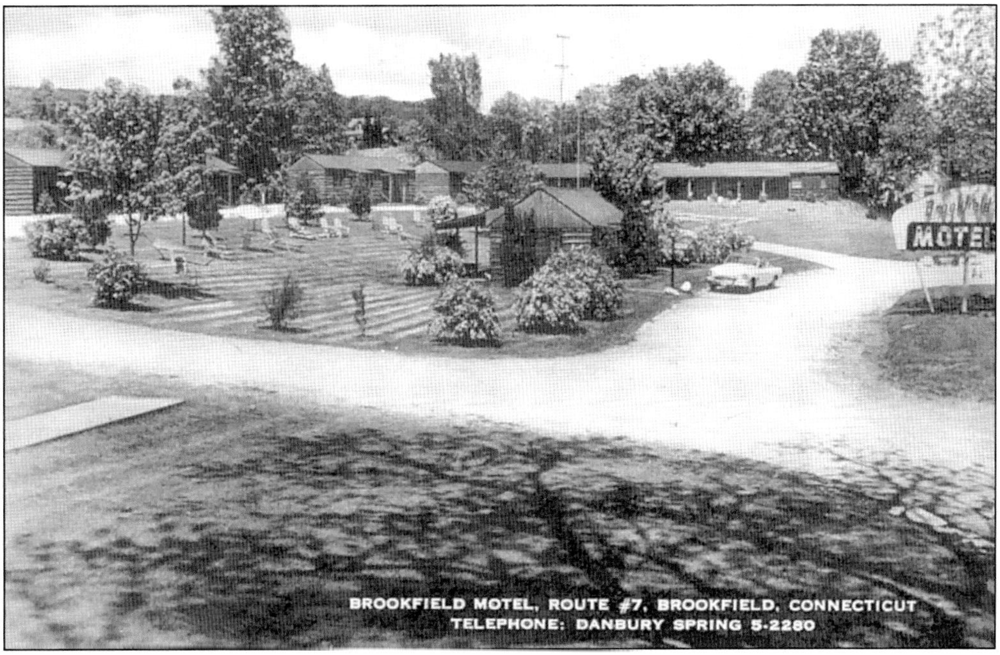

The Brookfield Motel and Cabins is yet another of the unusually large number of cabins once located in the town of Brookfield.

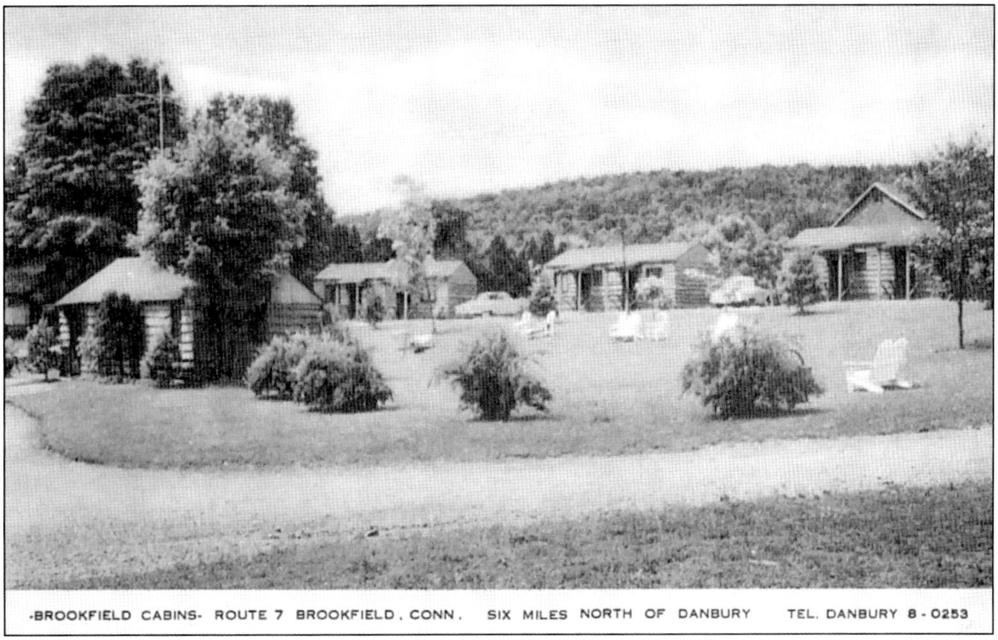

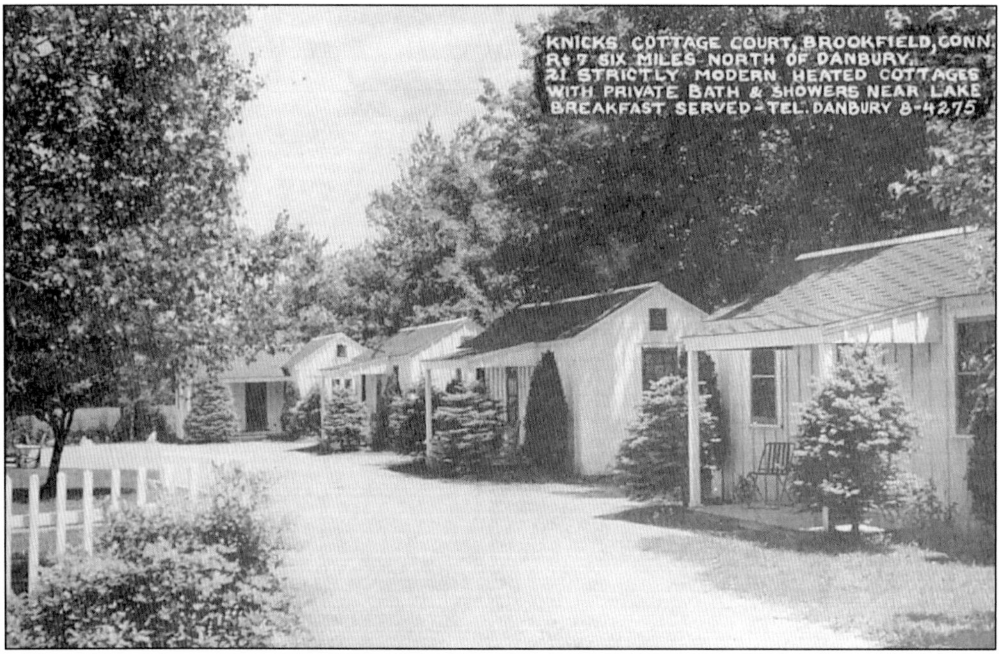

Currently for sale and in a dilapidated state, what is left of Knick's Cottage Court is located on the east side of old Route 7 (now Route 202), before Silvermine Road. The buildings were well maintained in this 1951 postcard.

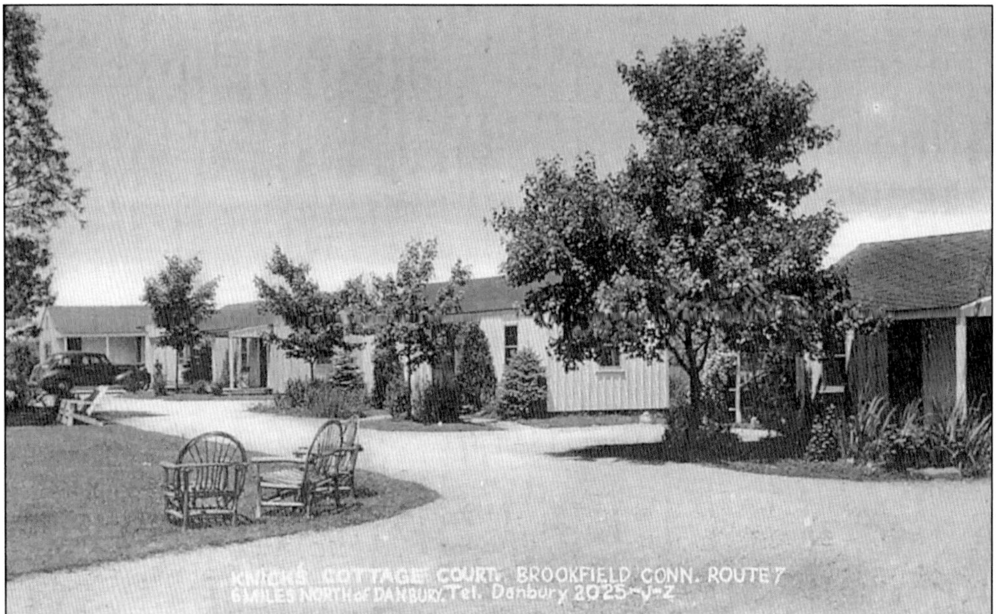

Knick's Motel continued in business longer than most roadside cabins in Brookfield. Originally, there were 21 cabins. Most recently, the cabins were rented on a long-term basis, operating as the Brookfield Motor Lodge.

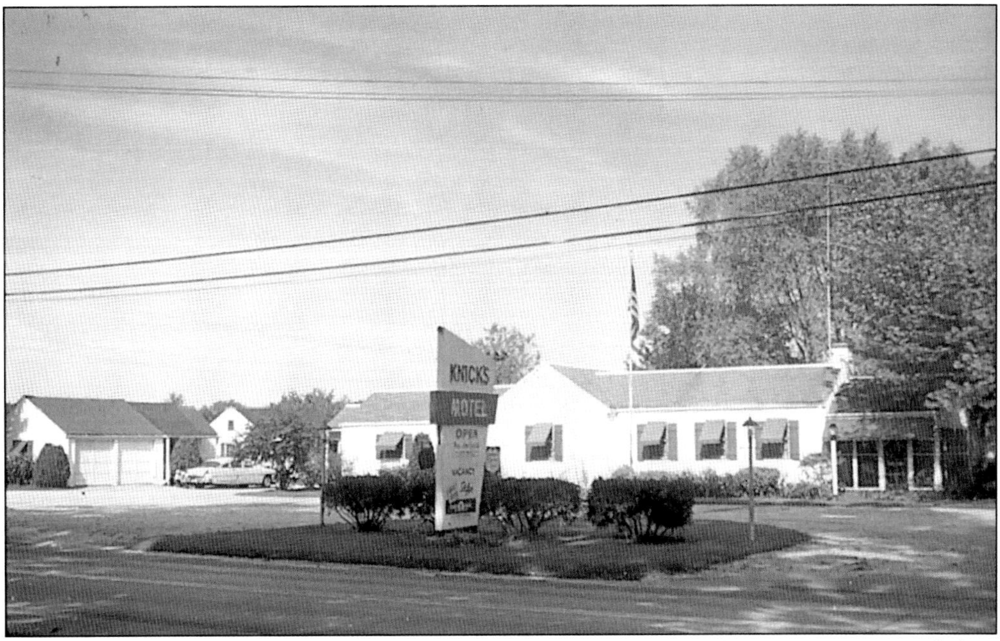

Knick's Motel was at one time owned by William and Mary Budd. It was recommended to travelers by Duncan Hines and boasted "individually controlled heat, showers, TV, and a lounge."

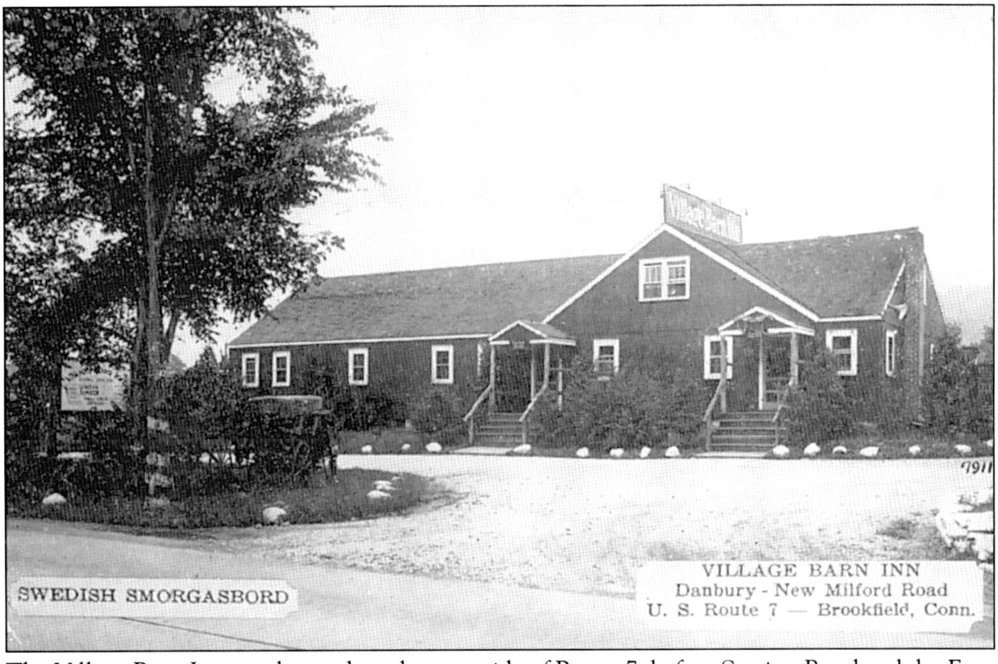

The Village Barn Inn was located on the west side of Route 7, before Station Road and the Four Corners. The Wilton Bulletin included advertisements for its smorgasbord in the early 1940s.

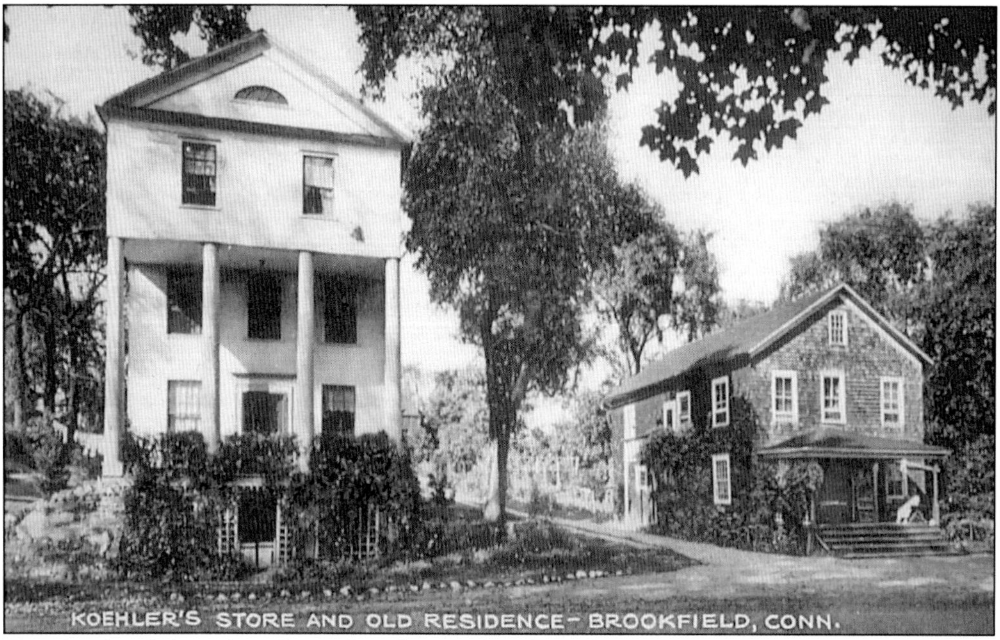

Travelers headed north on Route 7 and stopped at the red light at the Four Corners (intersection of Station Road) should look to the right. Just inside Station Road is the building (street number 283) that was formerly Koehler's Store and residence. Before that, it was a blacksmith shop.

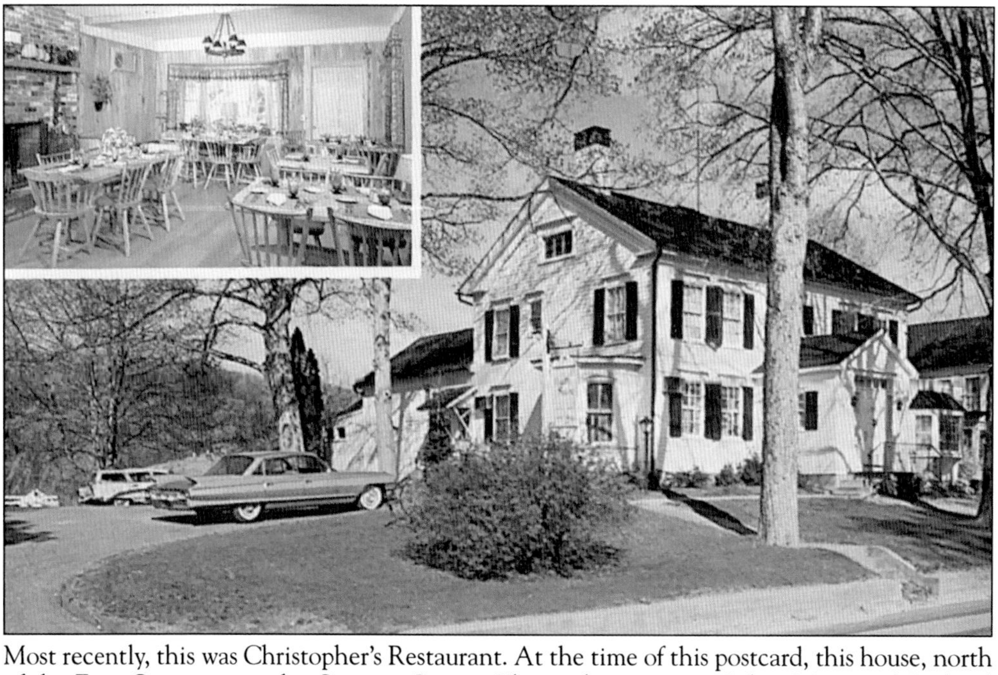

Most recently, this was Christopher's Restaurant. At the time of this postcard, this house, north of the Four Corners, was the Country Squire. The innkeepers were John, Mary, and Richard Ciccarone. The Country Squire, billed as an early American inn, had four dining rooms, one of which was furnished with Hunt Country Furniture from nearby Wingdale, New York. The card was published by Fred's Studio at 60 Sugar Hollow Road (Route 7) in Danbury.

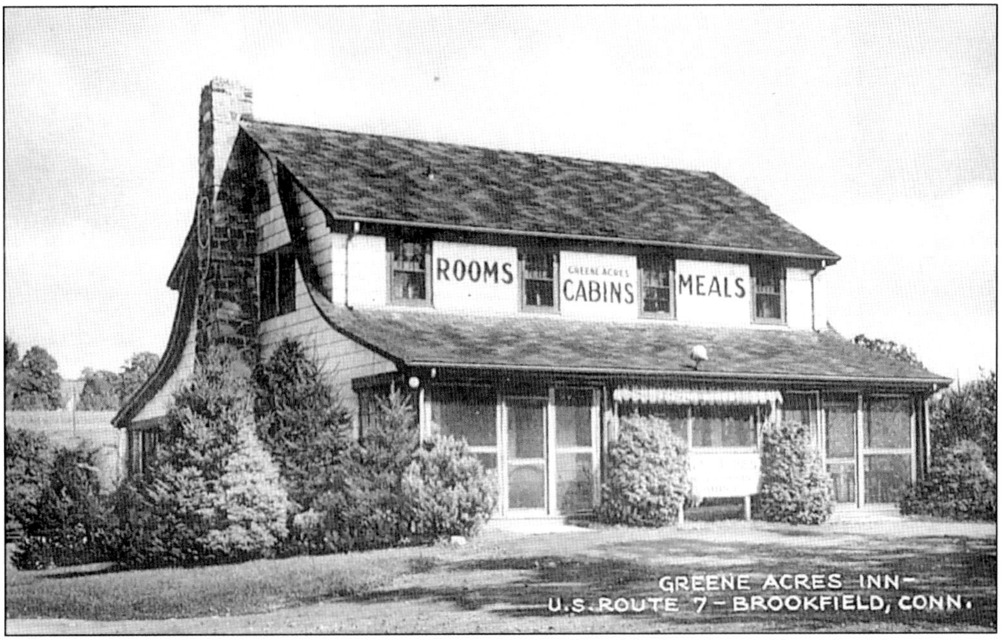

Today, the lawn of Green Acres Inn (857 Federal Road) is filled with small out-buildings, wares of the Barn Yard. A close look reveals that several cabins are still standing, mostly hidden at the rear of the property. Built in the early 1930s, Green Acres Inn was still a going concern in the 1960s, when weekend drives north on Route 7 were popular.

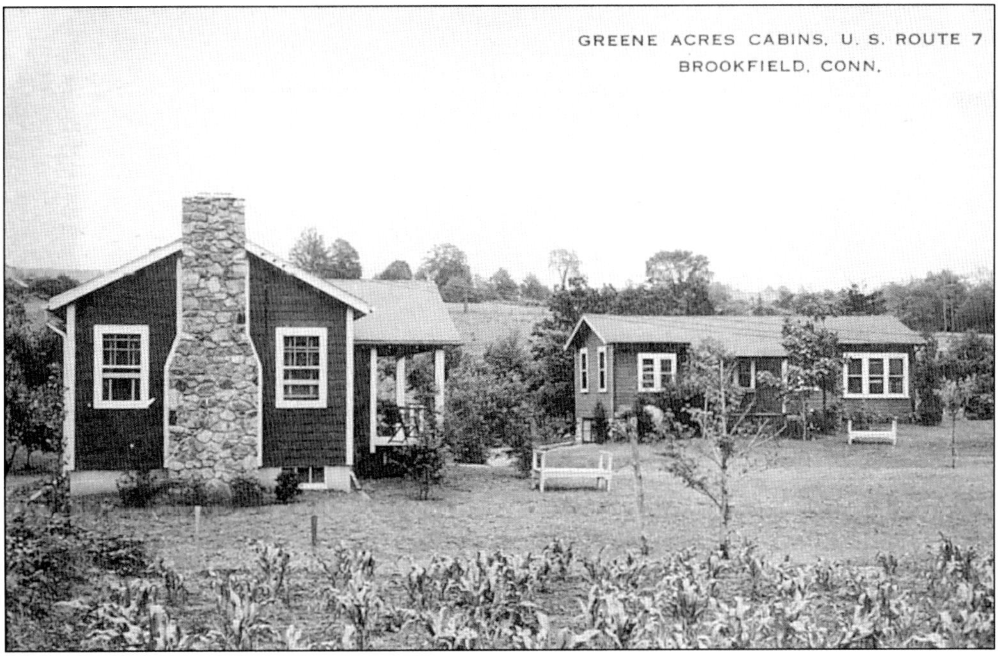

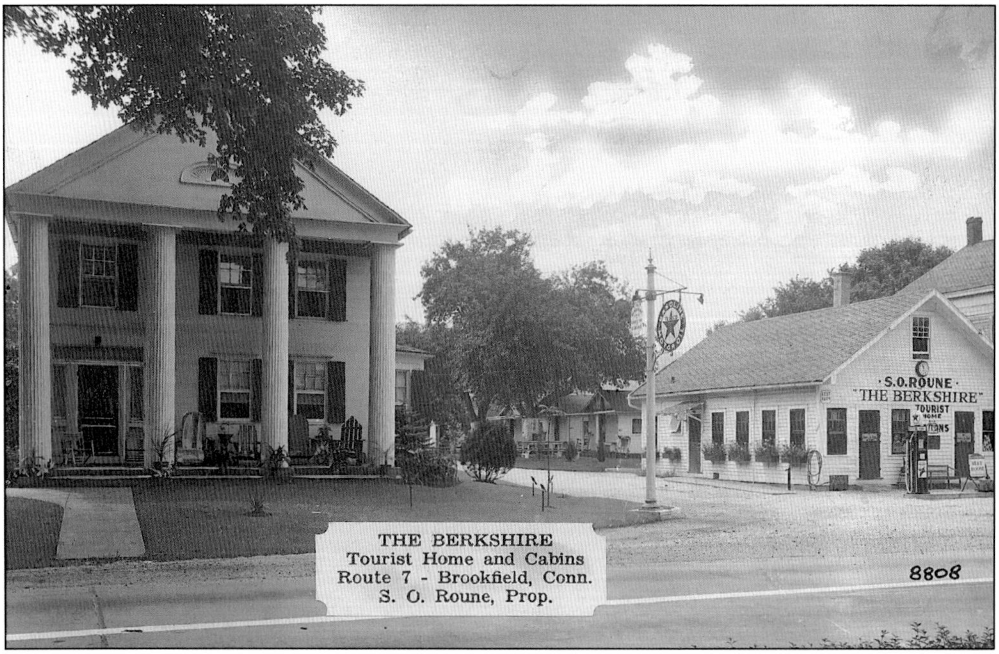

Cabins lined up behind the building on the right, which is now the Village Liquor Shoppe. Only two cabins remain as residences. The house on the left was built in 1825 by Henry Burwell. Called the Pillars, it now houses the law office of Peter B. Buscemi at 846 Federal Road.

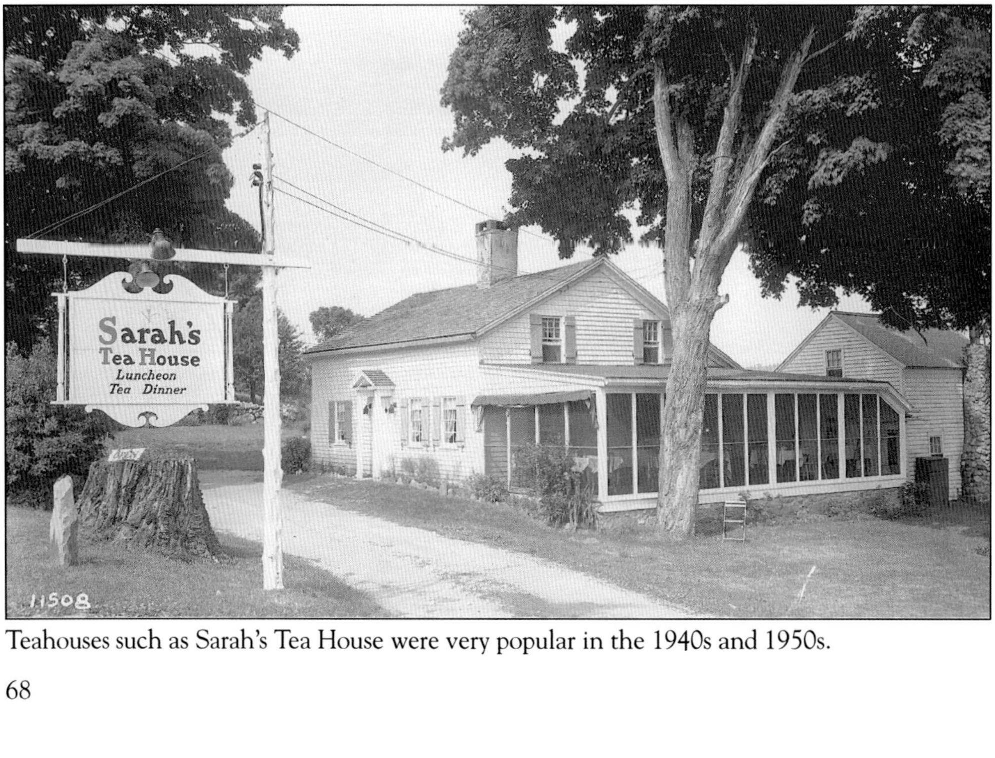

Teahouses such as Sarah's Tea House were very popular in the 1940s and 1950s.

Six

New Milford Including Gaylordsville

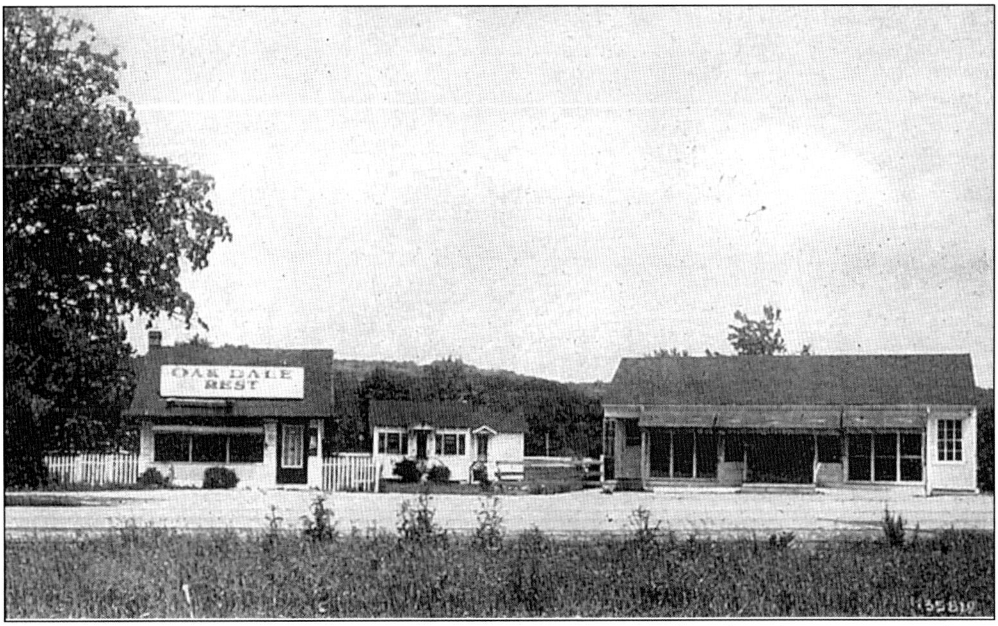

New Milford has been the commercial center for a rural, agricultural, and tourist area. This is why its enterprises, such as the Oakdale Rest with food and cabins, have been such an asset.

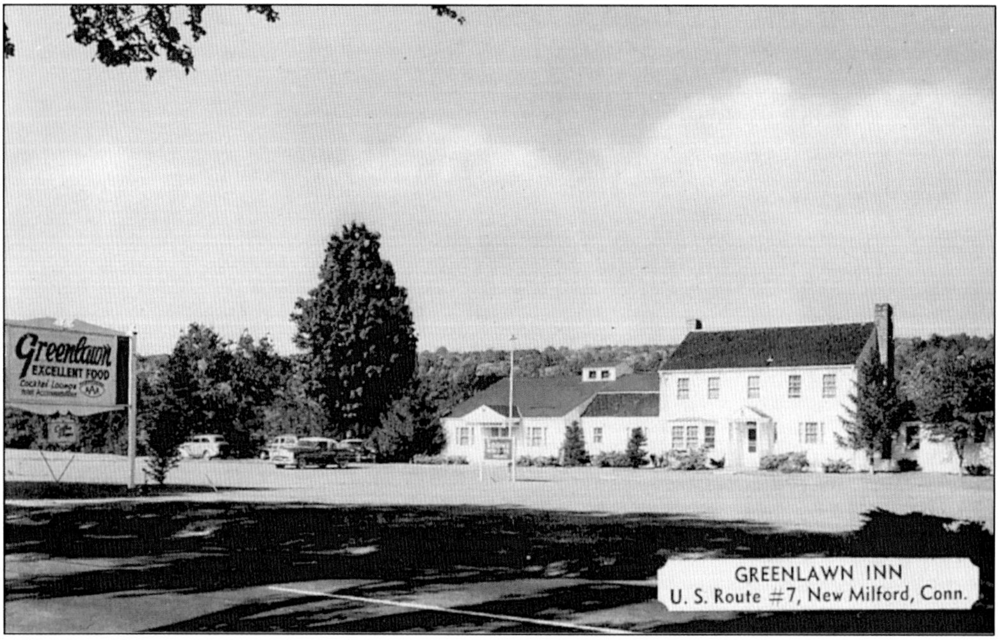

The Greenlawn Inn had three dining rooms, a "mural bar," and guest rooms. Behind it was a 500-foot terrace along the Housatonic River. It now houses the Town and Country Shops, sellers of used furniture and antiques.

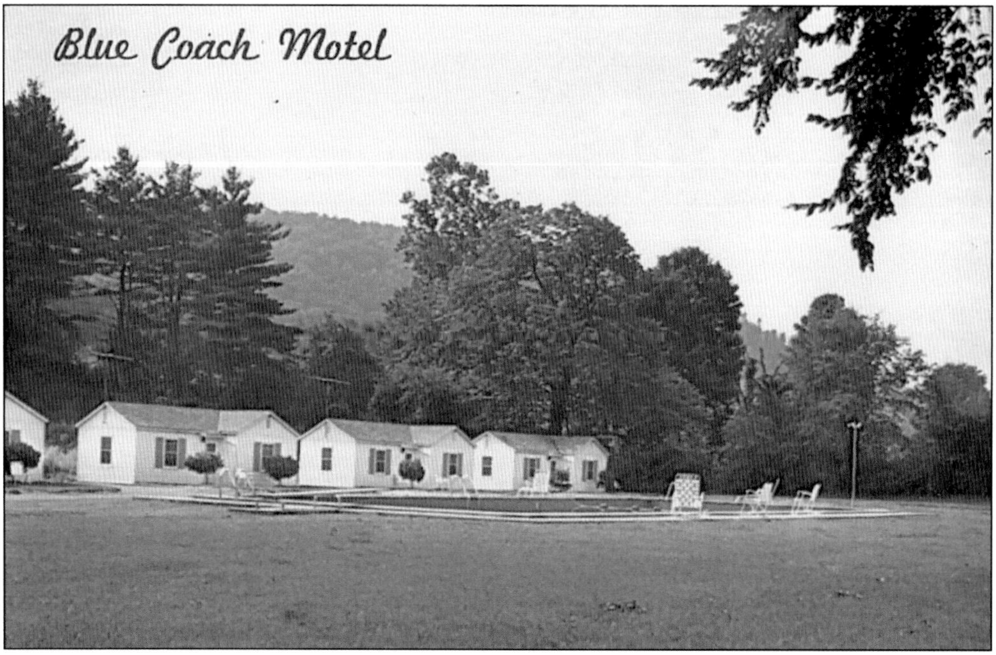

Across the street from the Greenlawn Inn was the Blue Coach Motel. Remnants of the sign show a blue coach, and the large cabins are now long-term rentals. It once had an Olympic-sized pool. This Dexter Press photo was taken by Leonard Bourdette of Danbury.

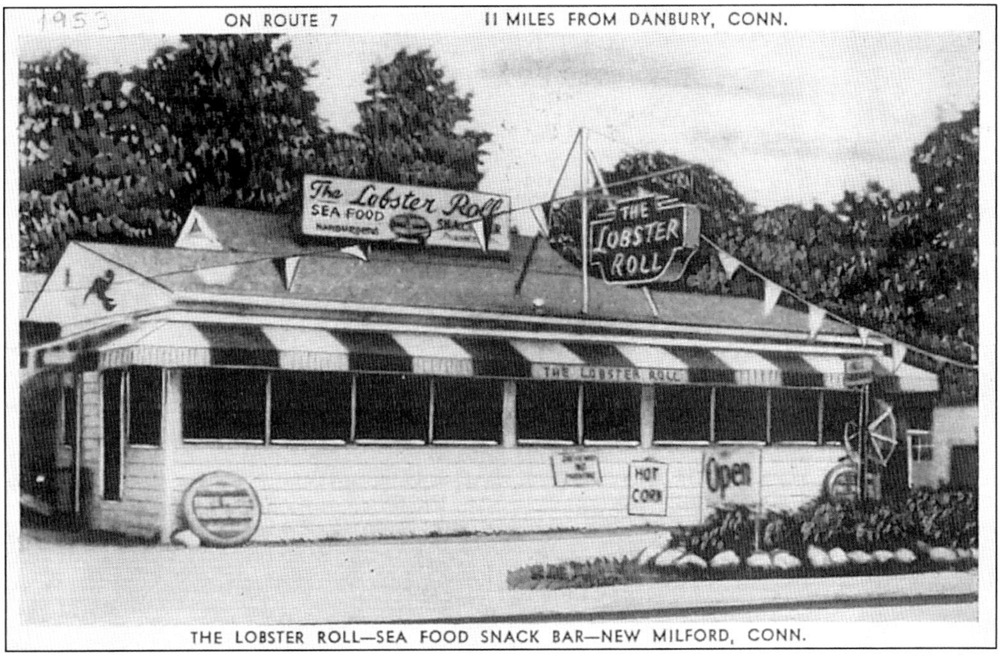

Roadside stands such as the Lobster Roll were once common along Route 7 in New Milford.

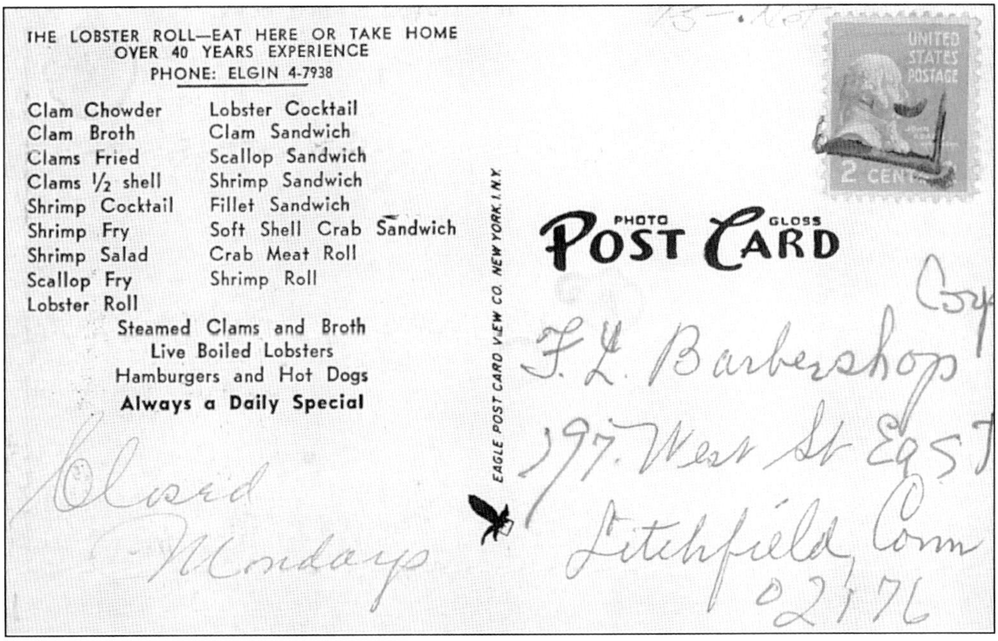

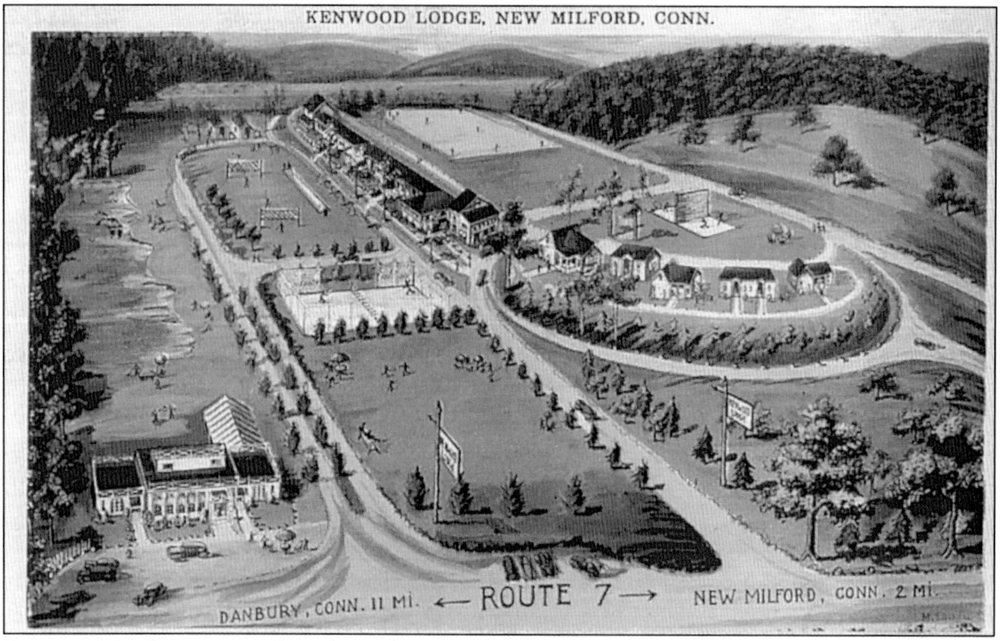

Kenwood Lodge appeared to have been a family vacation site with accommodations and entertainment for all ages. It must have been located somewhere between lower Sunny Valley Road and Sullivan Road.

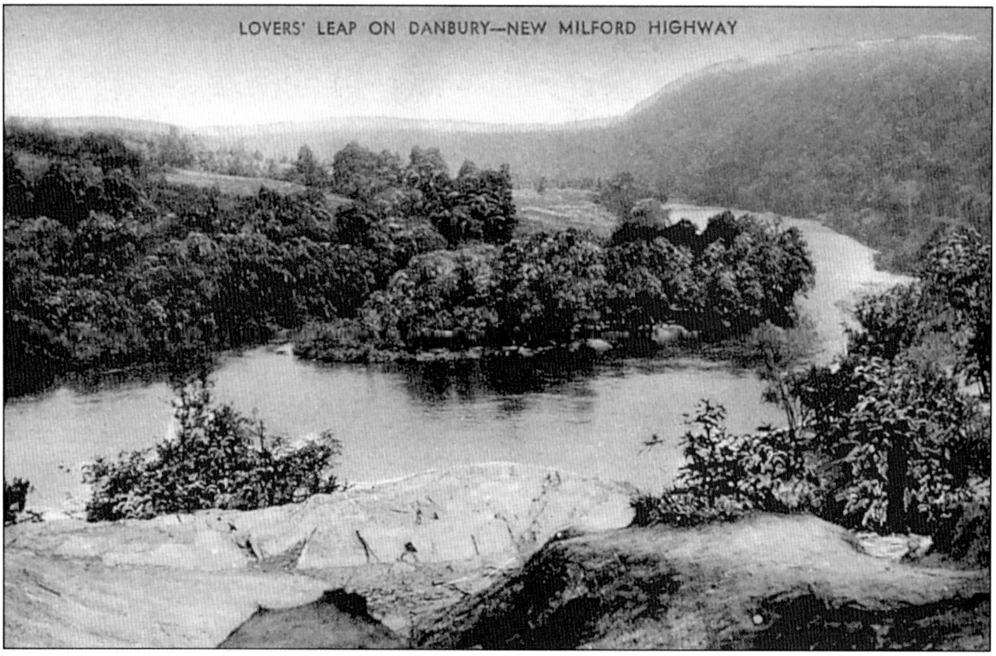

Lovers Leap, overlooking Lake Lillinonah just east of Route 7, was named for a romantic Native American legend of tragic love. Lovers Leap Road is now blocked off to cars, but hikers may walk to the top.

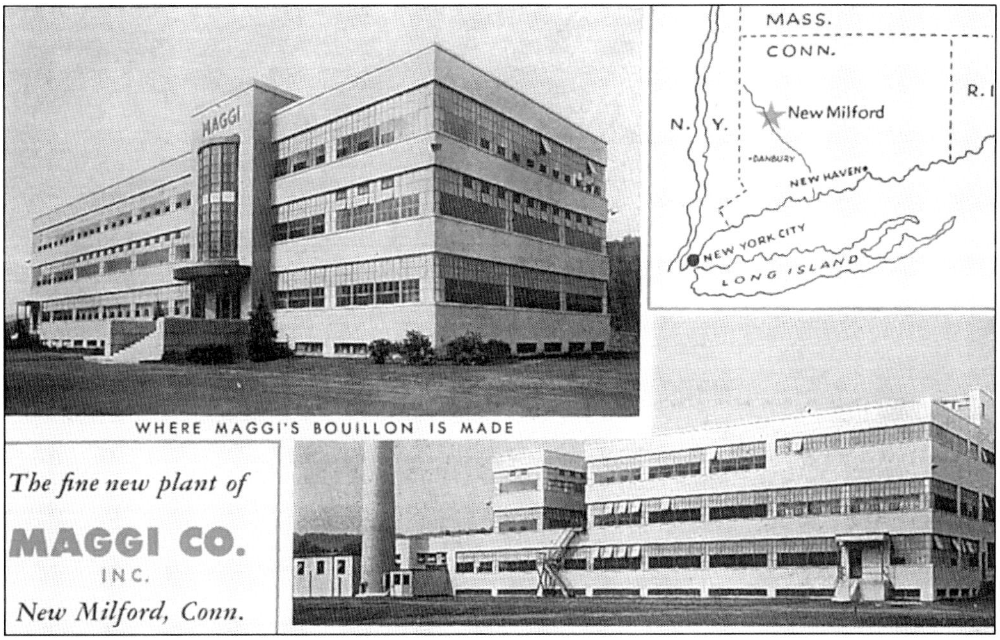

The Maggi Company, makers of well-known seasonings, was located across the Housatonic River, visible from Route 7.

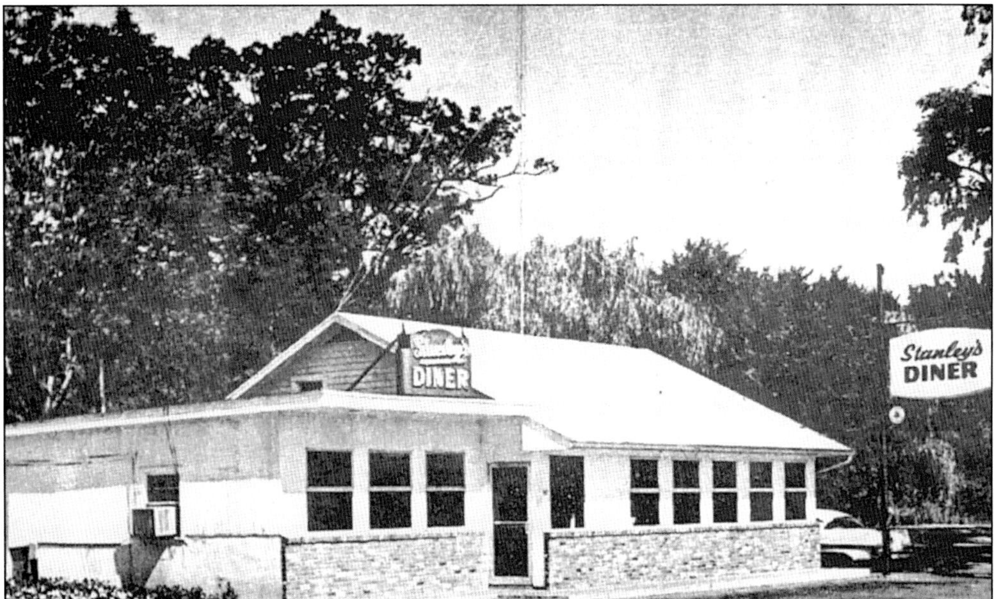

For many years, Stanley's Diner was a conveniently located restaurant just north of upper Sunny Valley Road on the west side of Route 7. It operated into the early 1970s and was "famous for its home-baked pies and biscuits."

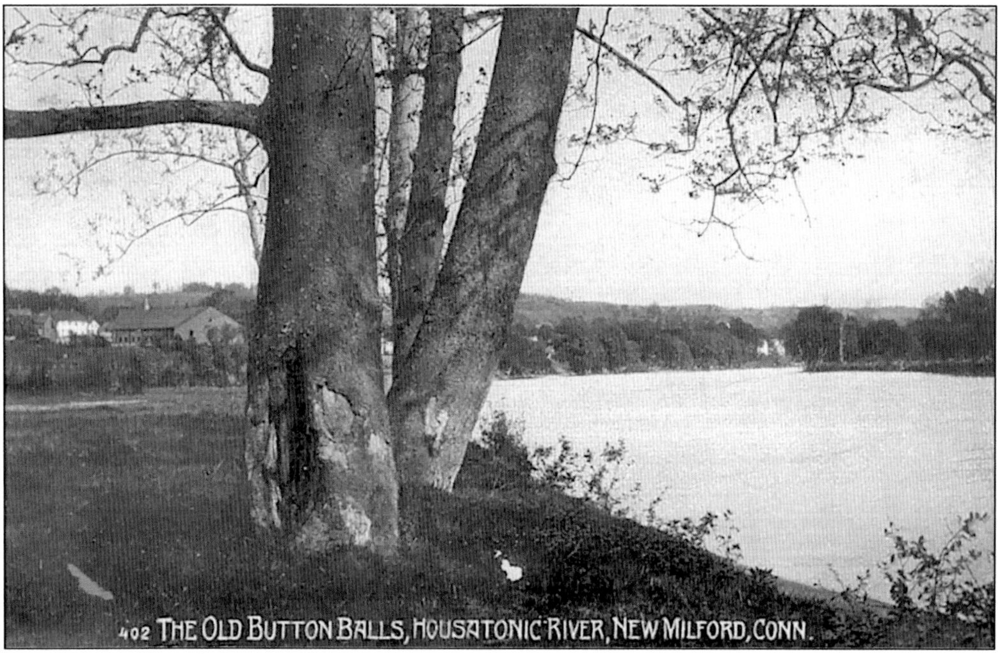

Buttonball trees, also called sycamore trees, grow quickly in wetland areas like those along the Housatonic River, as seen in this 1907 postcard.

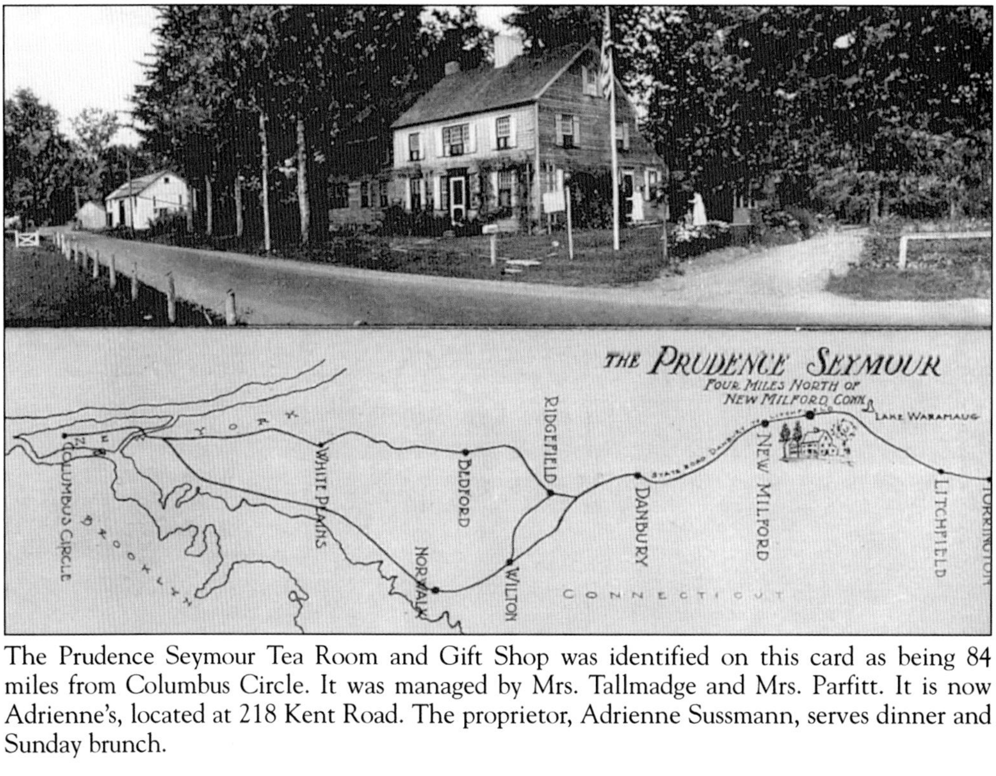

The Prudence Seymour Tea Room and Gift Shop was identified on this card as being 84 miles from Columbus Circle. It was managed by Mrs. Tallmadge and Mrs. Parfitt. It is now Adrienne's, located at 218 Kent Road. The proprietor, Adrienne Sussmann, serves dinner and Sunday brunch.

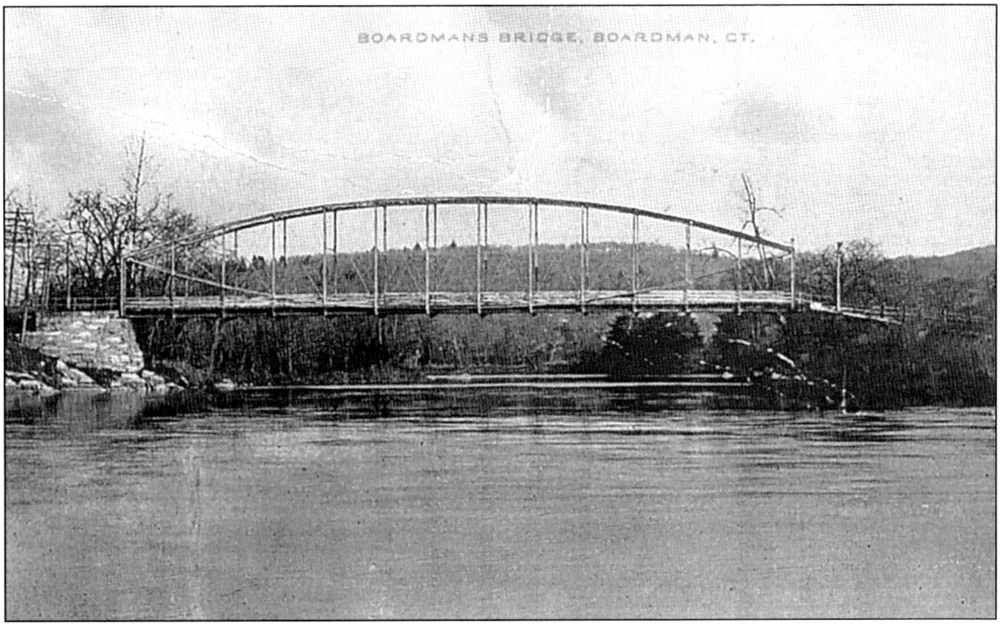

Now just a foot bridge with a modern bridge next to it, Boardman's Bridge was built in 1888. Metal plaques at each end of the bridge proudly proclaim that it was built by the Berlin Iron Bridge Company of East Berlin, Connecticut. Patents for these types of bridges were granted to Douglas and Jarvis in 1878 and 1885. The plaques include the names of three selectman, P.N. Paul, J.L. Buck, and F.E. Starr.

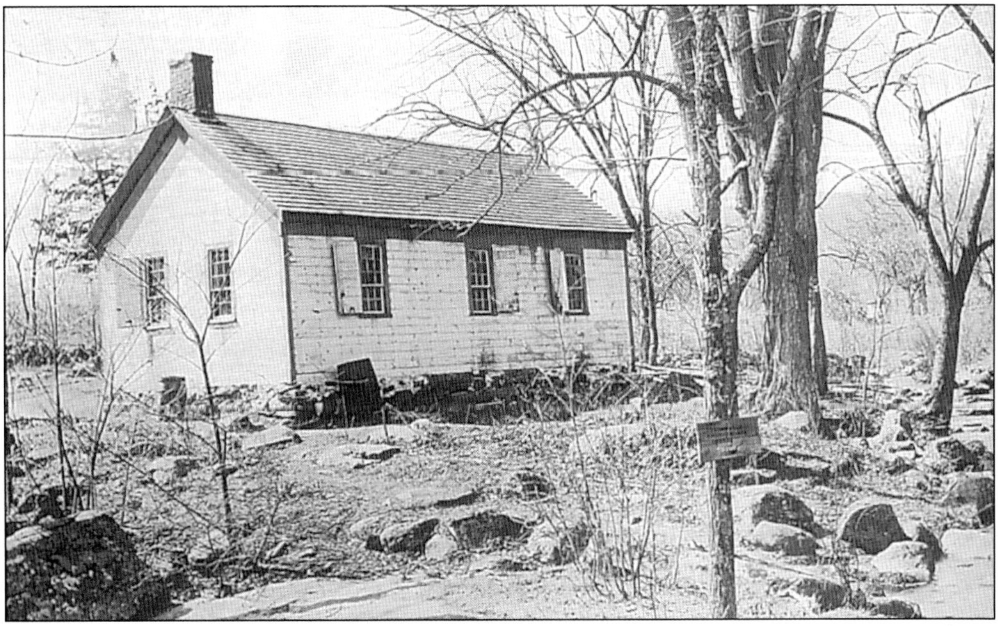

This old one-room school is located on the west side of Route 7 just before Route 37. A front entrance with separate doors was added later.

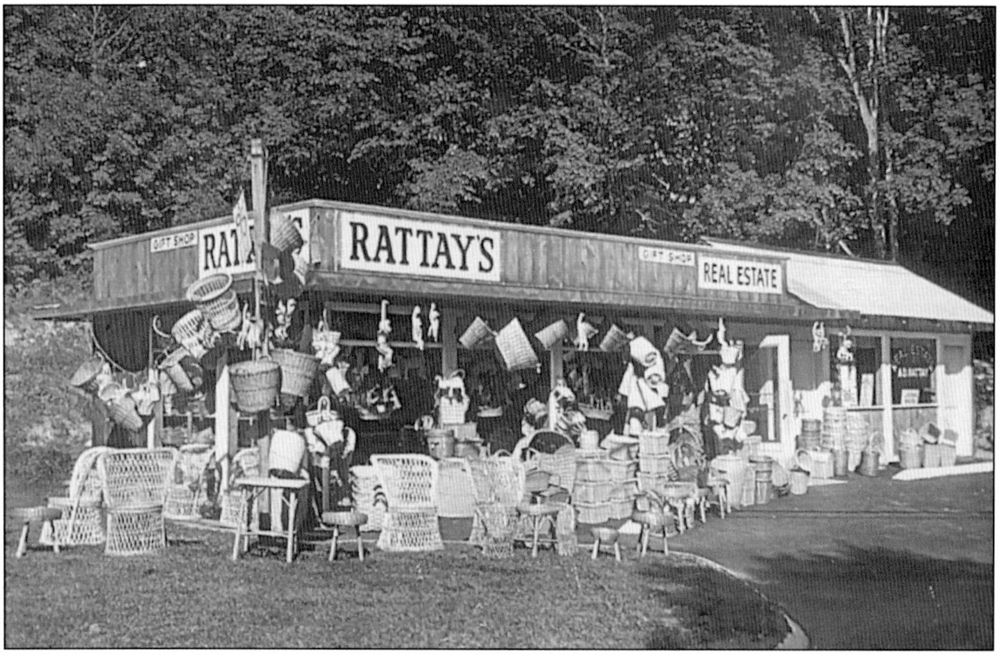

In the 1960s, "Rattays for Rattans" was on the west side of Route 7 at the corner of Eastview Drive. It was in direct competition with the Basket Shop in Gaylordsville.

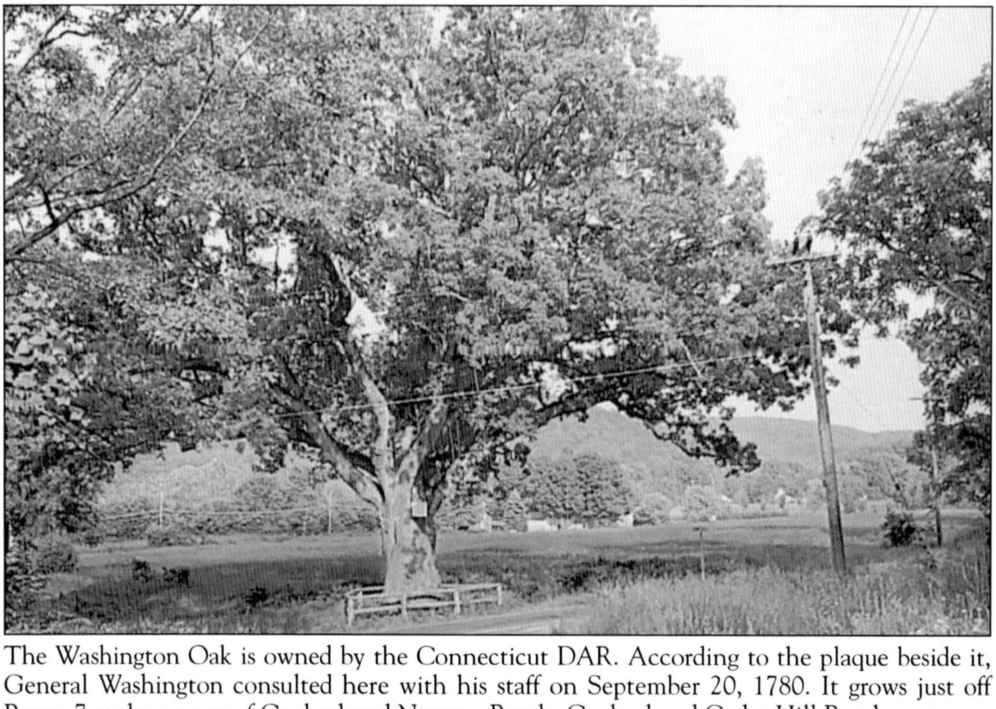

The Washington Oak is owned by the Connecticut DAR. According to the plaque beside it, General Washington consulted here with his staff on September 20, 1780. It grows just off Route 7 at the corner of Gaylord and Newton Roads. Gaylord and Cedar Hill Roads appear to be part of the original path of what is now Route 7.

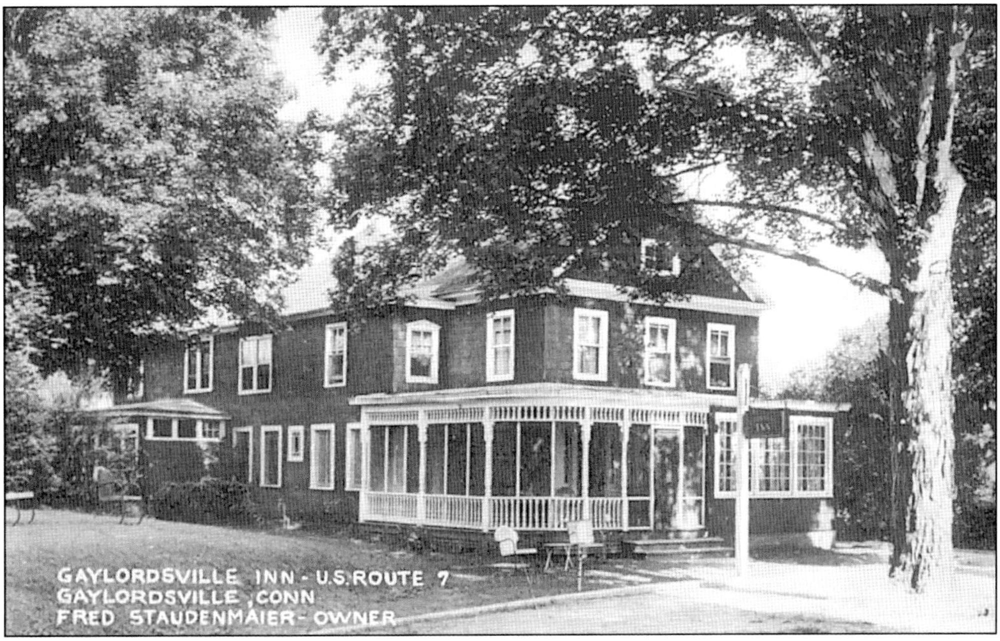

The Gaylordsville Inn was operated by the Baldwins after WWII. It is now the Gaylordsville Rest Home.

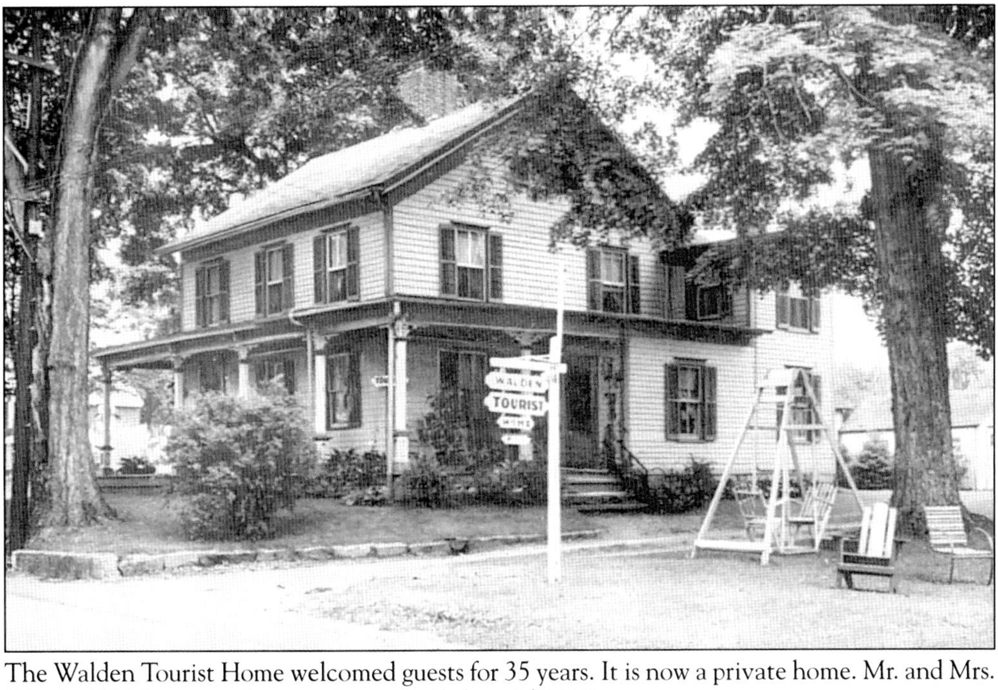

The Walden Tourist Home welcomed guests for 35 years. It is now a private home. Mr. and Mrs. Charles Walden were the proprietors until the mid-1960s.

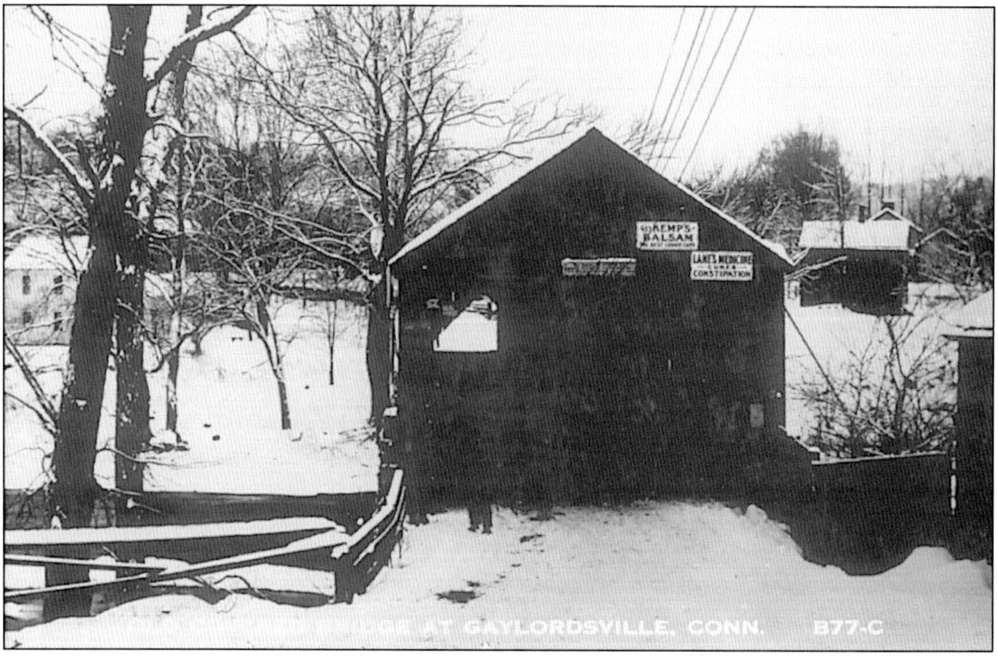

This bridge was used for approximately 50 years, until 1926 when a steel bridge was built.

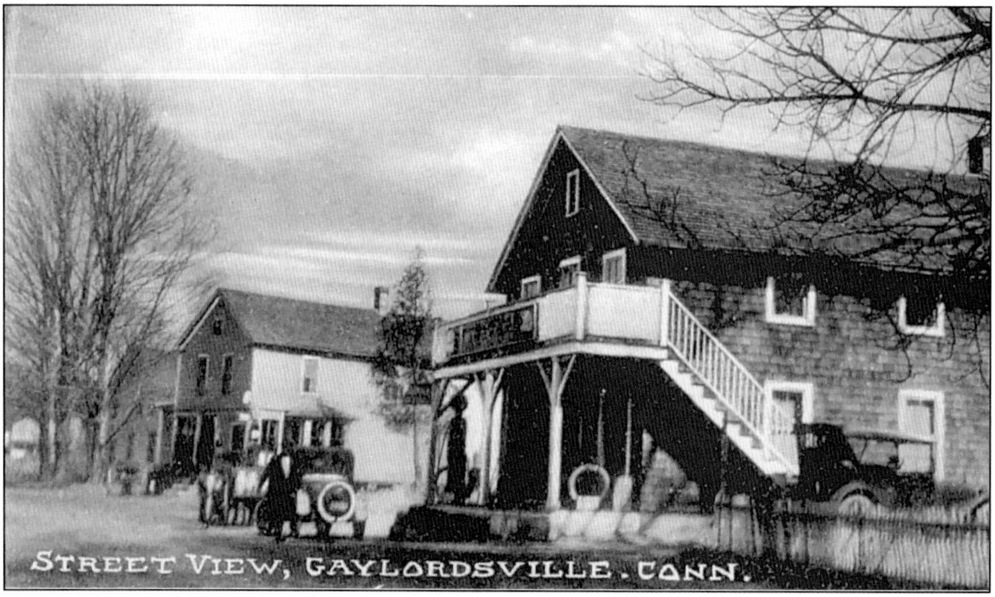

After you exited the covered bridge going north, these are the buildings that were visible, including Honan's Store.

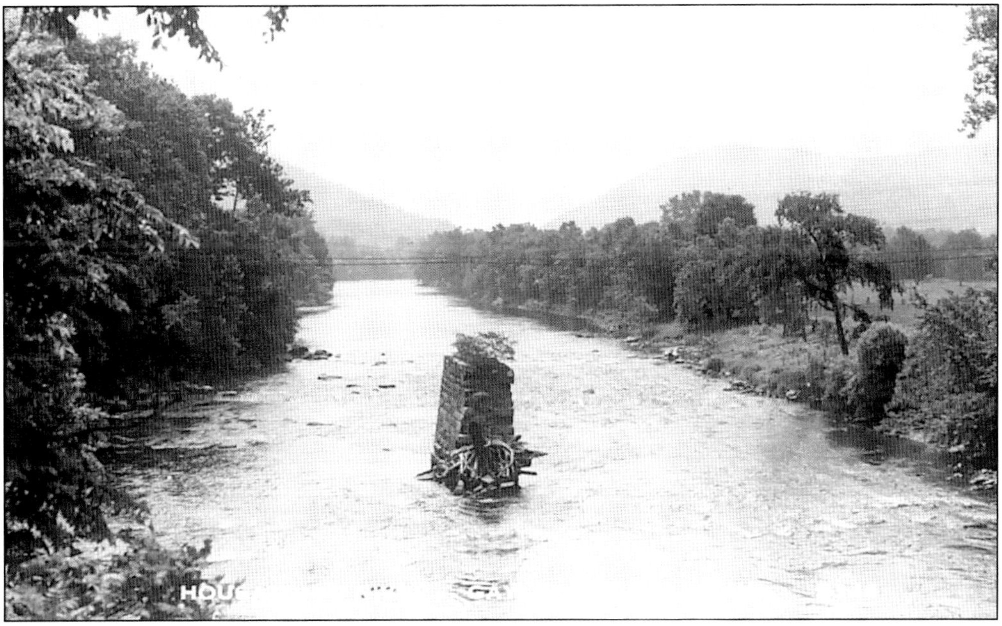

Now just a pile of stones, the pilings in the river show where the old covered bridge crossed at a different angle than the current one does. They finally crumbled in 1980.

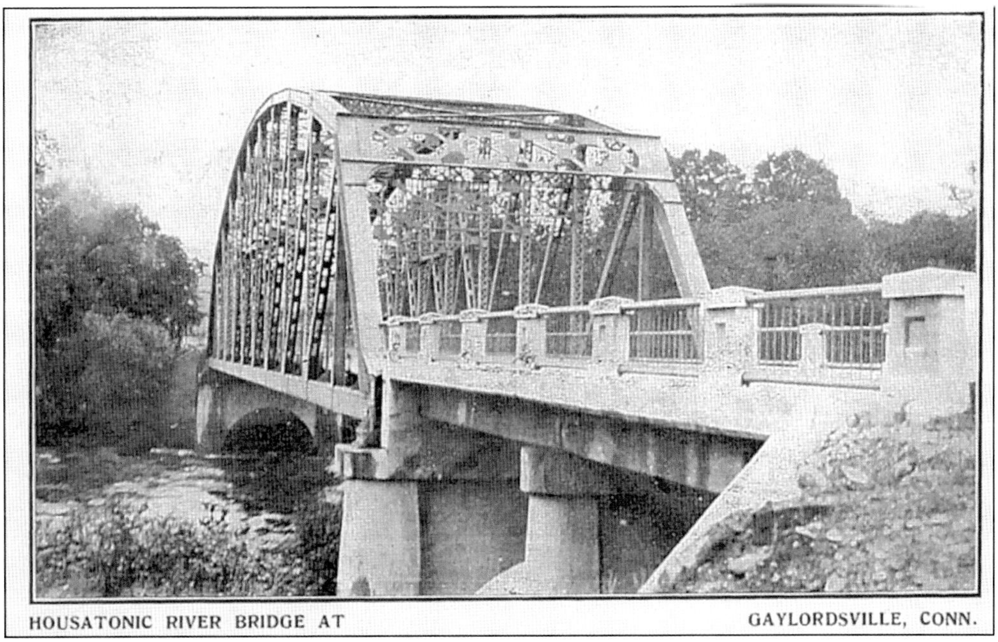

Since 1801, a series of bridges have crossed the Housatonic River. This one was replaced in the 1970s.

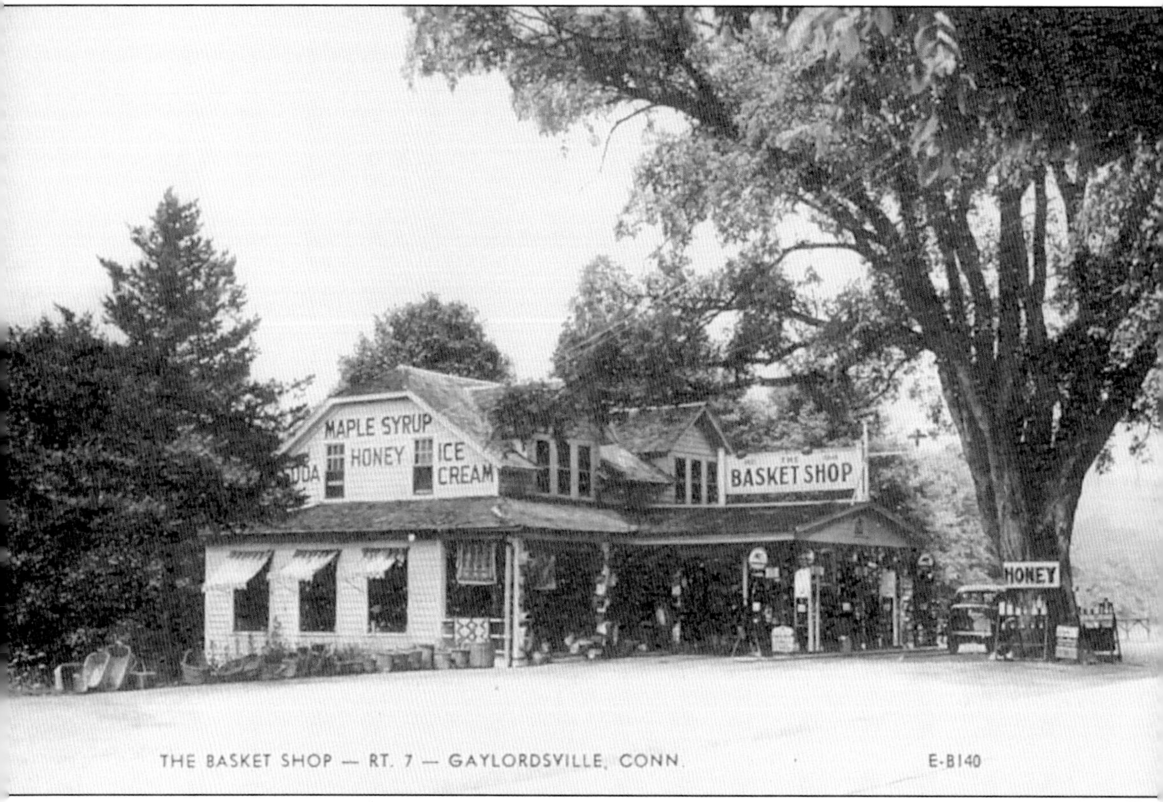

Although the huge tree in front is now missing, the Basket Shop is otherwise clearly recognizable in 1999. The Basket Shop was built in 1926 by George Ward. Tourists along Route 7 can still find a good selection of baskets, gifts, and refreshments.

Seven

KENT

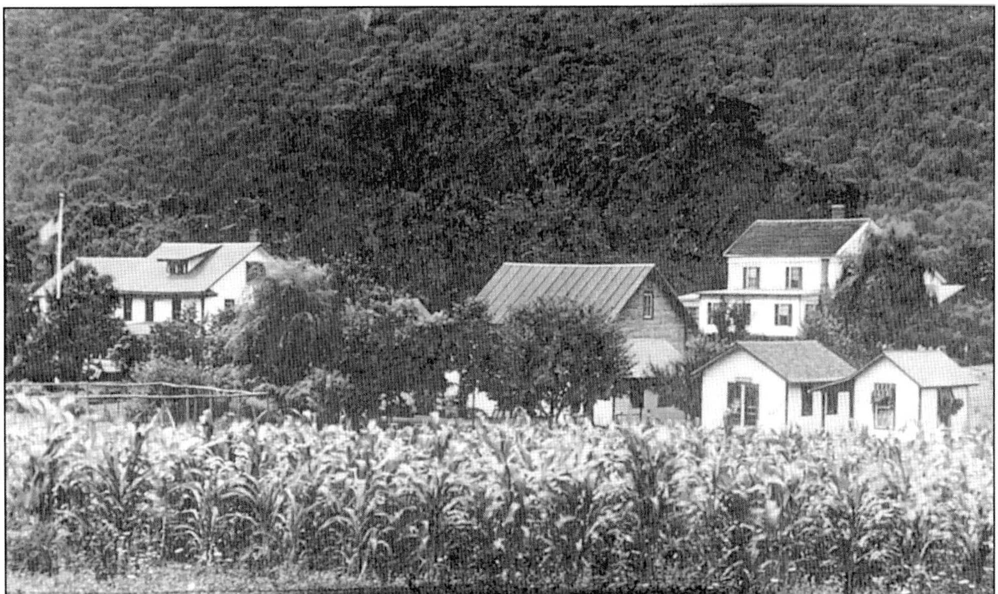

This unusual view shows the area behind Bulls Bridge Inn and gives us a picture of Kent, still in its agricultural heyday.

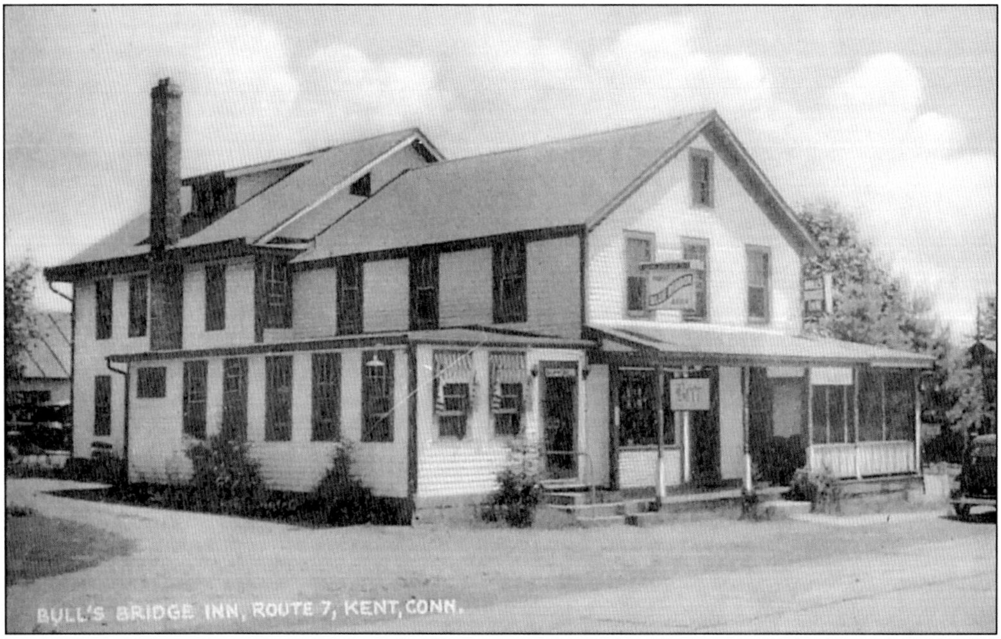

John Bull was a Tory during the Revolution. His inn and bridge have had a large part in the history of Kent and have managed to exist up to the present.

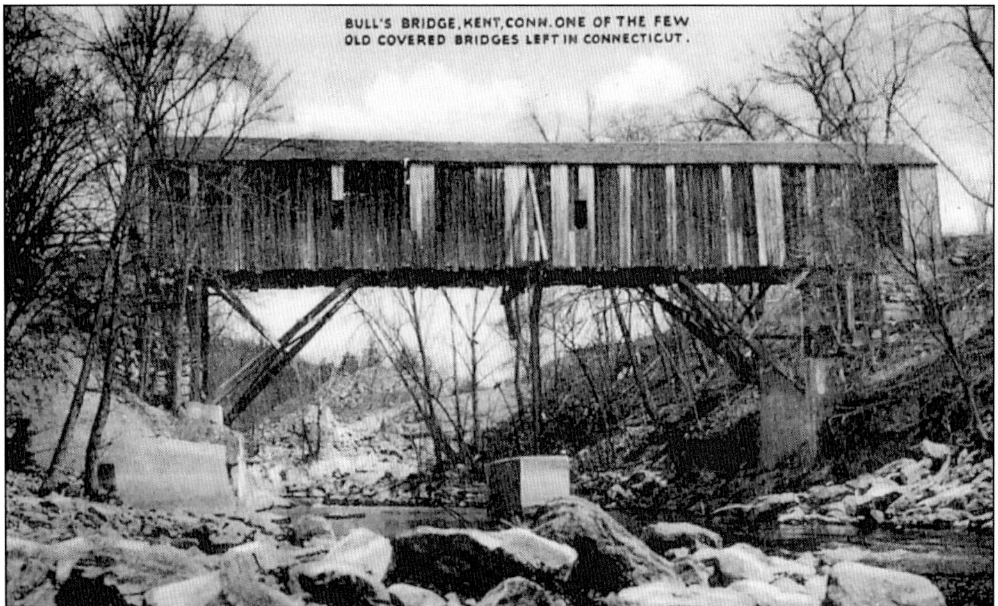

The wooden bridge just off Route 7 at Bulls Bridge Road is one of two covered bridges in continuous use in this region. Built around 1812, refurbished in 1981, it receives only one lane of traffic at a time.

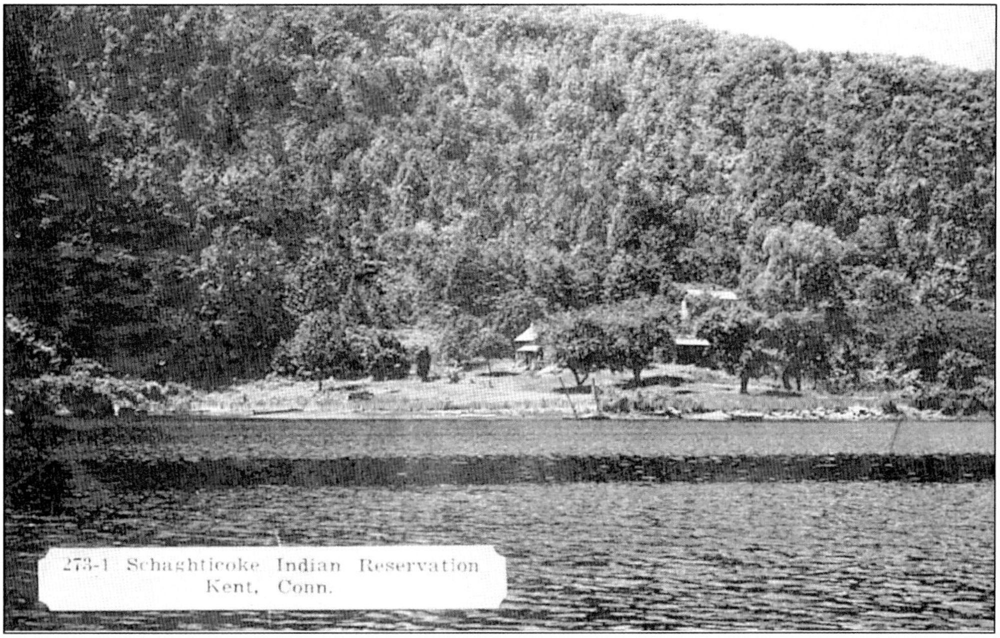

The Schaghticoke Indian tribe has had a long history in Kent. Their reservation is on the west side of the river before town and includes a burial ground. As a child, Virginia remembers going to the reservation with her father, talking to an older resident, and being fascinated by the fox he had in a cage.

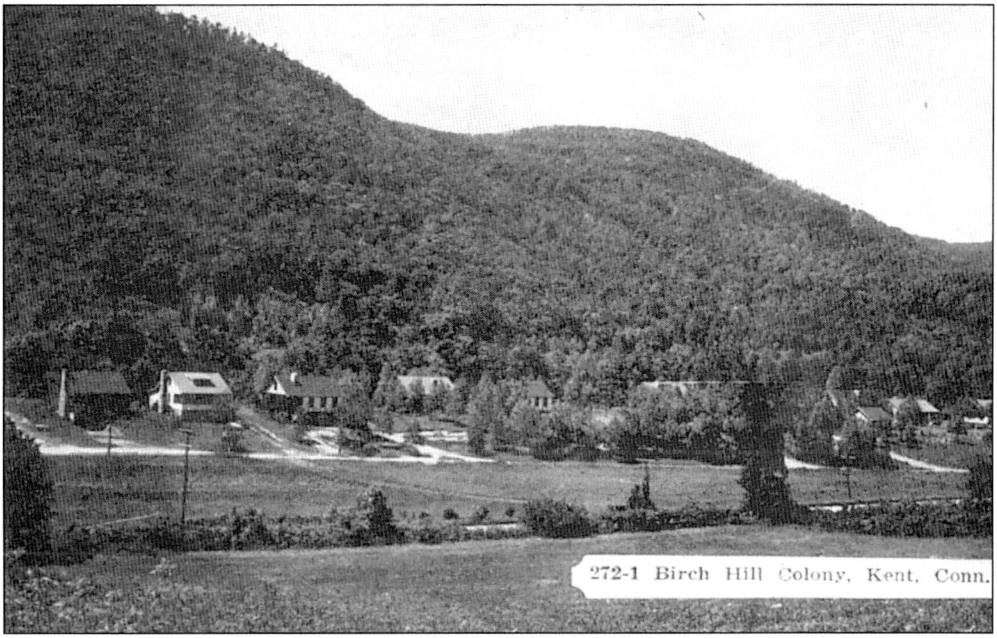

A group of small homes along the Housatonic signals the approach to the main village of Kent. This is the Birch Hill Colony where Birch Hill Lane and Birch Hill Court lead to former summer cottages.

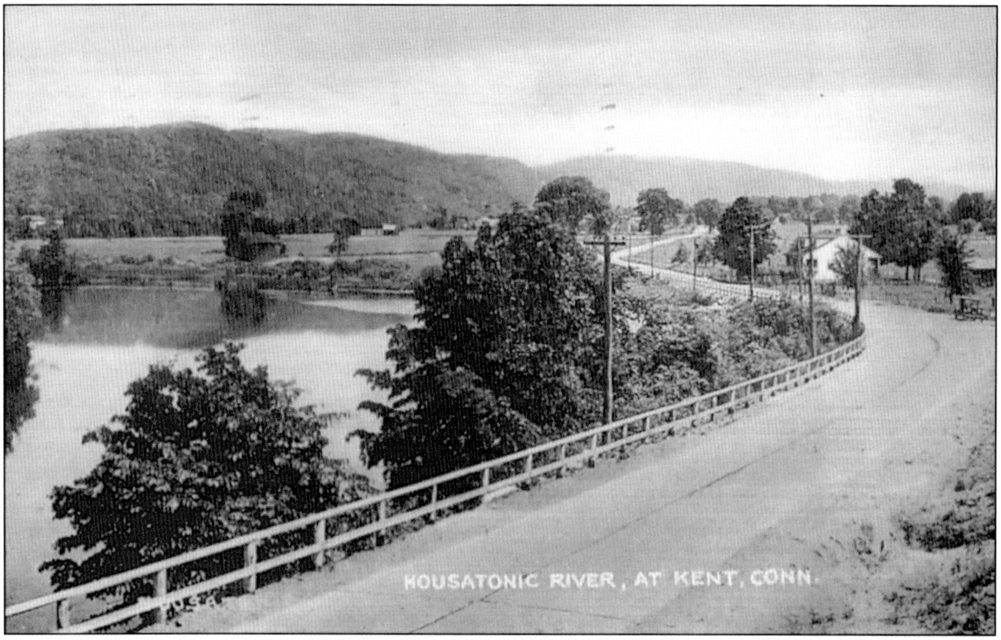

According to writer and life-long resident Phil Camp, the early road through Kent was on the west side of the village and was known as the Schaghticoke Trail.

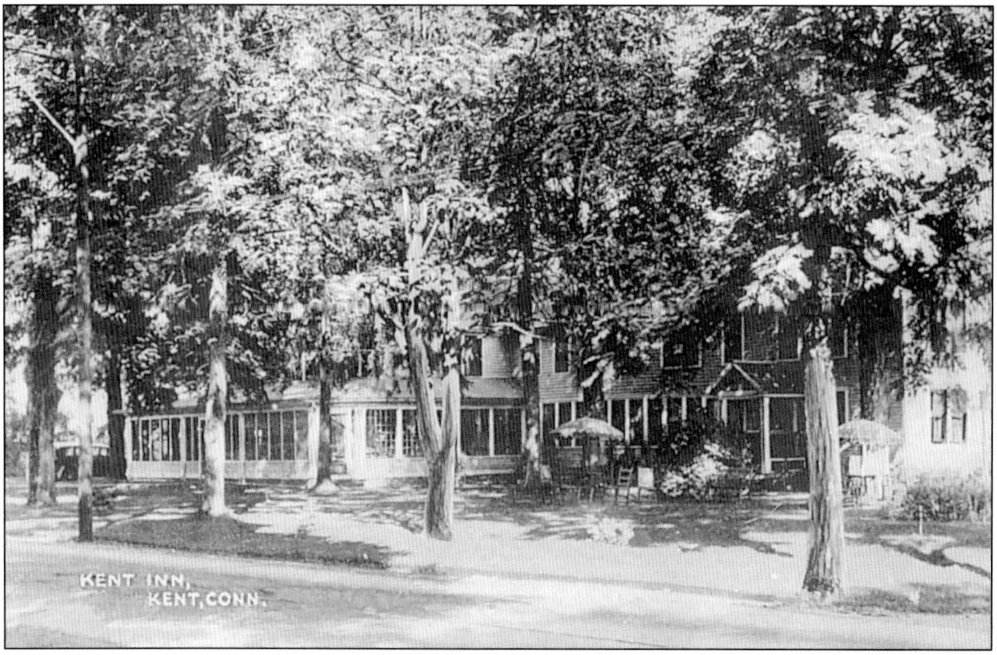

Several Main Street homes were turned into inns and restaurants to provide for tourists. The Kent Inn stood on the southeast corner of Route 341, where today there is a Mobil Station.

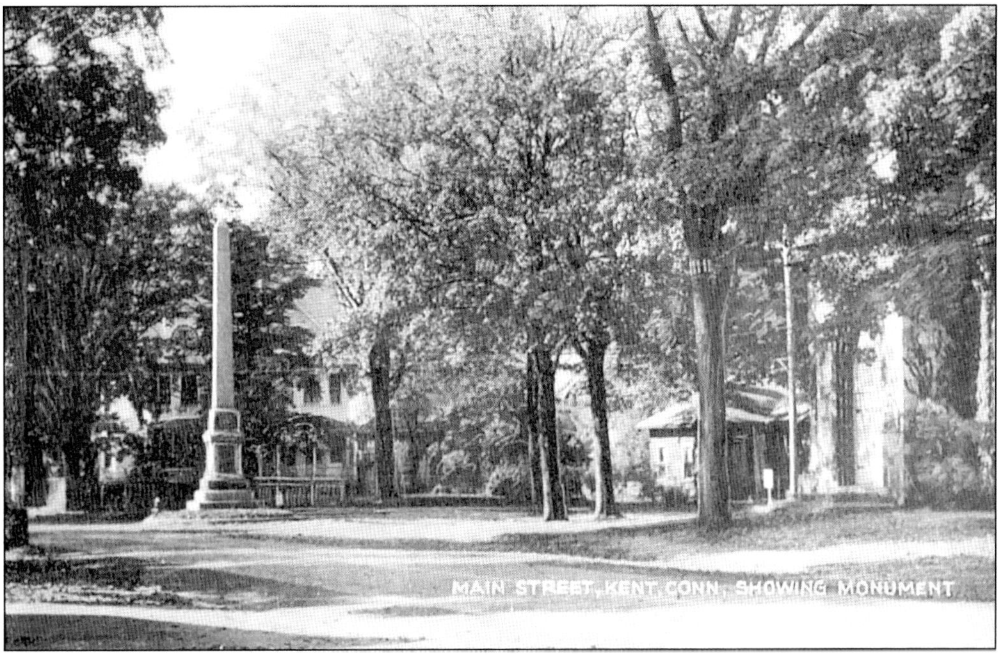

The commemorative monument stands at the major crossroads in town. It is a memorial to Kent veterans of the Civil War, erected in 1885.

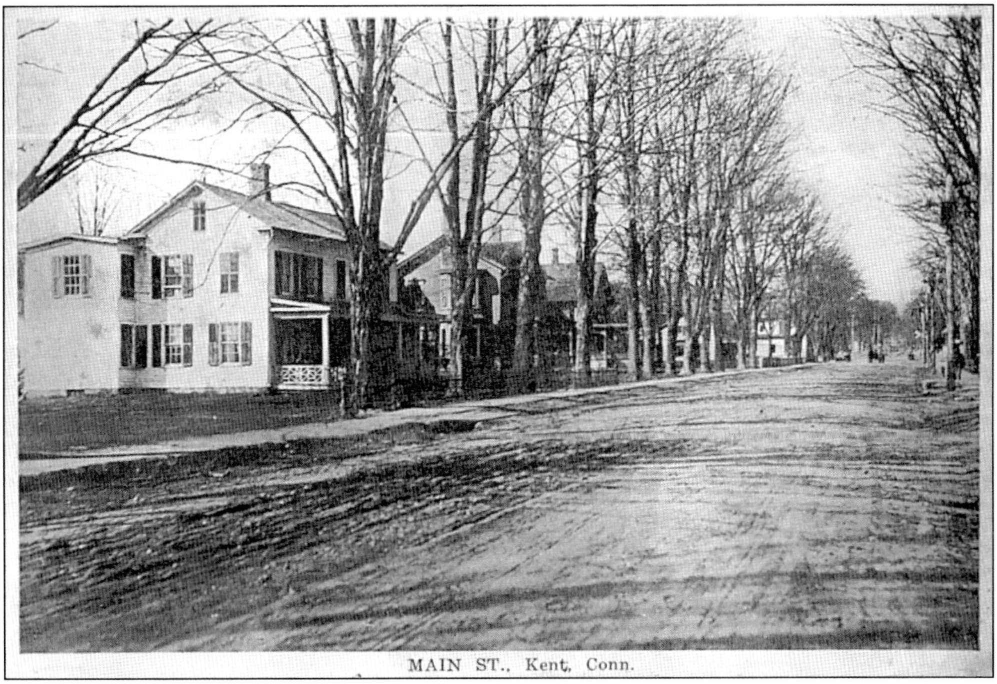

Main Street was still a dirt road in 1918.

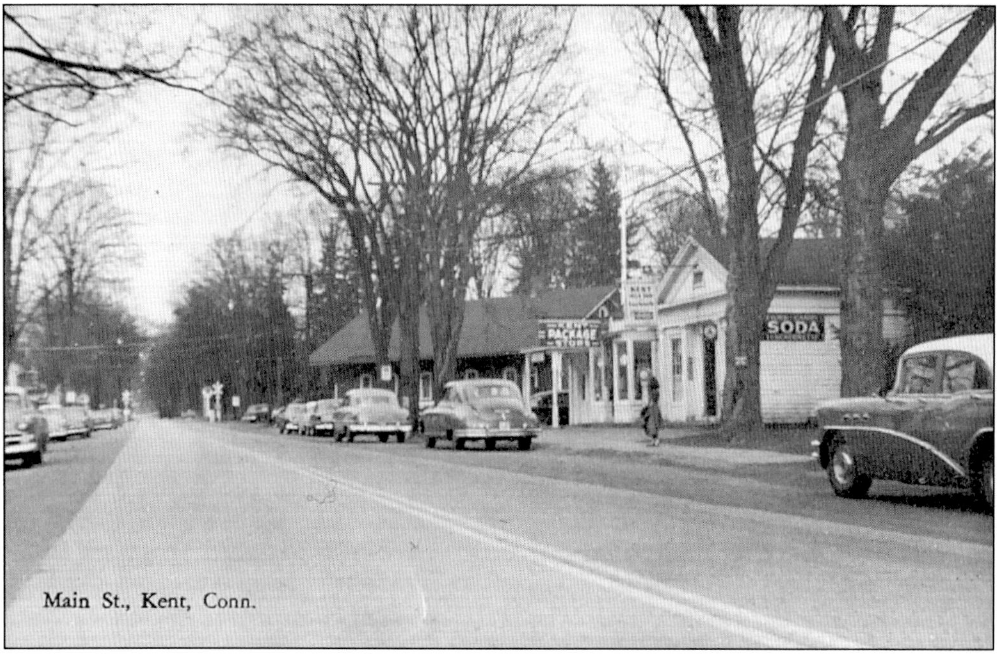

Further along Main Street we see the commercial area of the 1930s and 1940s.

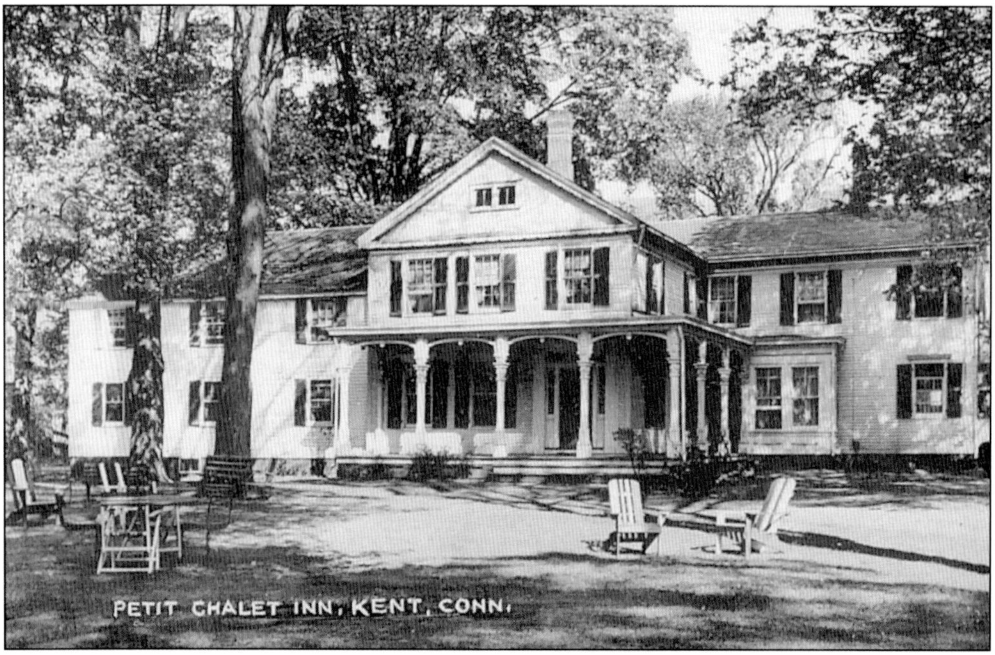

The Petit Chalet was formerly the John Judd House. It was located in the open field before the present liquor store. This card was sent by a young man about to register for the draft in 1940.

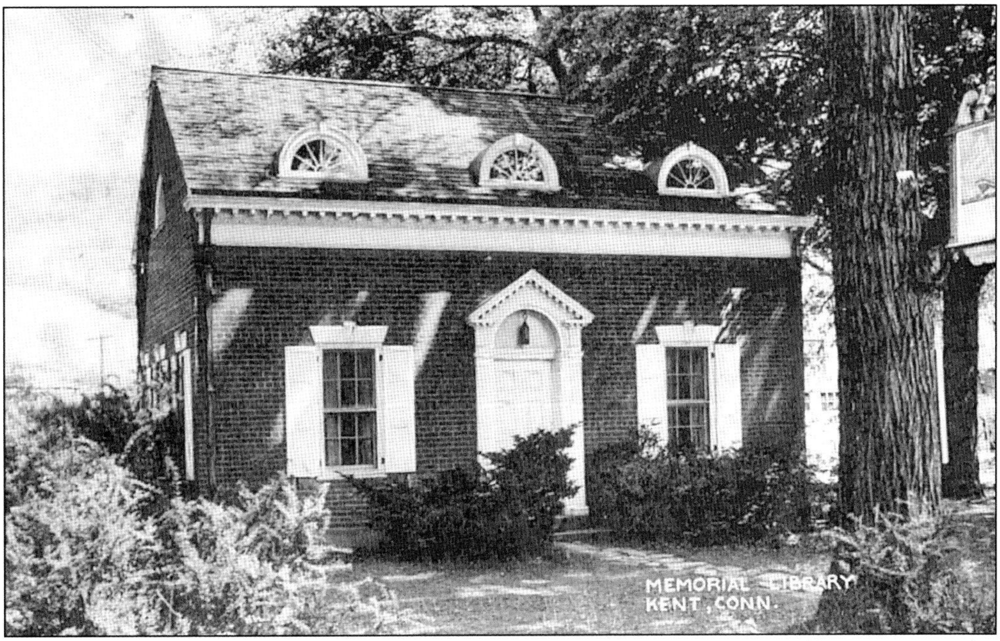

The Kent Public Library, shown here in 1954, still serves the reading public. Upstairs, the Historical Society maintains historical books, clippings, and photographs, presided over by town historian, Emily Hopson.

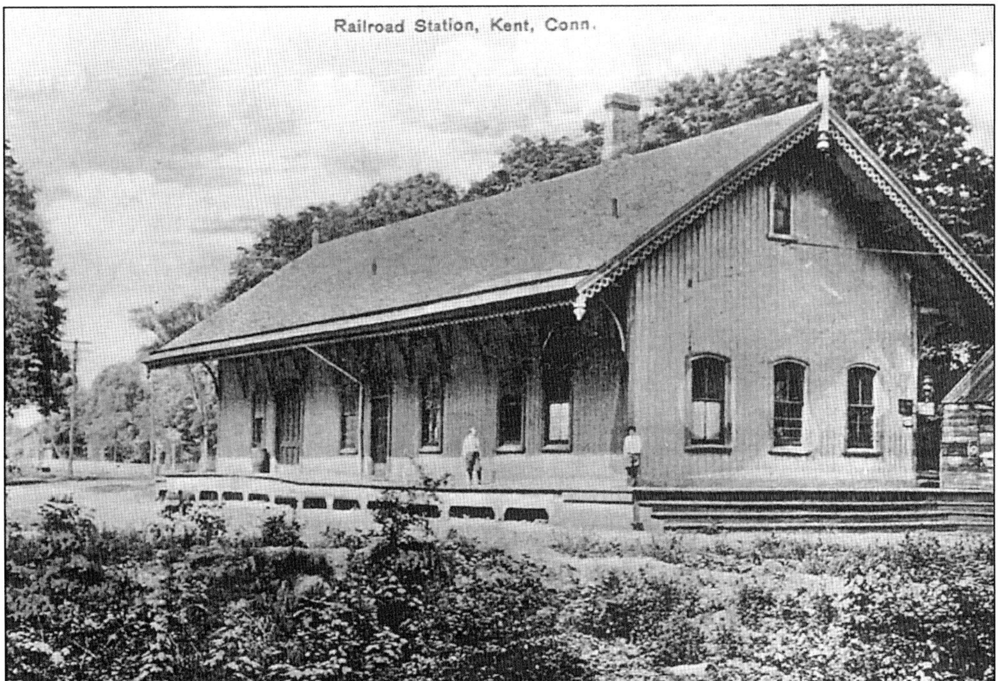

The Kent railroad station has served the area since the 1870s and now houses an ice cream shop.

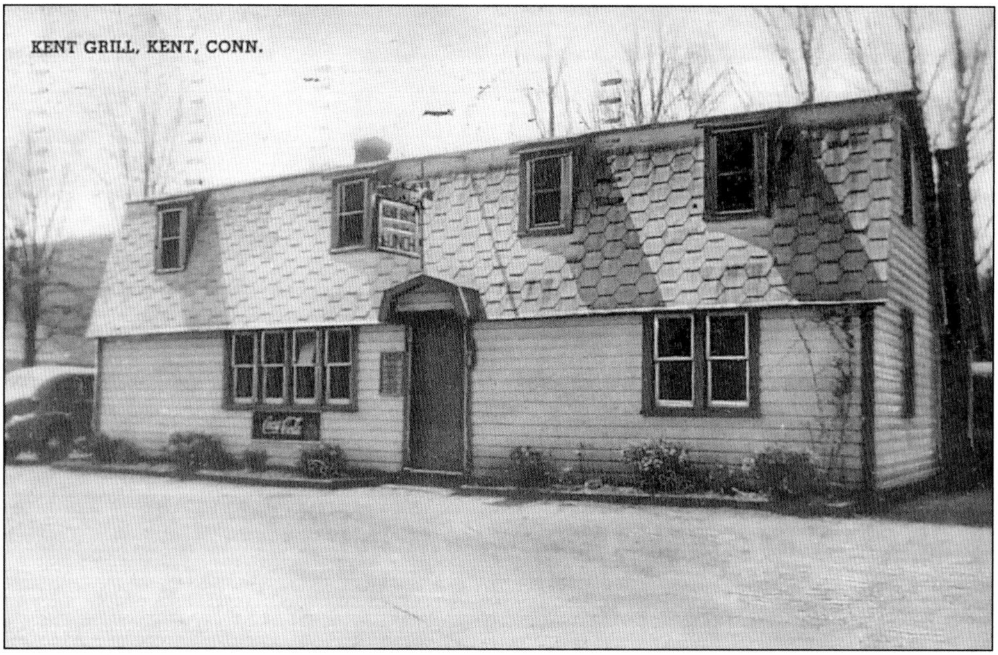

In 1940, the Kent Grill served "a sandwich or a meal."

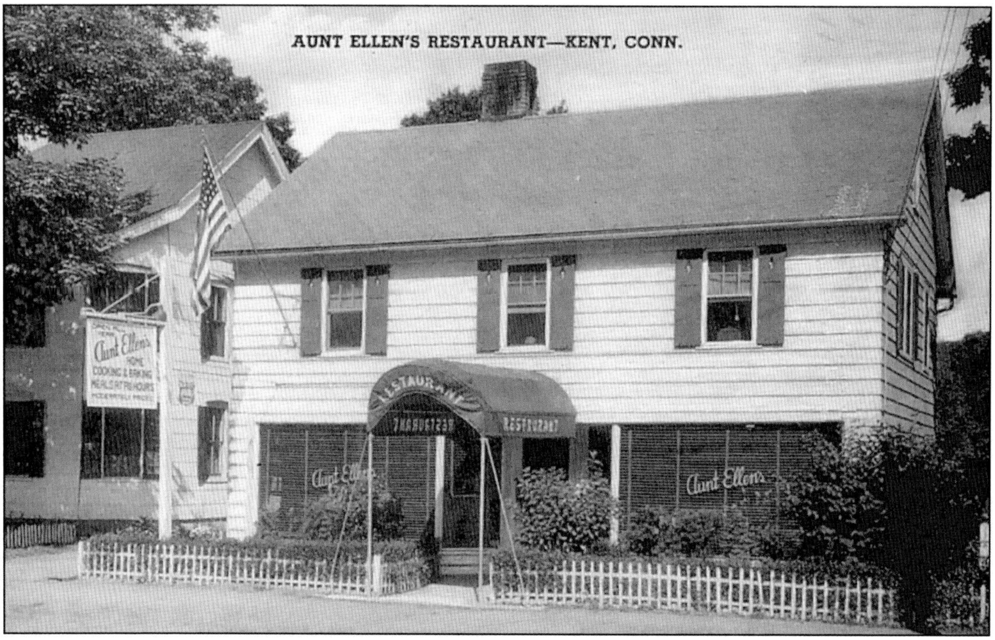

Aunt Ellen's was "opposite the railroad station, moderately priced," and baking was done on the premises. The building currently houses the office of dentist M. Monserrat.

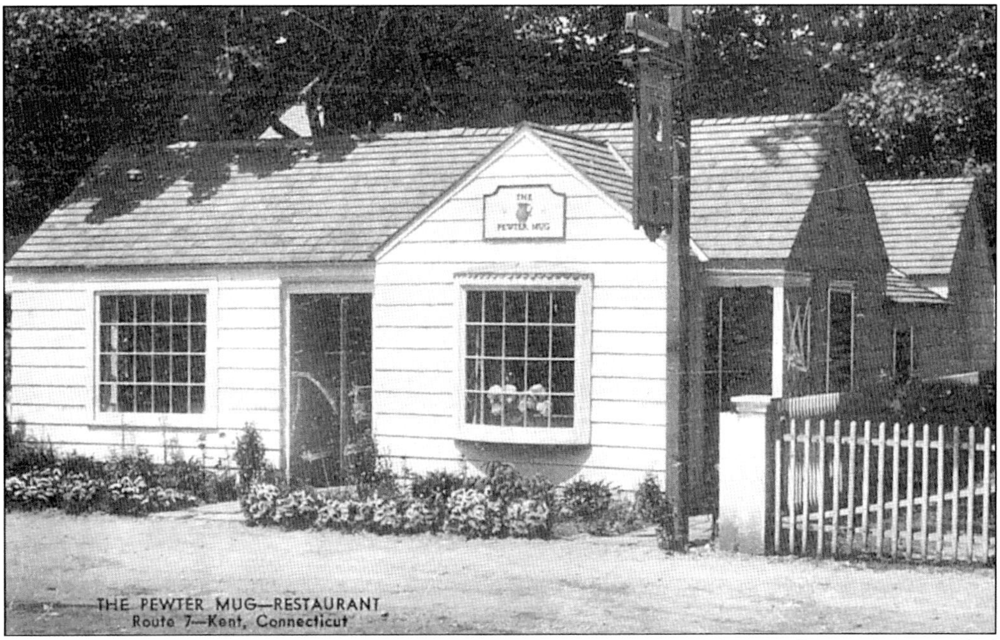

Just north of Aunt Ellen's was the Pewter Mug. "Located in the Berkshire Hills," it also provided home cooking and moderate prices. The building now serves as the Romantic Boutique.

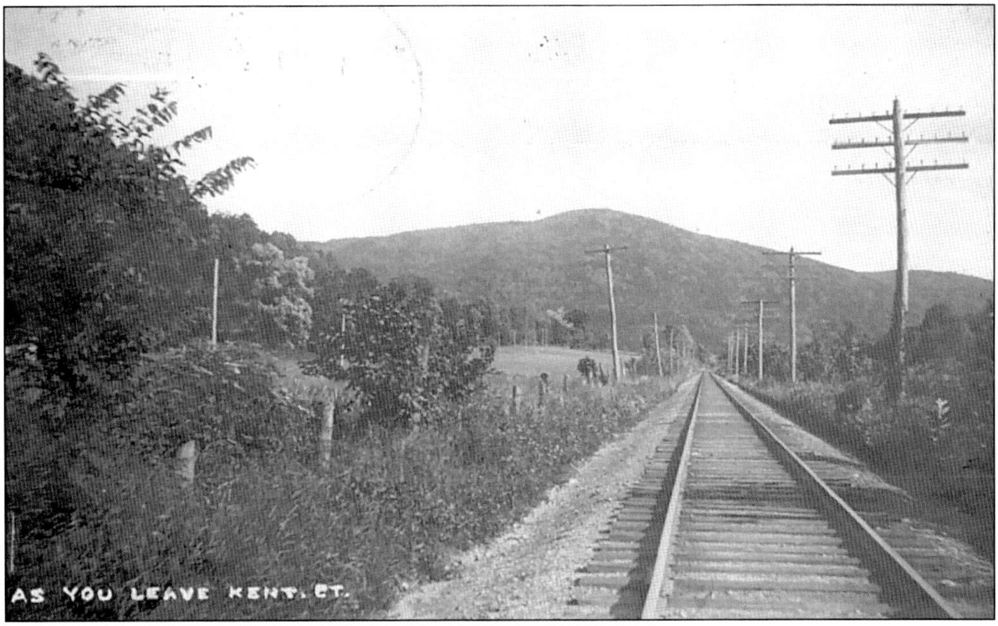

This real photo postcard was taken in 1907. The same panorama can be viewed today.

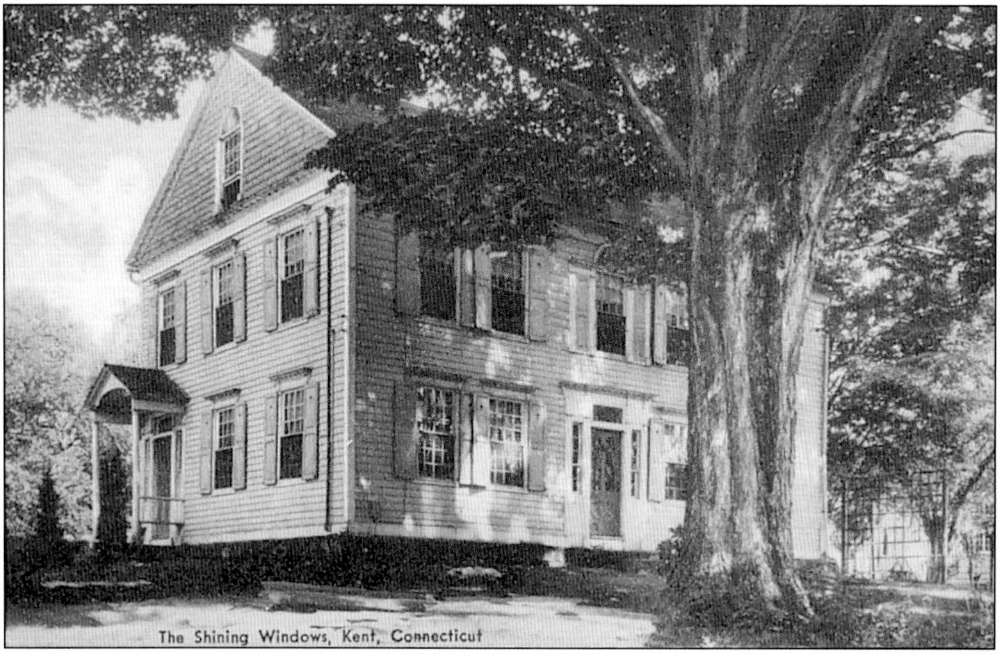

"An ancient house but comfortable, Here is found rest and food of the best, but at reasonable charges. Tel. Kent 120. 1 mile north of Kent." The writer of this card identified the house as "the old Robert's place, now the home of Mr. and Mrs. Len Howard."

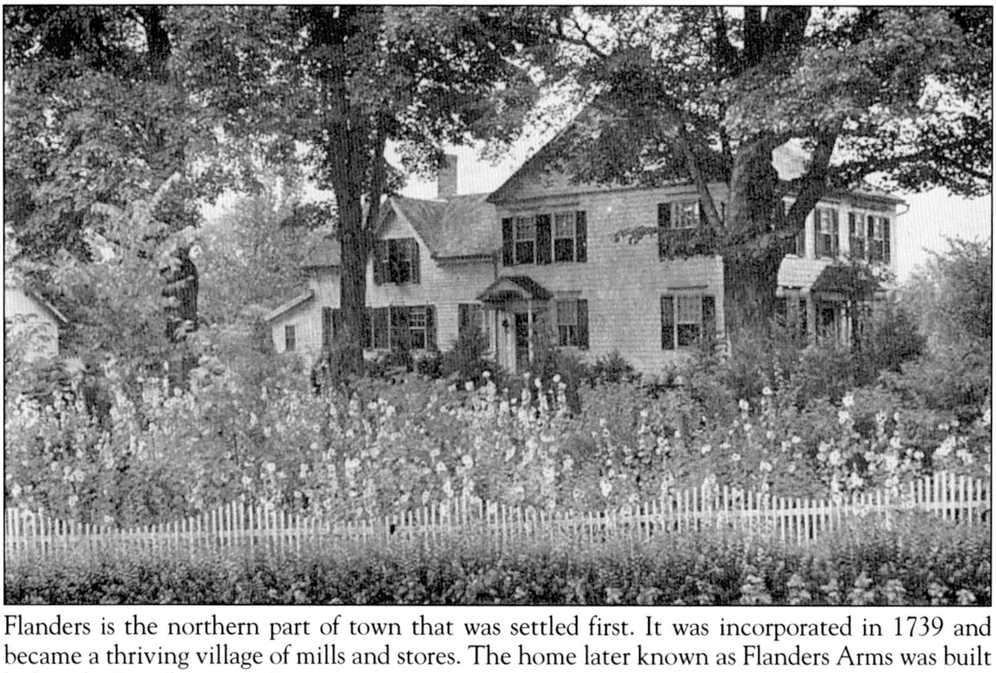

Flanders is the northern part of town that was settled first. It was incorporated in 1739 and became a thriving village of mills and stores. The home later known as Flanders Arms was built before the Revolutionary War.

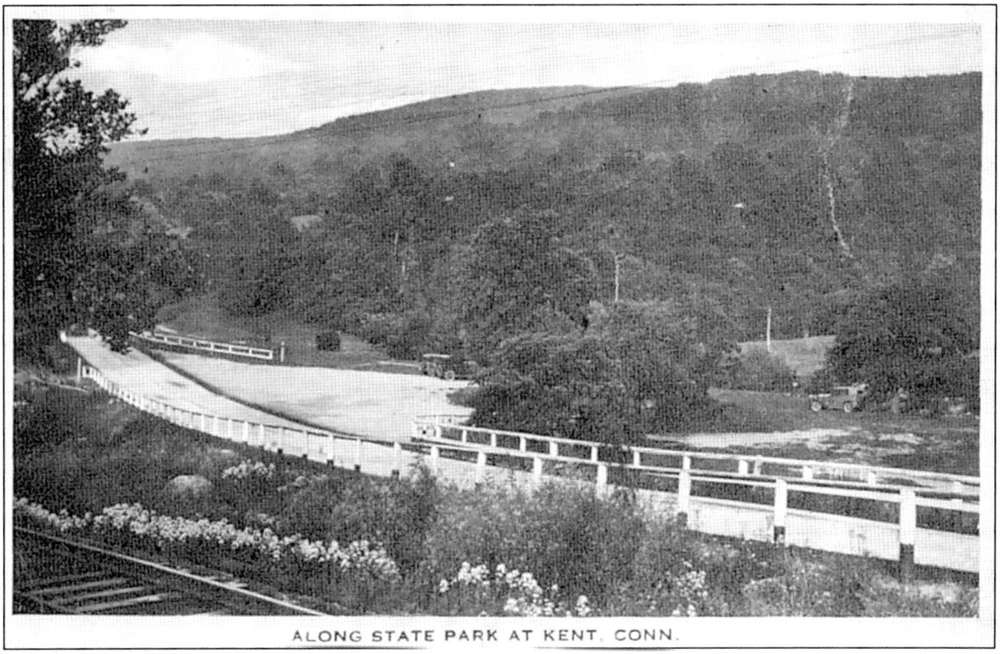

U.S. Route 7, shown here in 1930, continues along the railroad through the valley past Kent Falls State Park.

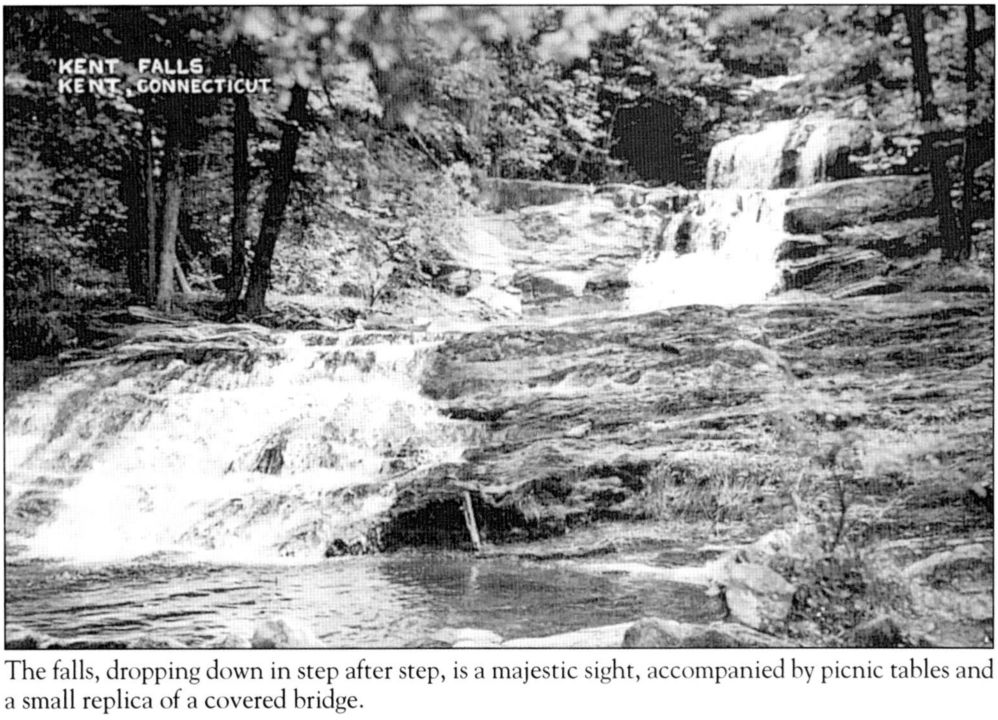

The falls, dropping down in step after step, is a majestic sight, accompanied by picnic tables and a small replica of a covered bridge.

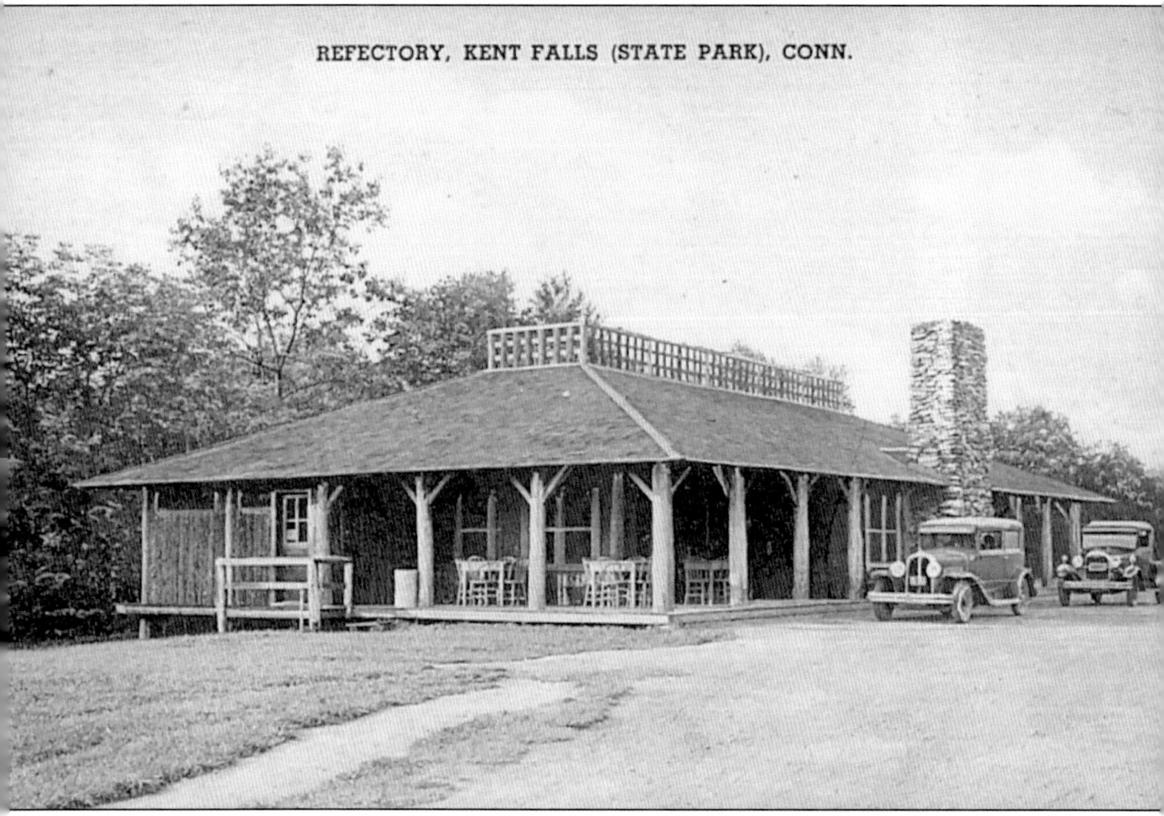

The Refectory was on the west side of Route 7 past the main entrance to Kent Falls State Park. Only the large, solid chimney remains. This card was published by the State Park and Forest Commission.

Eight

Cornwell Bridge and West Cornwall

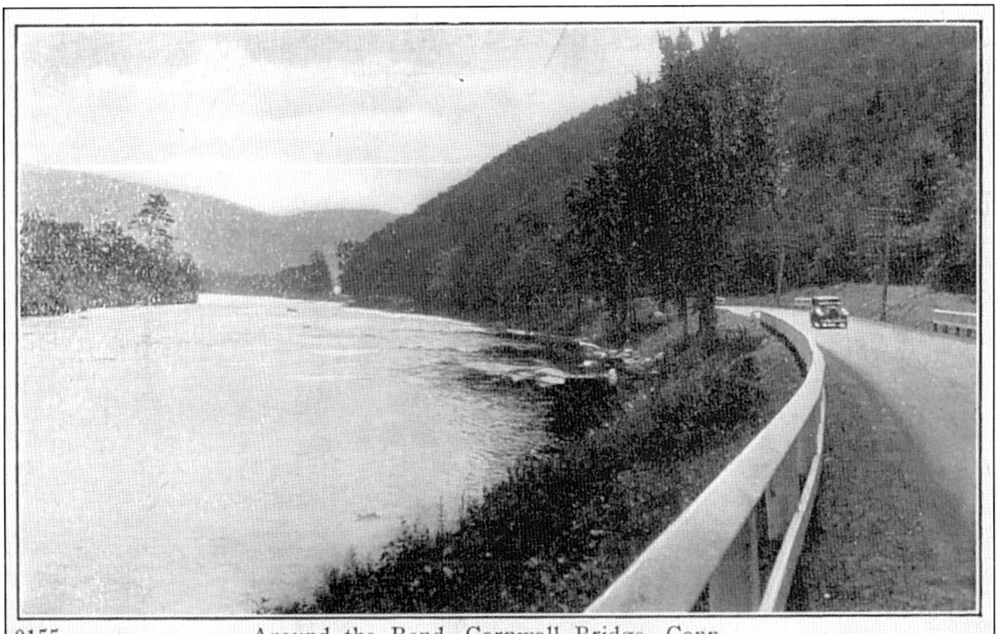

In 1731, the boundaries were established for Cornwall, although the name was not given until later. What is now Route 7, or the Ethan Allan Highway, follows the river, and here the scenery begins to reflect a change in topography.

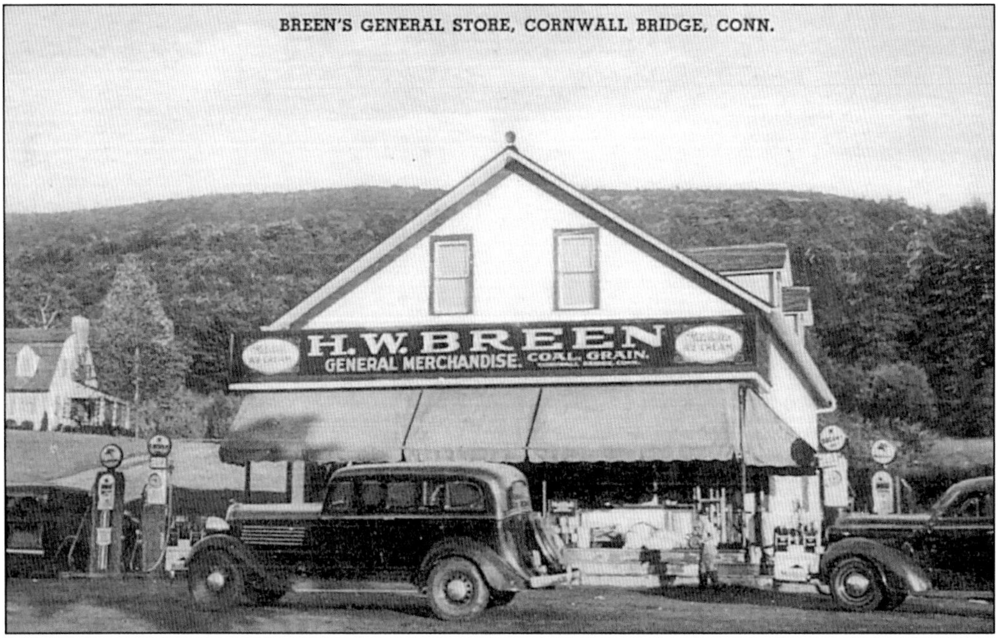

On the back of this card, an admirer wrote, "a grand general store and you'd be surprised at how modern it is inside. Has everything from thumb tacks to celery-loads of aisles to wander in. Mr. Breen is socially 'prominent' because he owns this grand place. He has a beautiful home, part of which you can see at the left of the picture." Today the tradition continues as Baird's Store.

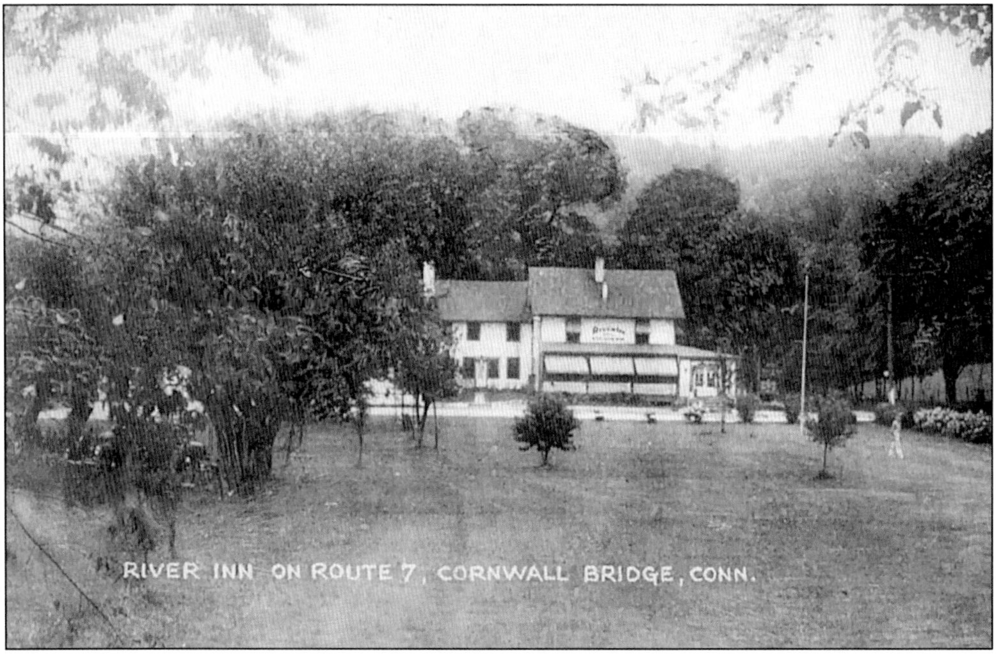

The River Inn would have had a strategic location for travelers through this region. A quiet night's rest and beautiful scenery would prepare vacationers for the next day's sight seeing.

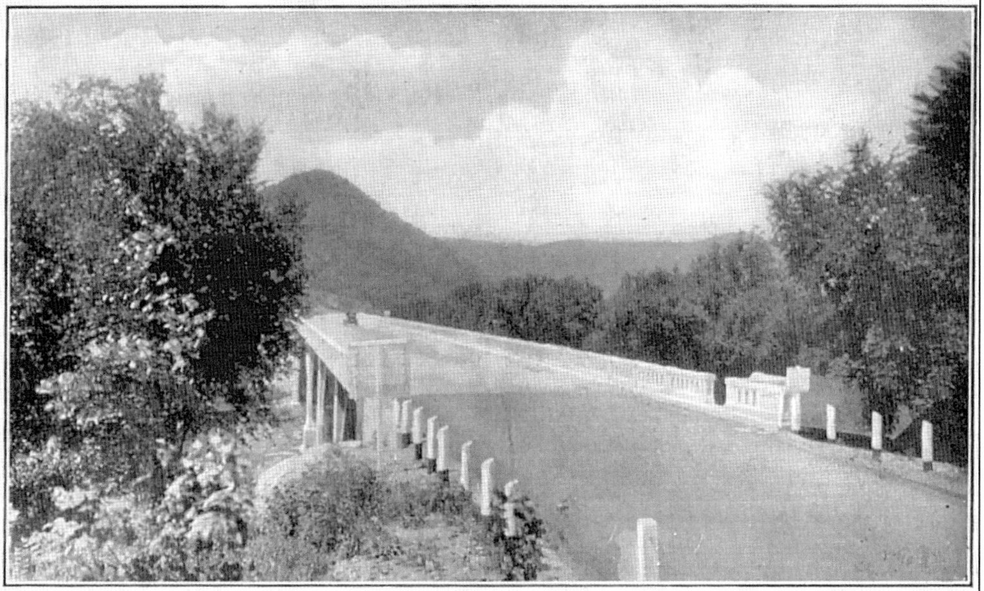

0160 Looking Across the Bridge at Cornwall Bridge, Conn.

Before this bridge was built, the town of Cornwall was located below it and was served by a covered bridge.

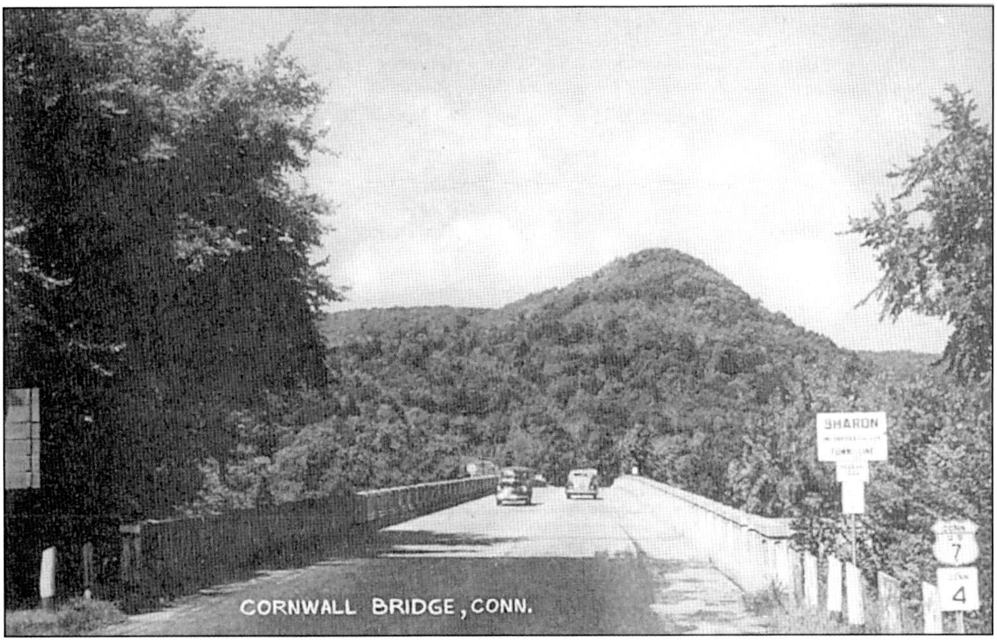

Not as isolated as it might seem at first glance, this road gives us several destination choices: Sharon, Lime Rock, or New York State.

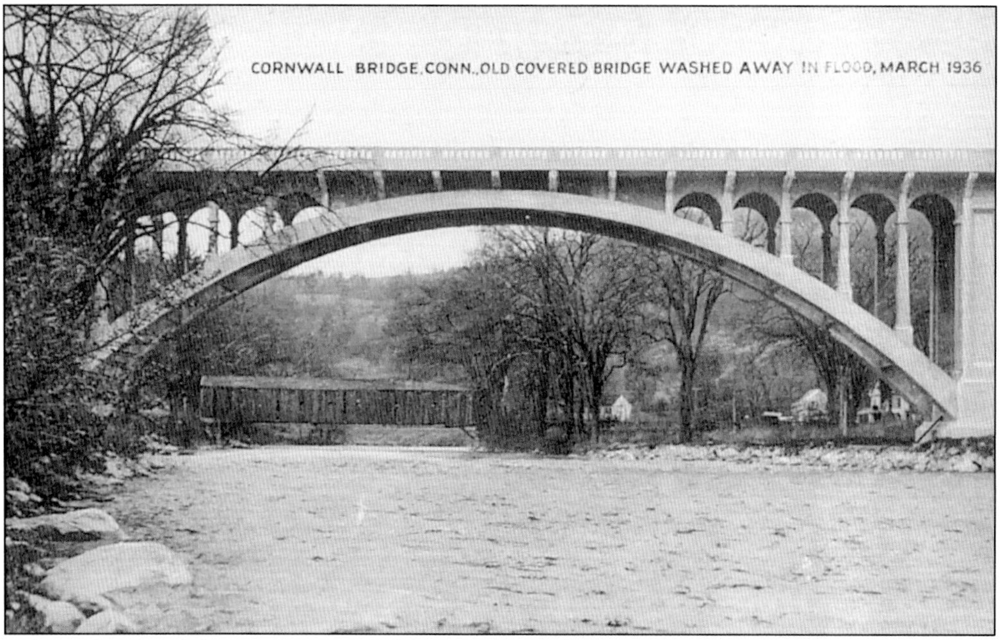

Taking the first left onto River Road before the bridge, one can see the vantage point from which this photograph was taken. The first right over the bridge leads to the opposite side of the river at the approximate location of the old covered bridge.

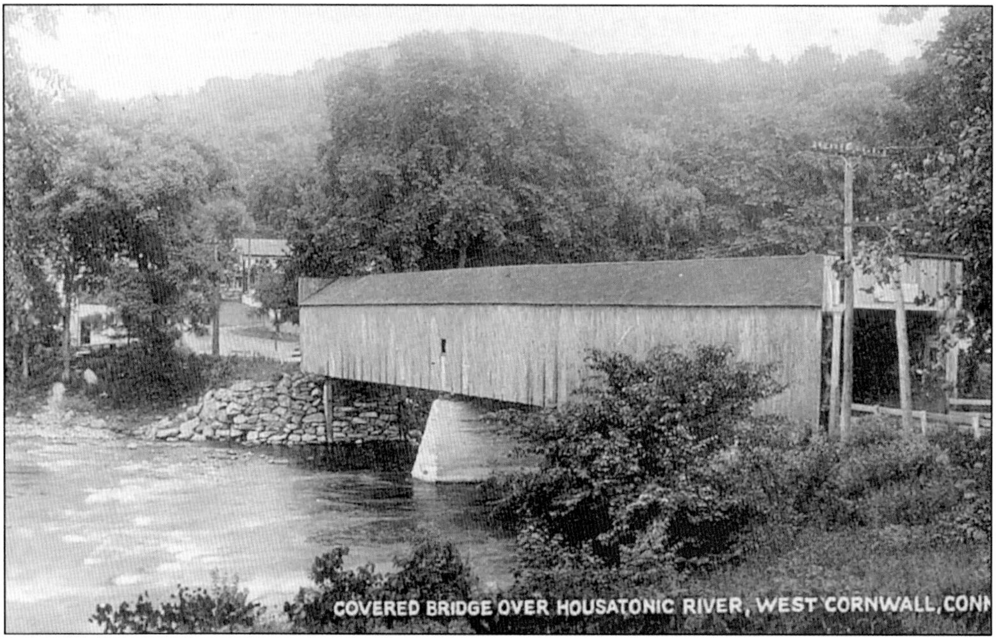

The bridge at West Cornwall was built in 1841. It is 12 feet wide, allowing only one lane of traffic. Listed on the National Register of Historic Places, it is the second covered bridge you can see as you travel north on Route 7.

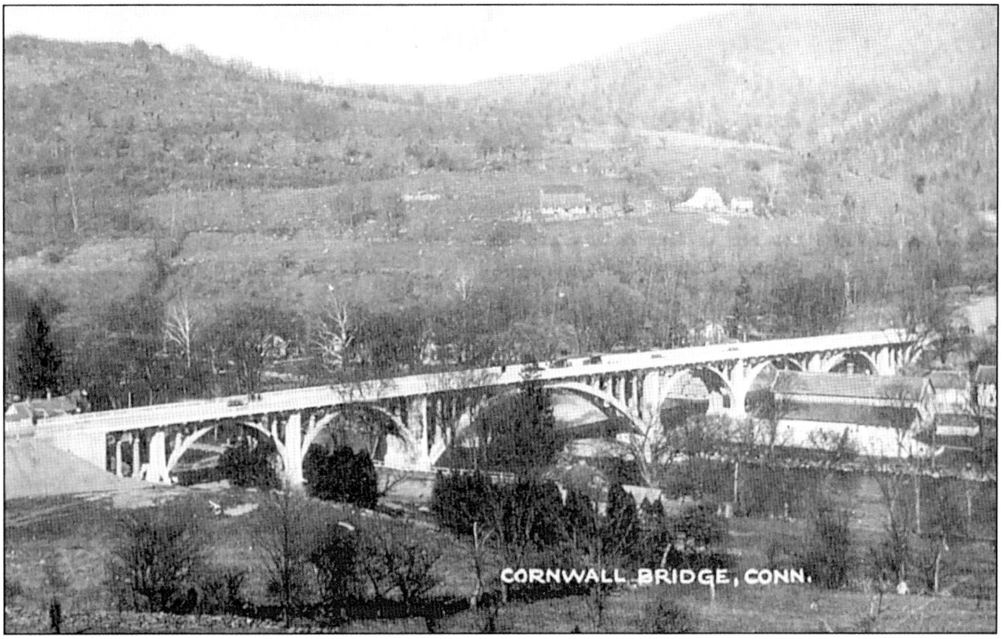

In order to see the Cornwall Bridge Railroad Station, one has to look down quickly while crossing the concrete bridge over the Housatonic River. The station was built in 1883, but its use as a station discontinued when rail service stopped in 1972. Most recently, it served as an antique shop.

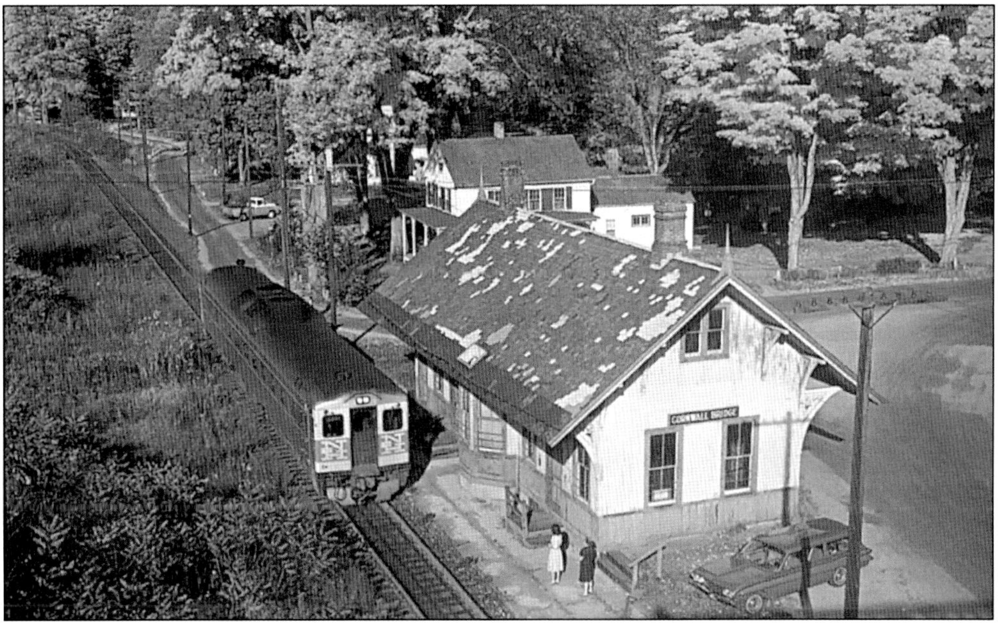

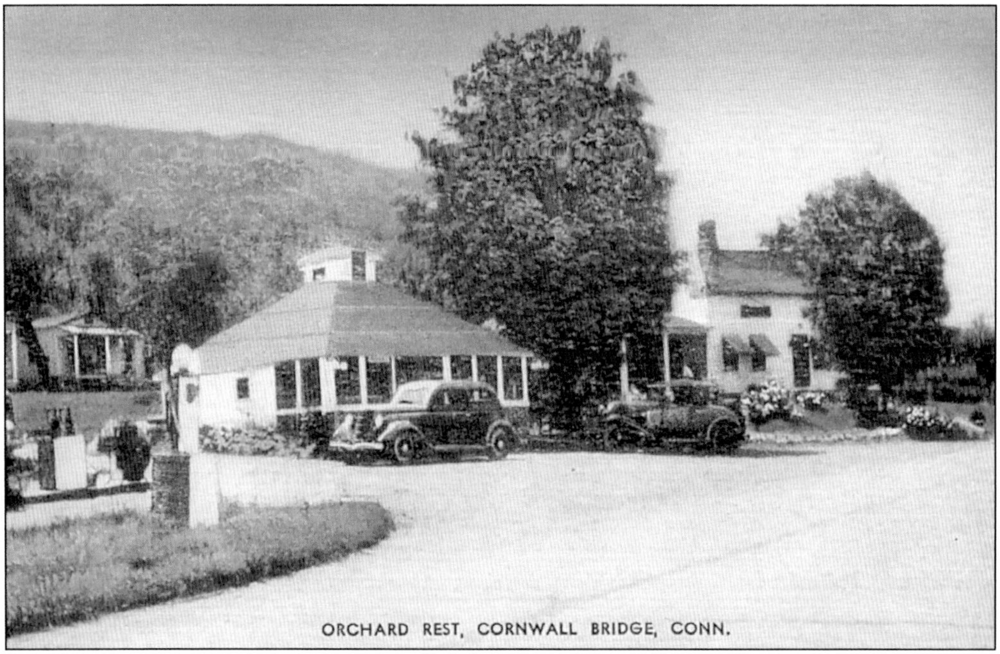

Orchard Rest was located north of Cornwall Bridge "in the beautiful Litchfield Hills." Mary J. Mitchell was the proprietor. There were five "modern heated cabins," and home-cooked meals were provided. The cabins are still visible behind the home and bait shop across from Housatonic Meadows State Park.

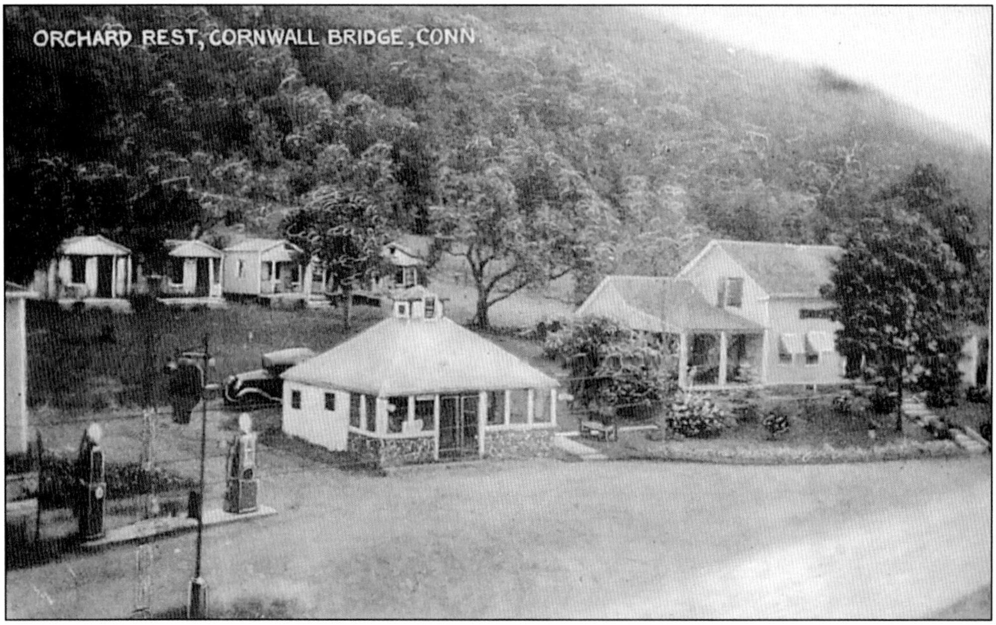

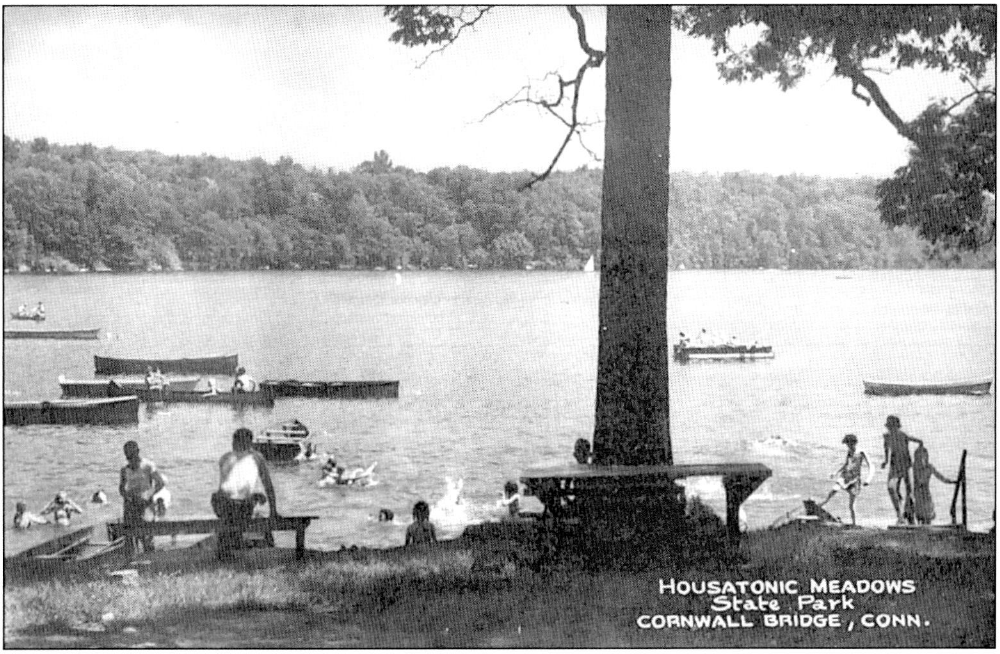

One of several state parks accessed by Route 7, Housatonic Meadows offered swimming, boating, and picnicking. Like the other state parks, the land was set aside at an early date and today includes both picnic and camping areas.

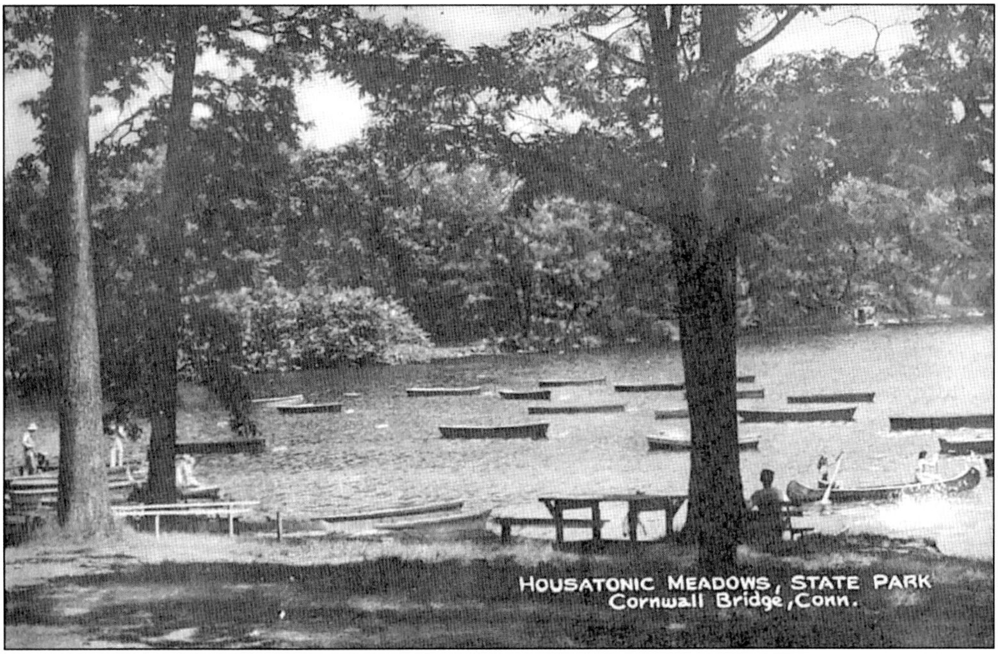

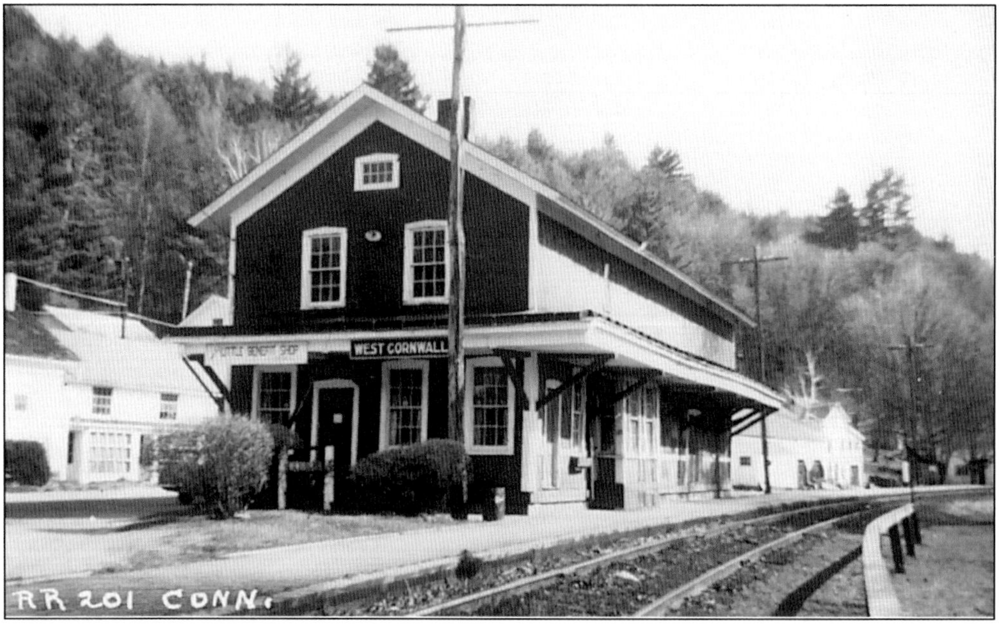

West Cornwall Station was once the designated pick-up for the milk cans from nearby dairy farms, until refrigerated tank trucks took over the job. Students also took the train from here to high school in New Milford or Canaan. It is now a private home just over the covered bridge at Railroad Square.

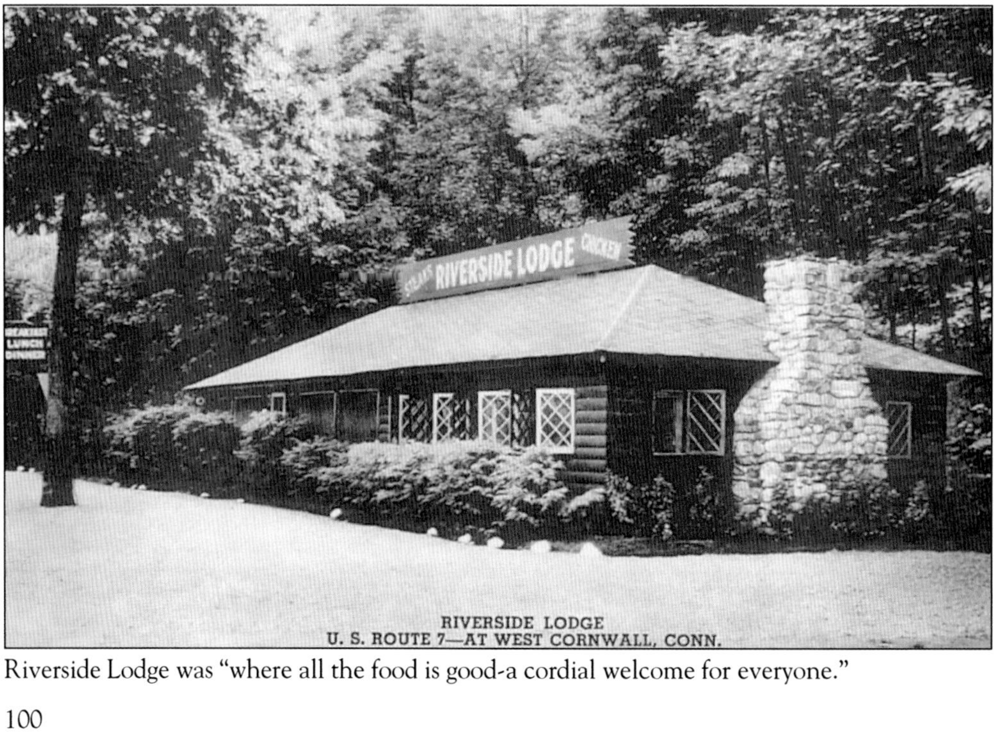

Riverside Lodge was "where all the food is good-a cordial welcome for everyone."

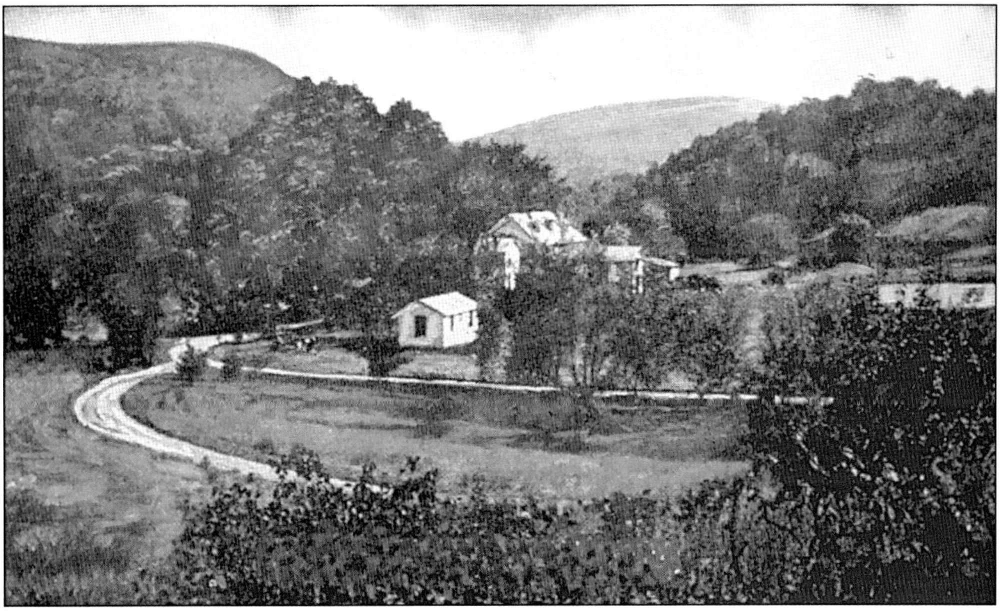

Pine Crest and Pine Villa both operated on the same property.

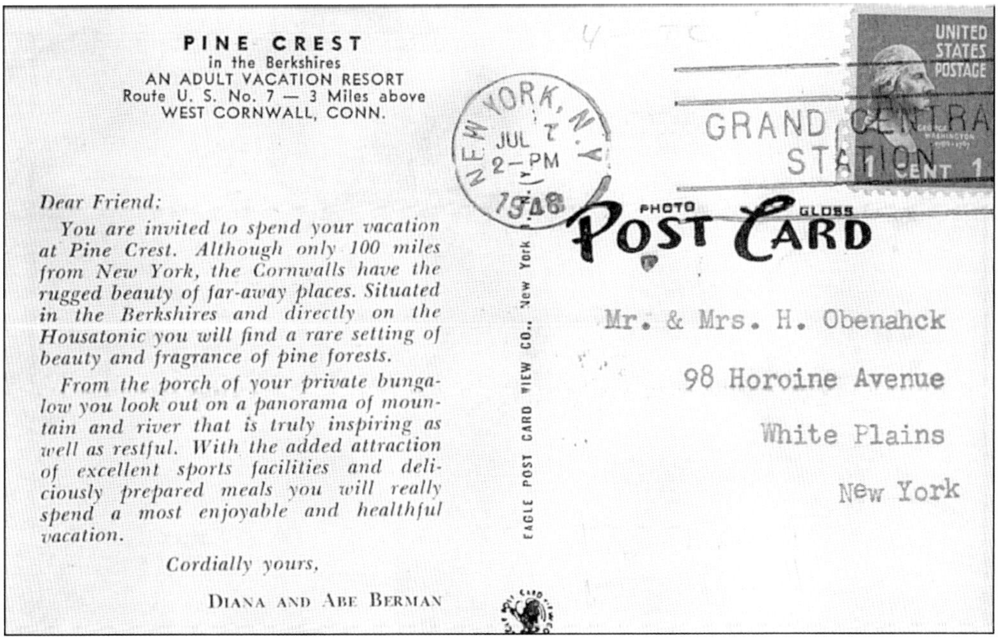

PINE CREST
in the Berkshires
AN ADULT VACATION RESORT
Route U. S. No. 7 — 3 Miles above
WEST CORNWALL, CONN.

Dear Friend:

You are invited to spend your vacation at Pine Crest. Although only 100 miles from New York, the Cornwalls have the rugged beauty of far-away places. Situated in the Berkshires and directly on the Housatonic you will find a rare setting of beauty and fragrance of pine forests.

From the porch of your private bungalow you look out on a panorama of mountain and river that is truly inspiring as well as restful. With the added attraction of excellent sports facilities and deliciously prepared meals you will really spend a most enjoyable and healthful vacation.

Cordially yours,

DIANA AND ABE BERMAN

EAGLE POST CARD VIEW CO., New York

NEW YORK, N.Y.
JUL 7
2-PM
1948

GRAND CENTRAL
STATION

UNITED STATES POSTAGE
1 CENT 1

PHOTO GLOSS
POST CARD

Mr. & Mrs. H. Obenahck
98 Horoine Avenue
White Plains
New York

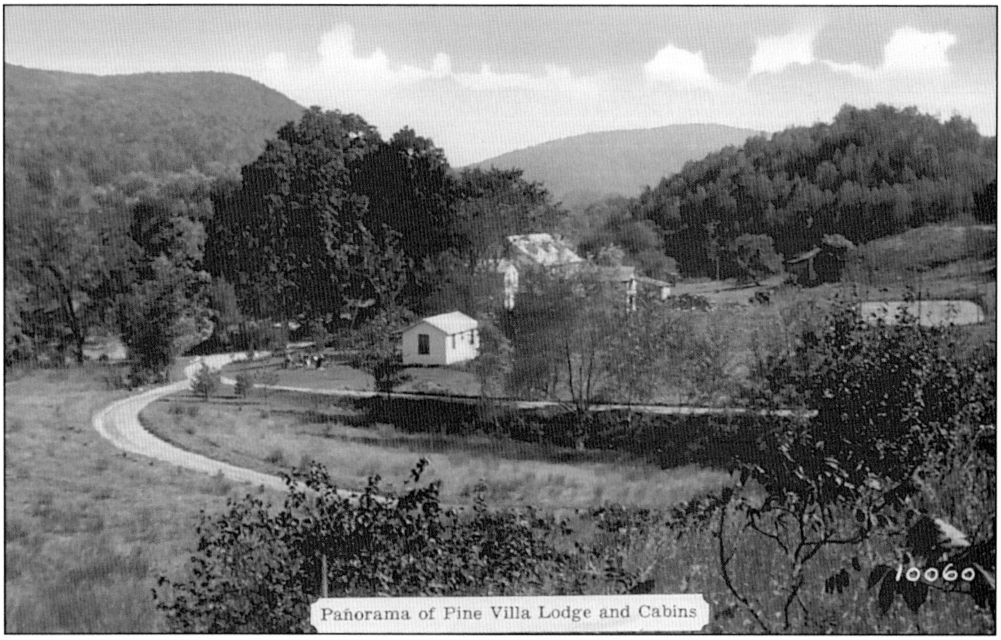

Pañorama of Pine Villa Lodge and Cabins

Part of the original property now serves as the location of Housatonic Anglers, which provides guide services, fly fishing instruction, and guest cottages.

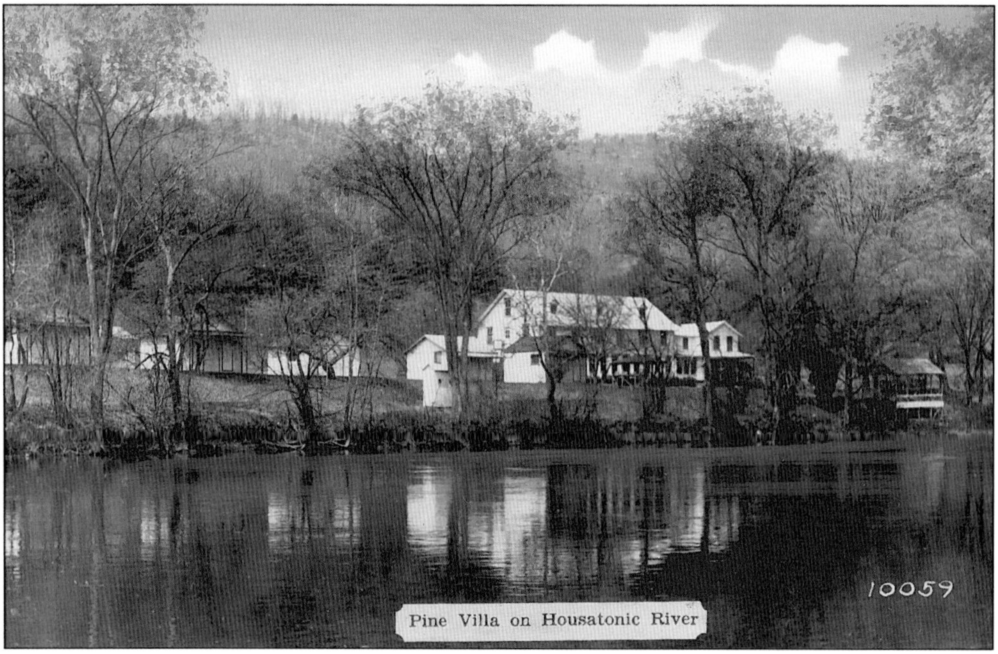

Pine Villa on Housatonic River

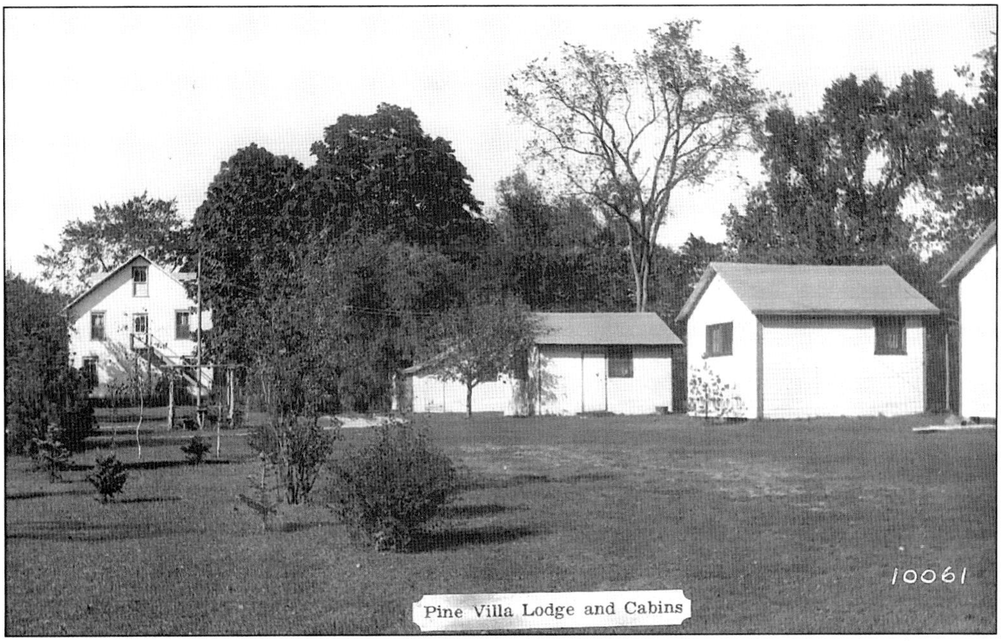

This photo and the previous two were original photos used by Dexter Press to create advertising postcards.

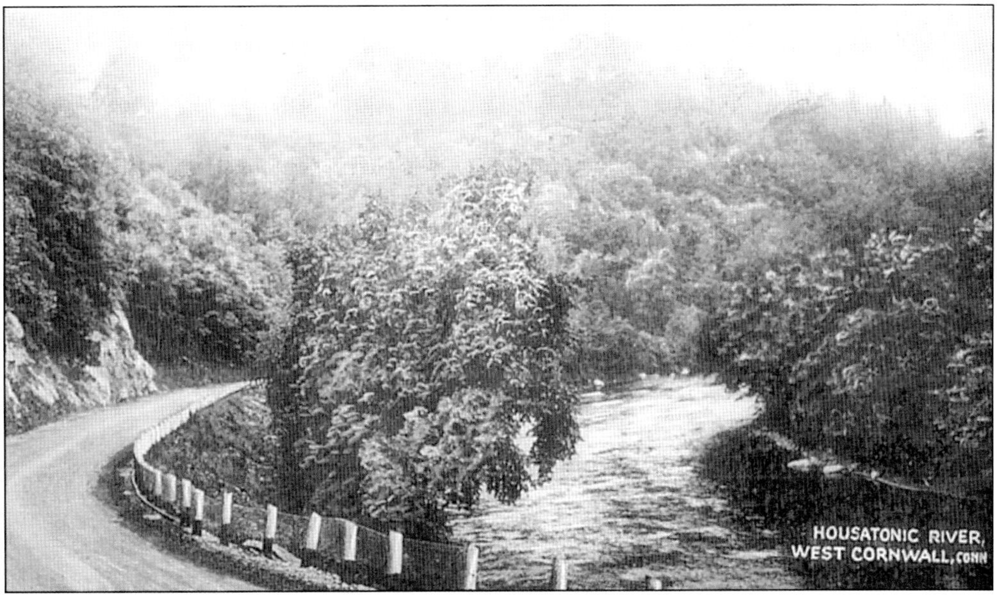

Even in 1999, a drive along the Housatonic River can still lead one to imagine being in the wilderness.

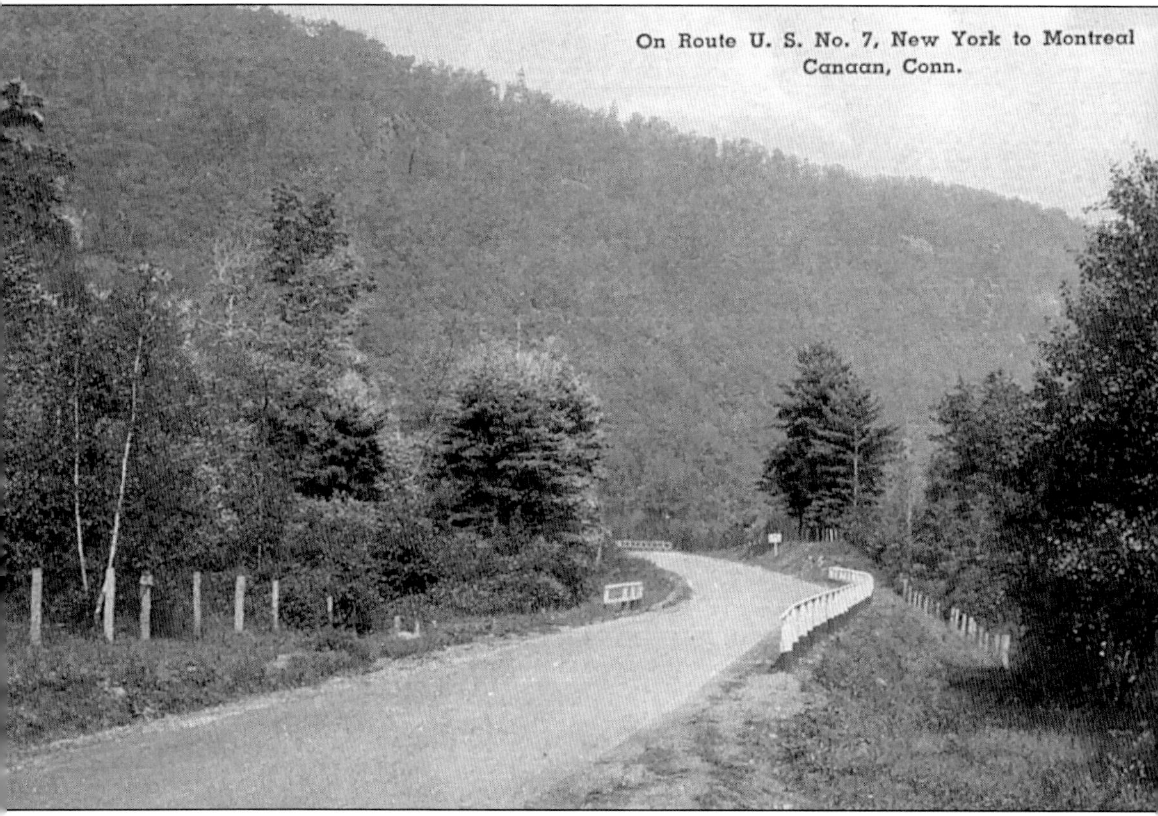

Route 7 continues to provide a way to Canaan or on to Montreal.

Nine

FALLS VILLAGE AND CANAAN

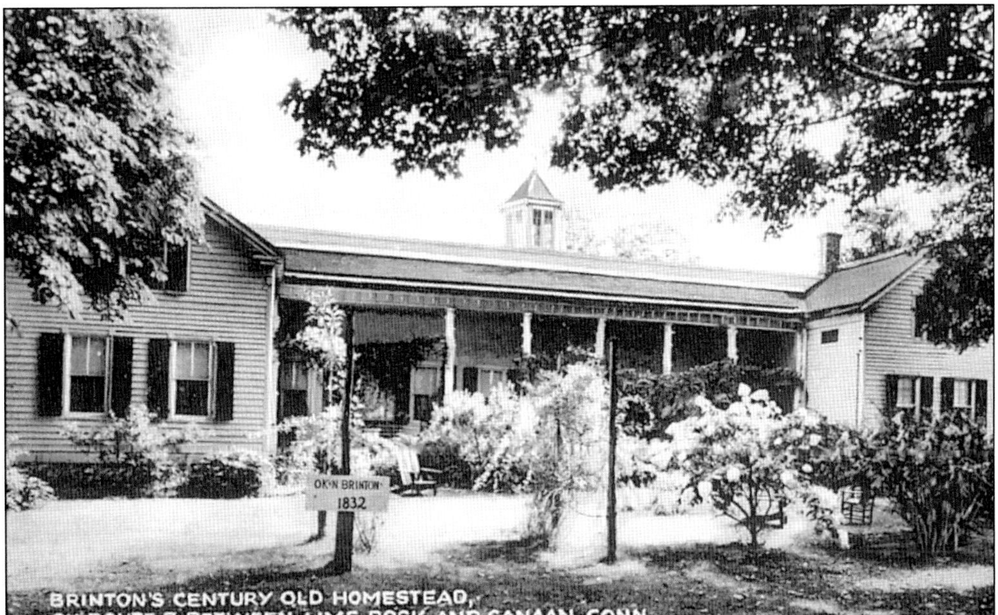

This home was built in 1832. It has been lovingly restored and kept up. Note the rustic posts supporting the porch roof. The house sits on a slight rise, at a curve of the road at the corner of Kellogg Street and Route 7. Brinton Hill Road is nearby on the other side of Route 7.

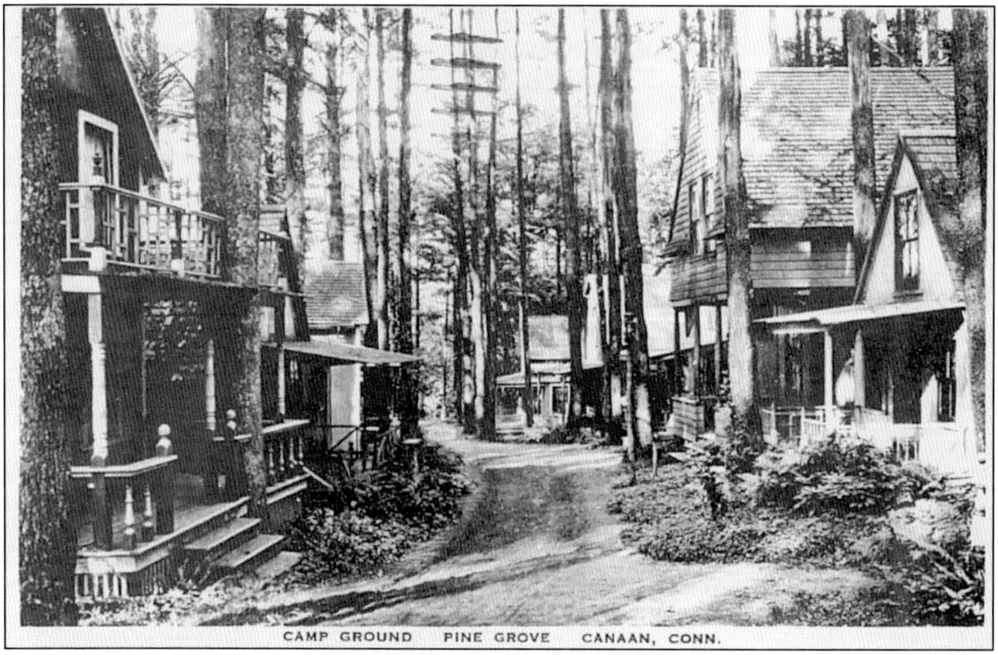

In his book *Country Depots in the Connecticut Hills*, Robert F. Lord shows a small station, Pine Grove, just south of Canaan. It served the Pine Grove Methodist Summer Camp Meeting. First tents, then summer homes, and finally a hotel were built around the chapel. This card was sent in 1943. Notice the porch built around a tree on the left.

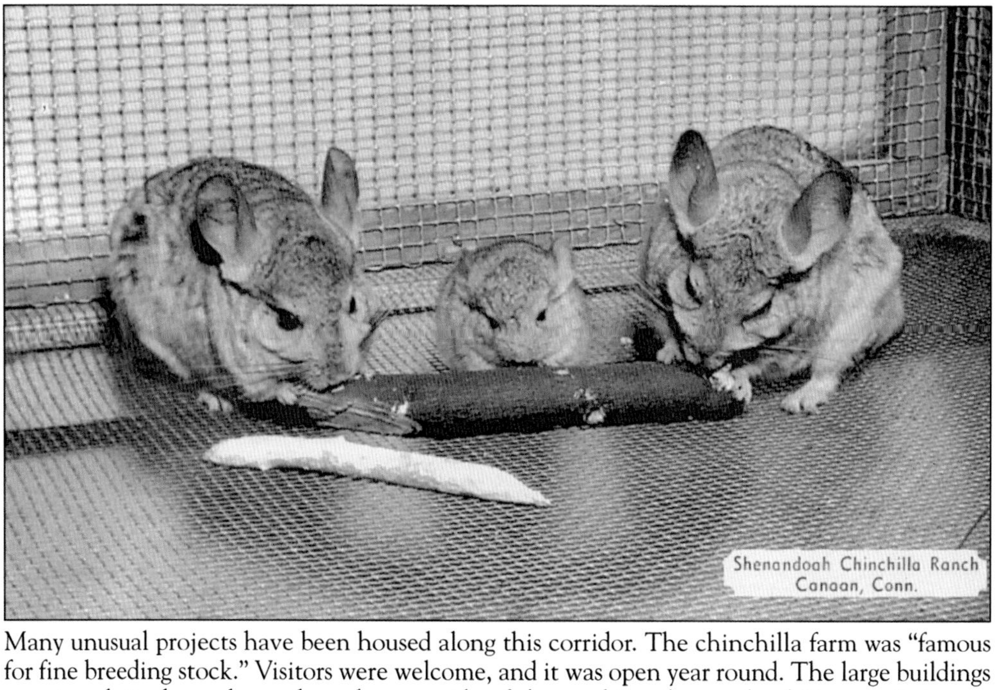

Many unusual projects have been housed along this corridor. The chinchilla farm was "famous for fine breeding stock." Visitors were welcome, and it was open year round. The large buildings remain relatively unchanged on the east side of the road 2 miles south of Canaan. It is now called Mountain Side.

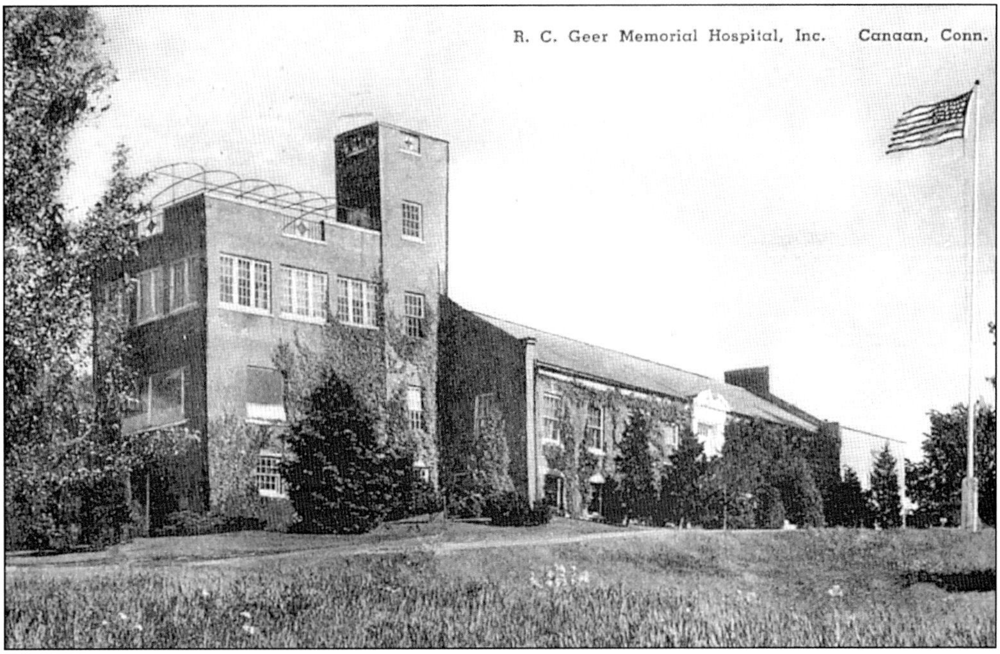

The R.C. Geer Hospital was the nearest source for medical care in a large area of northwestern Connecticut. This picture shows the hospital in 1946. It is currently the Geer Nursing and Rehabilitation Center and Adult Day Center.

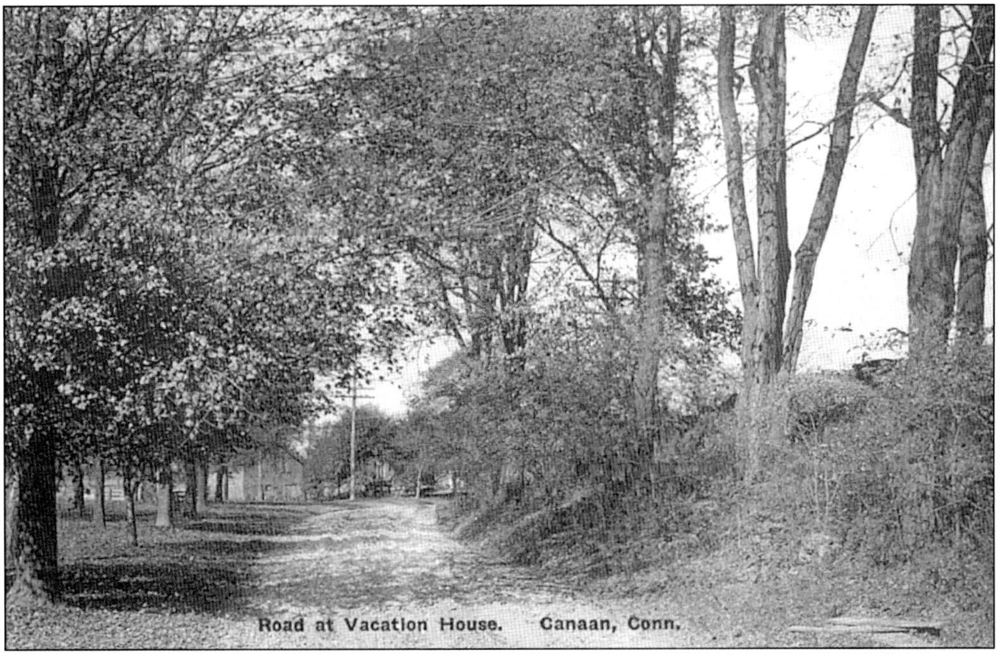

In 1915, Route 7 was still a dirt road. A camper at Vacation House, the Girls' Friendly Society Camp, wrote home to Meriden, "This is the house where I'm staying." The Girls' Friendly Society was a youth group of the Episcopal Church.

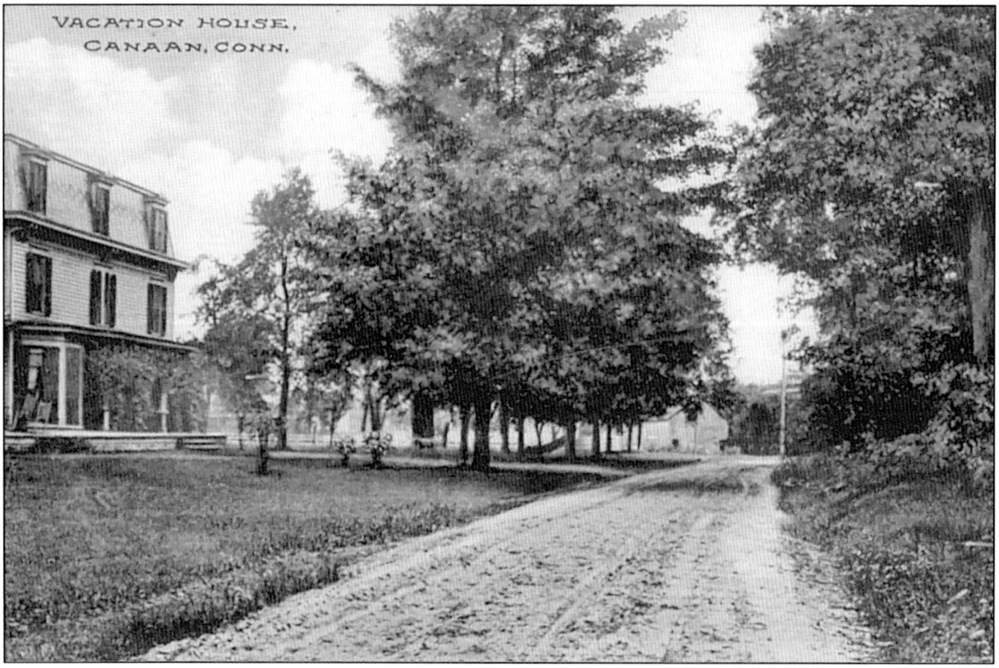

Vacation House, including 10 acres, was originally the home of Mary Watson Ward, given to the Episcopal Church by her daughter Mrs. R.L. McClain in 1901.

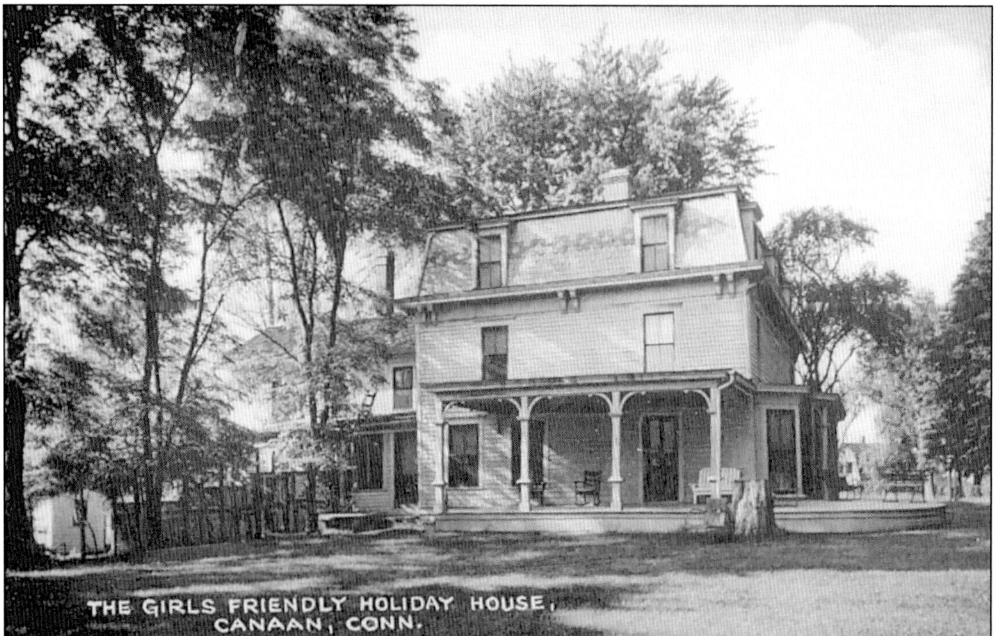

Holiday House, as it was later called, operated as a camp from 1902 until 1966, when the house did not meet modern safety codes.

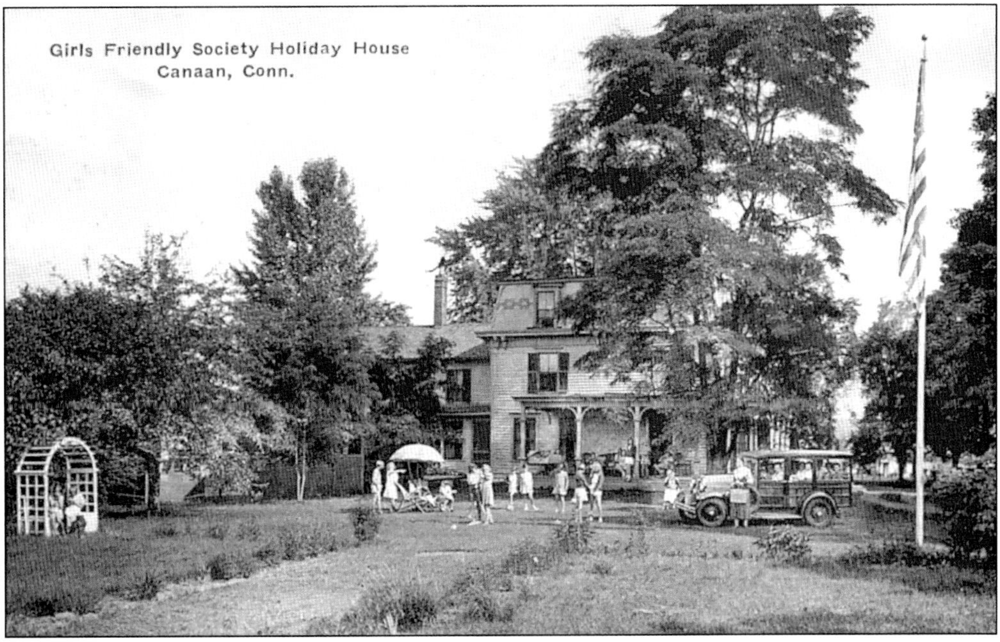

The gardens were located south of the house next to Route 7. In later years, they were replaced by a lawn. The flagpole remained, and campers attended the raising and lowering of the flag each day.

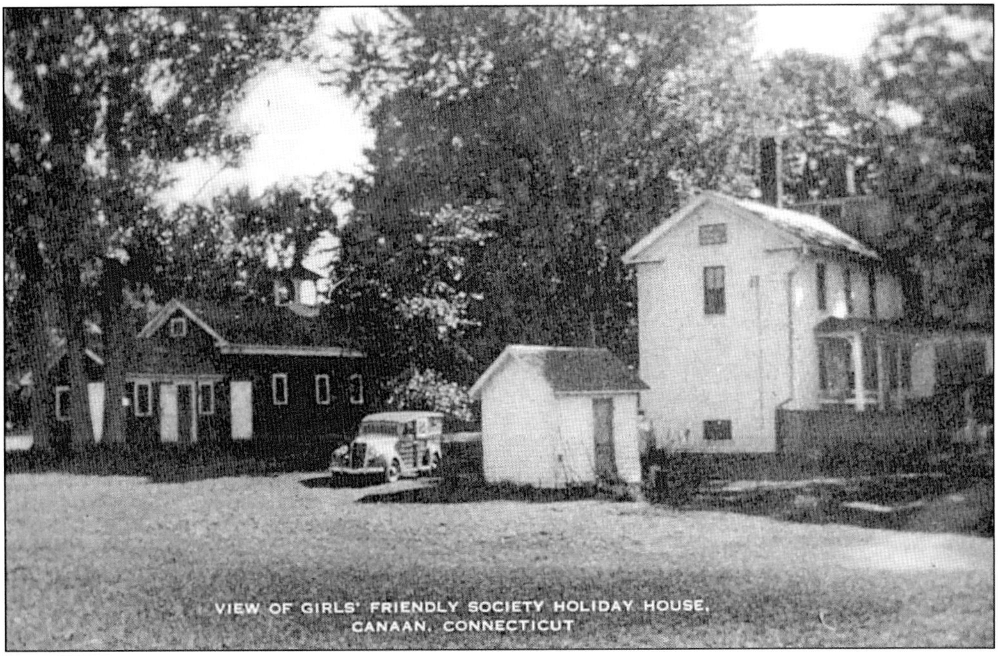

The main house, shown to the right, included the dining room, sitting rooms, and campers and counselors rooms on the second and third floors.

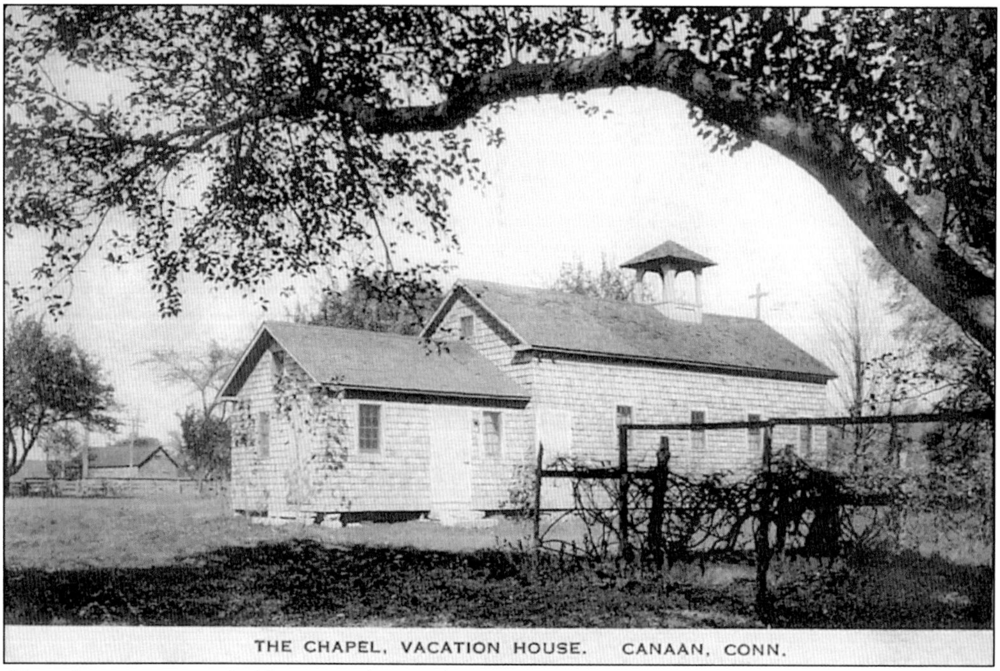

Chapel services were held twice a day, and communion was held on Wednesday. This card was sent in 1920 to Mrs. Jennings on Flax Hill in South Norwalk.

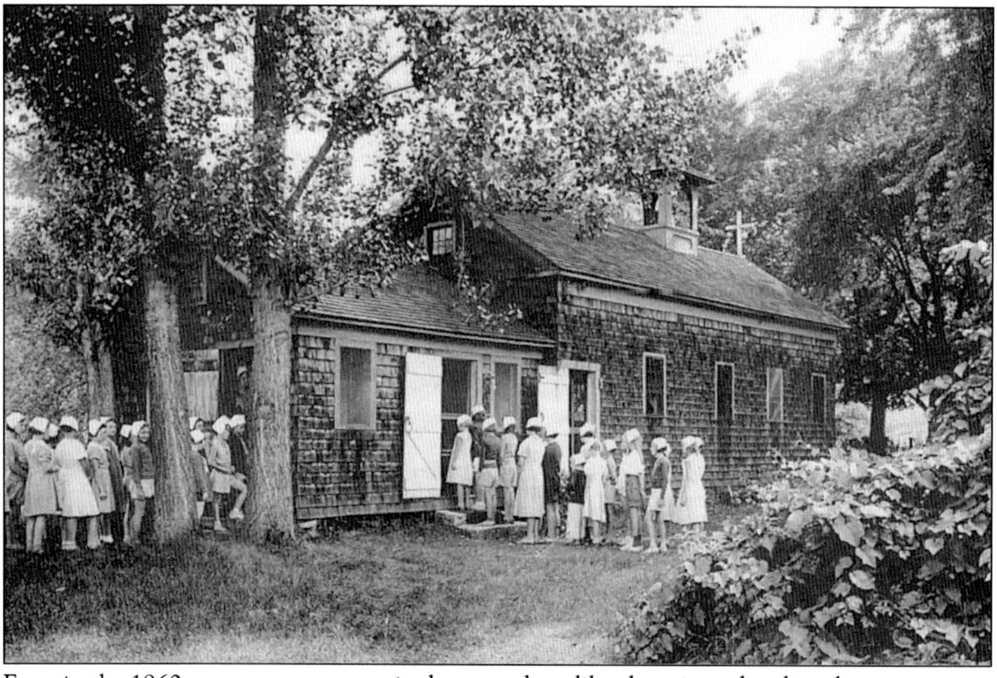

Even in the 1960s, campers were required to wear hats like these into the chapel.

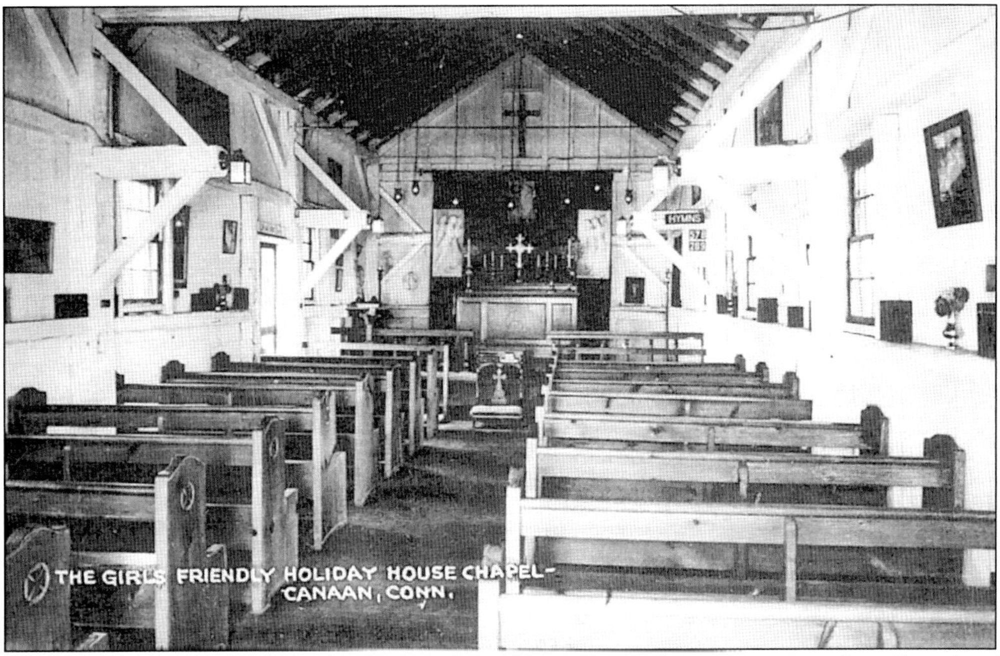

Hymns and religious songs were an important part of the services in the Chapel of Transfiguration.

Behind Joan Bepler is the small building that served as the camp store. It was open twice a day, and campers could not have more than two sweets per day. The building remains today as an outbuilding for the Seventh Day Adventist Church, now on the property at the corner of Route 126. Another small outbuilding remains, which was the craft house for the camp.

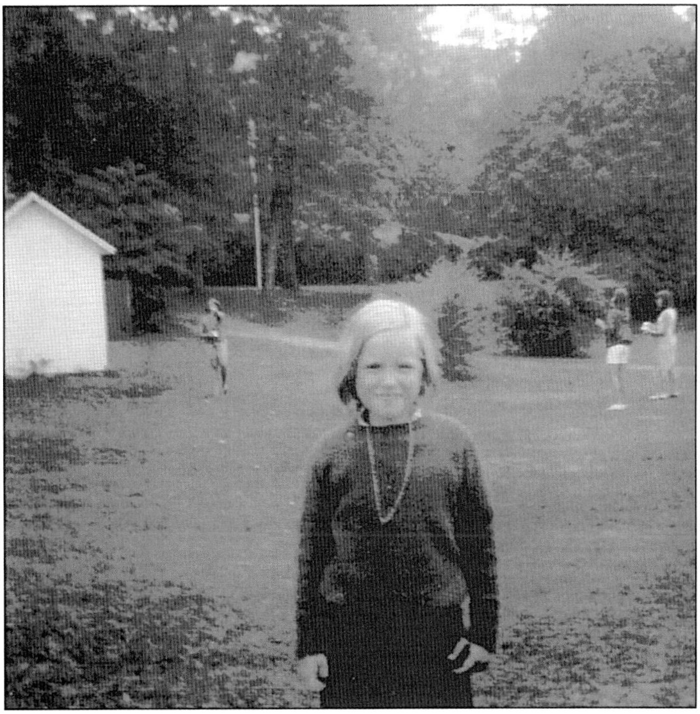

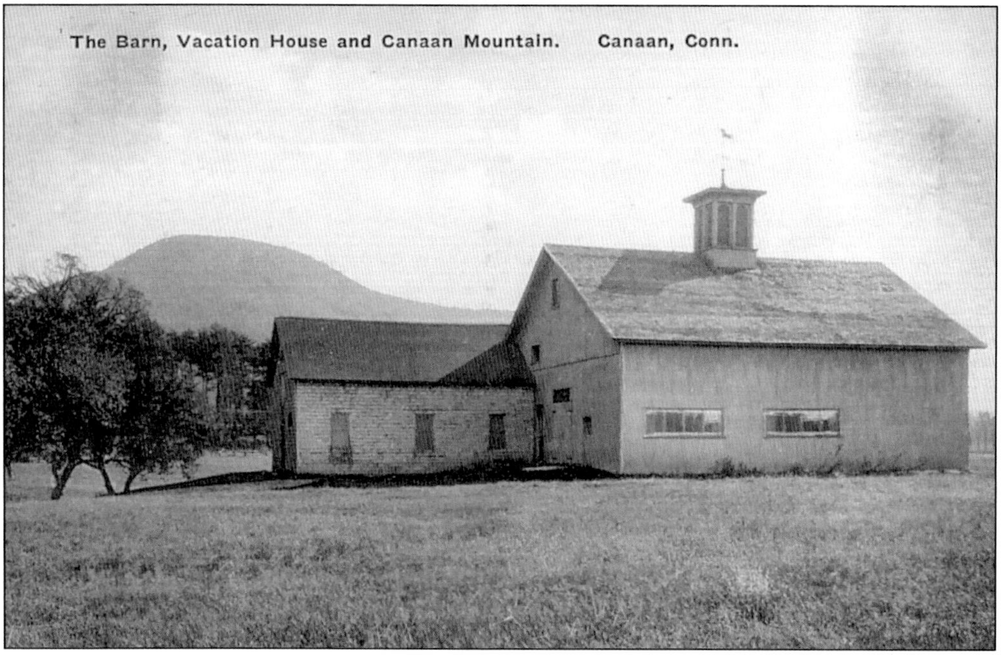

This earlier view clearly shows the characteristic architecture of a Victorian barn. Later changes to the barn included the addition of windows, a stage, a fireplace, and the removal of the cupola.

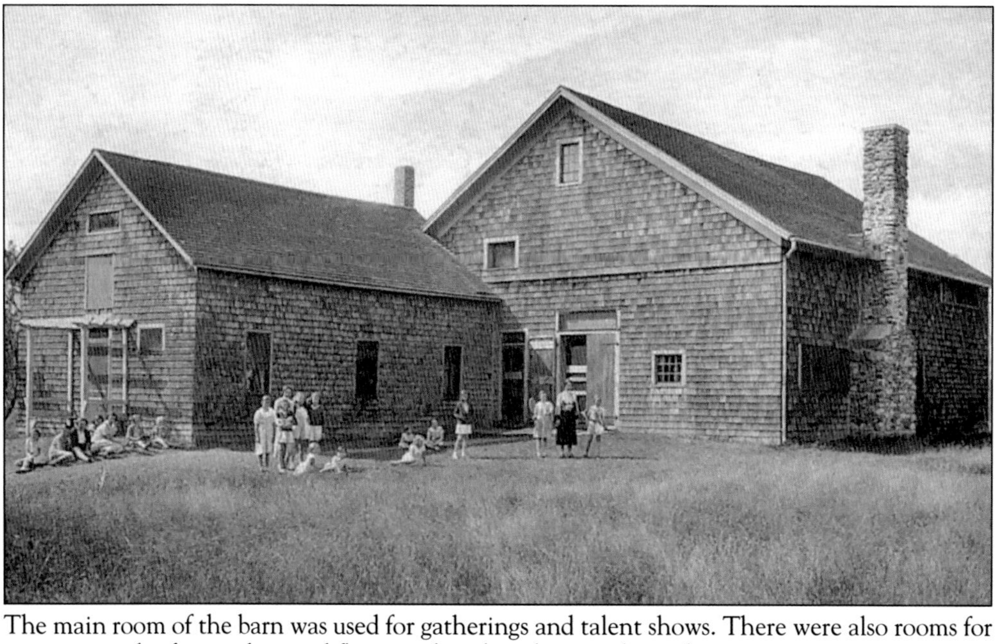

The main room of the barn was used for gatherings and talent shows. There were also rooms for campers on the first and second floors and in the adjoining bungalow.

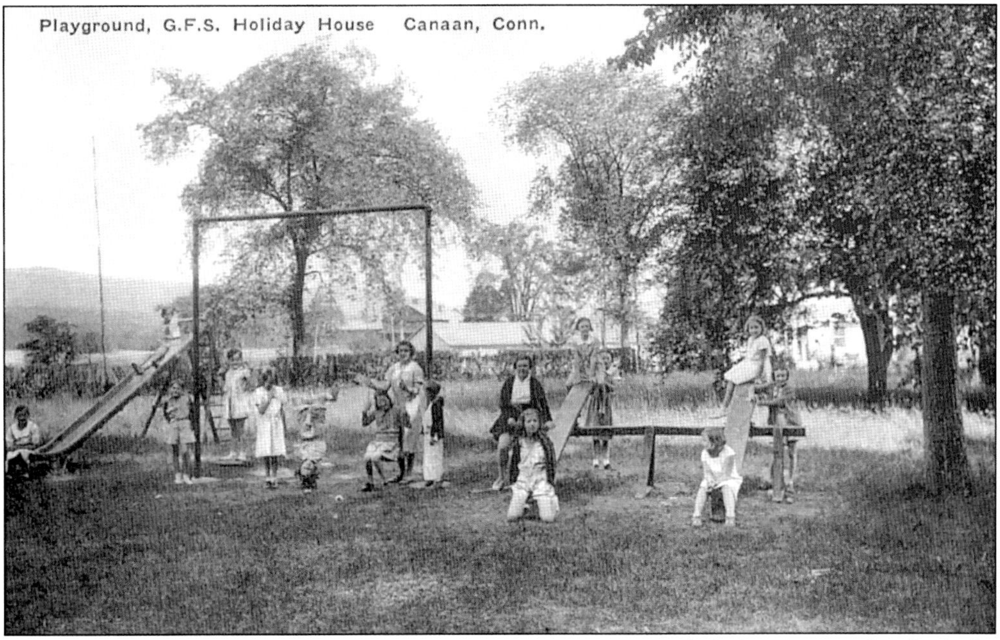

This shows the playground in 1937. Other playtime activities included archery and volleyball.

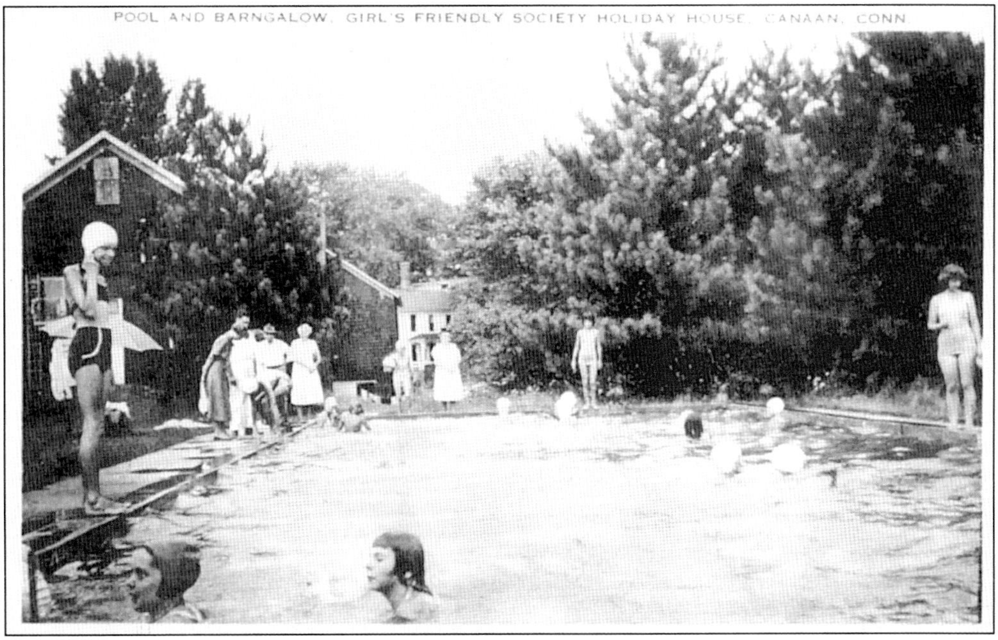

The Anna Freeman Memorial Swimming Pool was located behind the barn. Campers signed themselves in and out of the pool with the use of metal tags on a wooden board. A buddy system was also required. On Saturday evenings, camp sessions were tearfully culminated with an awards ceremony, at which campers floated their own candle in the water.

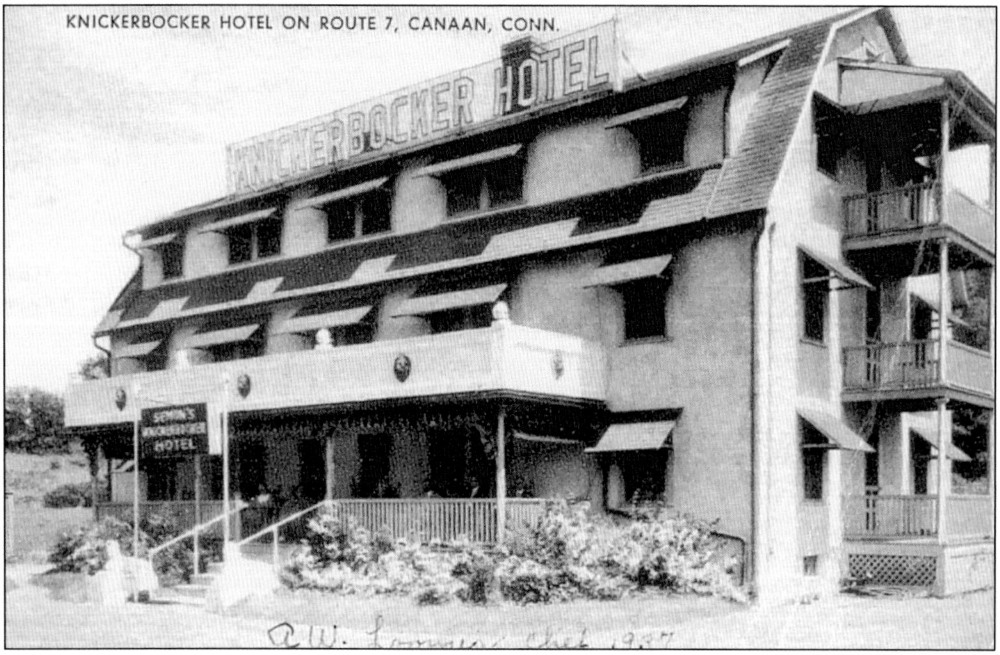

The Knickerbocker Hotel may have been the A.W. Loomis Club in 1937.

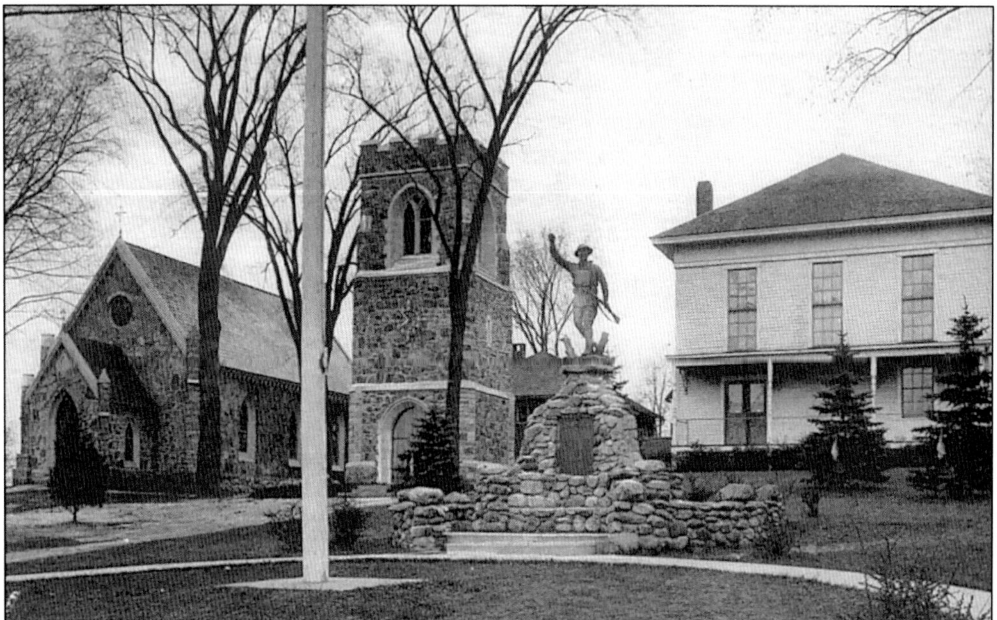
CHRIST EPISCOPAL CHURCH, CLOCK TOWER, WORLD WAR MEMORIAL AND TOWN HALL CANAAN, CONN.

This is the oldest church in Canaan. The building was started in 1846 and finished on a budget of $2,000. The stone was quarried locally and is called Cannaanite. The clock tower was built much later, in 1931. It was outfitted with a Seth Warner clock and four bells. Girls' Friendly Society campers walked to town to attend this church at Main and Granite Avenues.

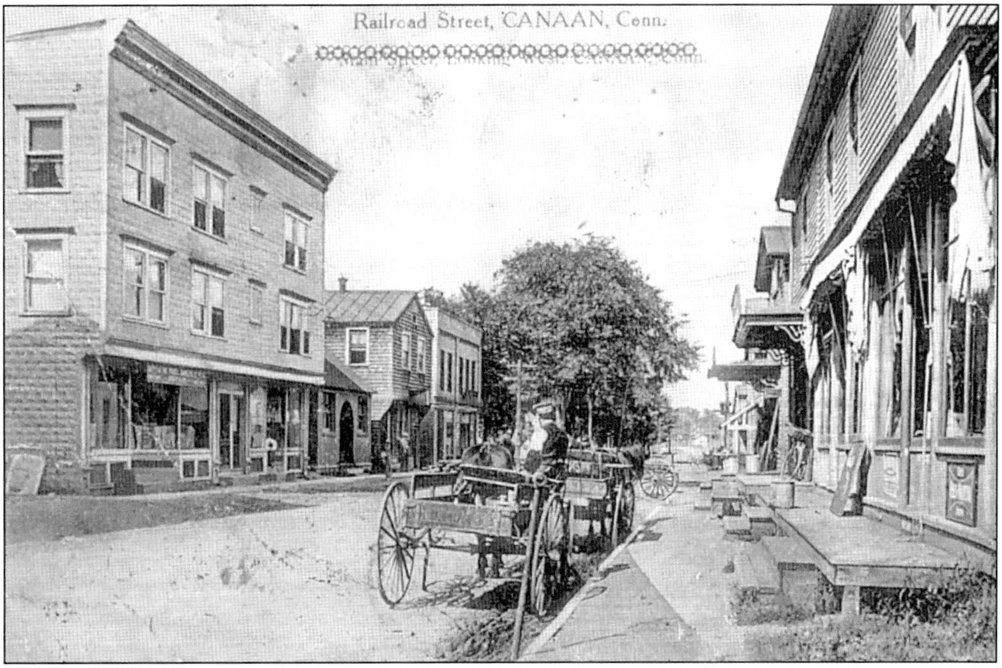

In 1911, the town has the look of the western frontier. The Canaan Railroad Station, located to the left of Railroad Street, currently houses Keilty's Depot (pub), Sidetracks Gifts, and the Housatonic Railroad Company.

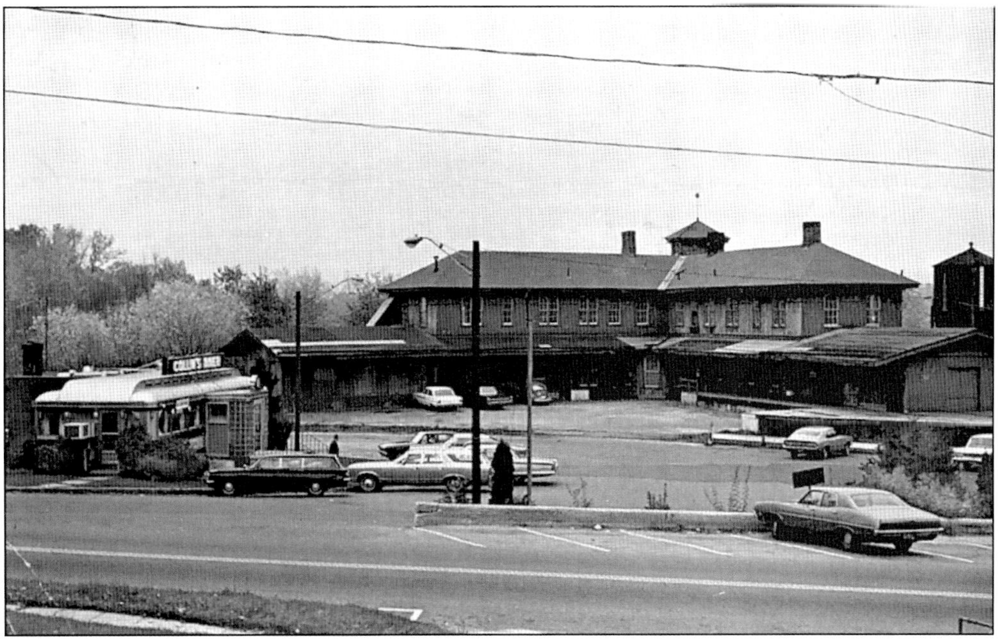

Collins Diner is located next to the historic railroad station. The diner has been operating since 1941 and is on the National Register of Historic Places.

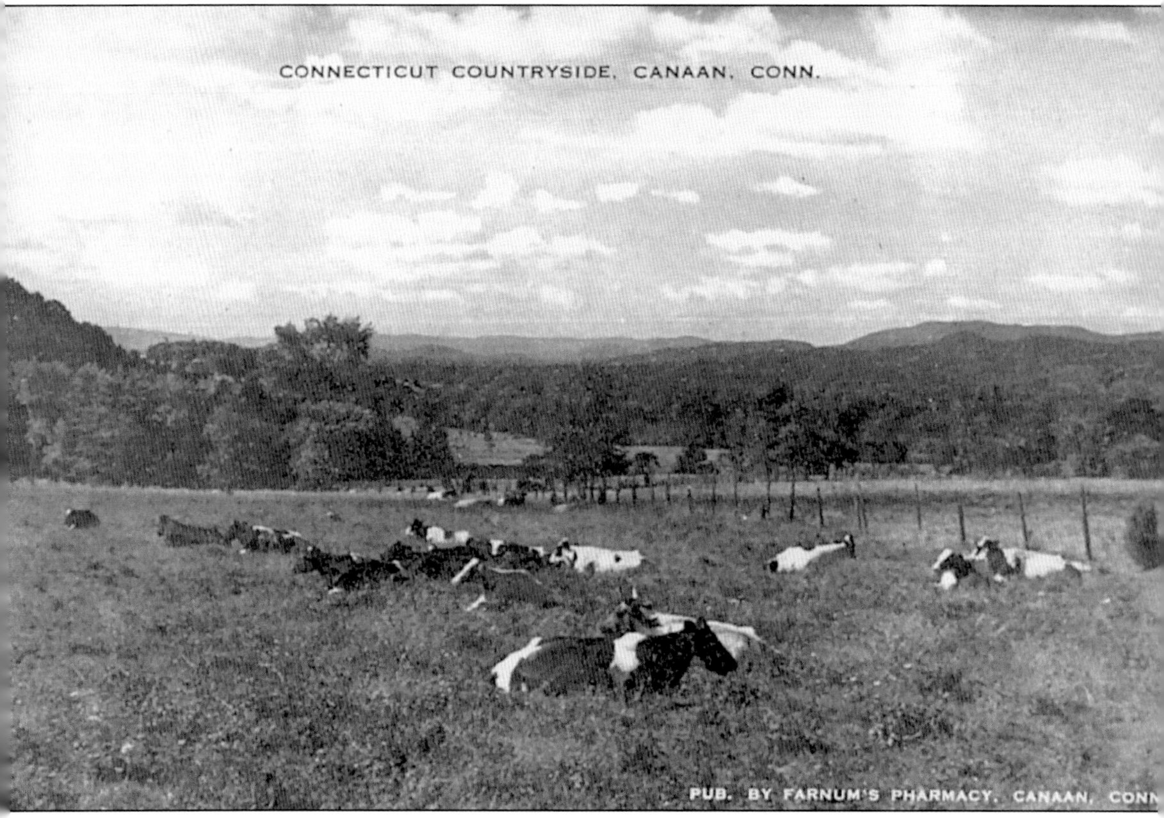

This sight, once commonplace along Route 7, can still occasionally be seen.

Ten

GOING TO CAMP

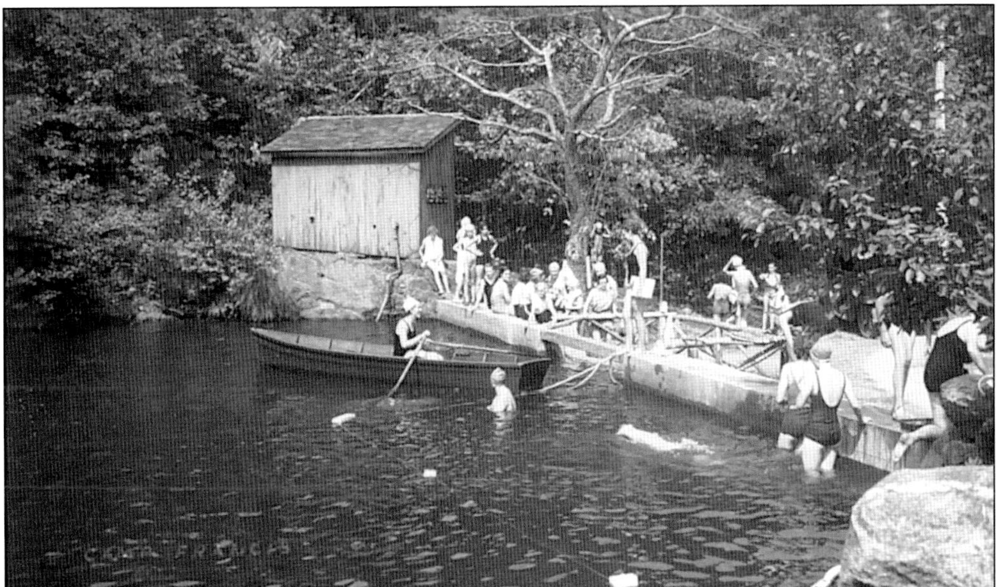

The dam at the pond at Camp Frances in Kent still exists, but it is doubtful that anyone swims from it.

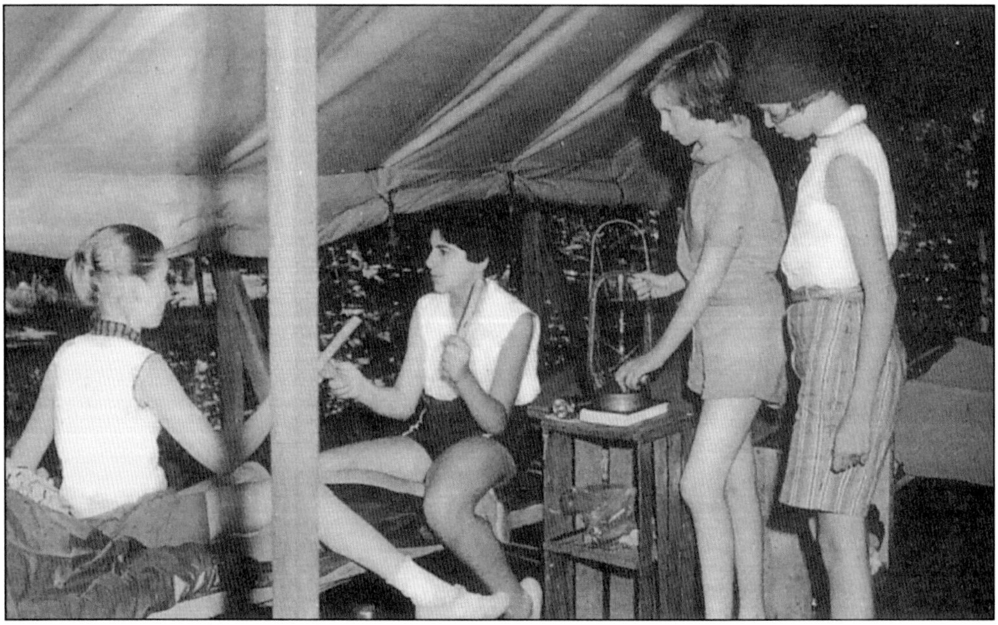

Camp Frances is still operated as a Girl Scouts camp for troops from Connecticut. It is located off Kent Hollow Road.

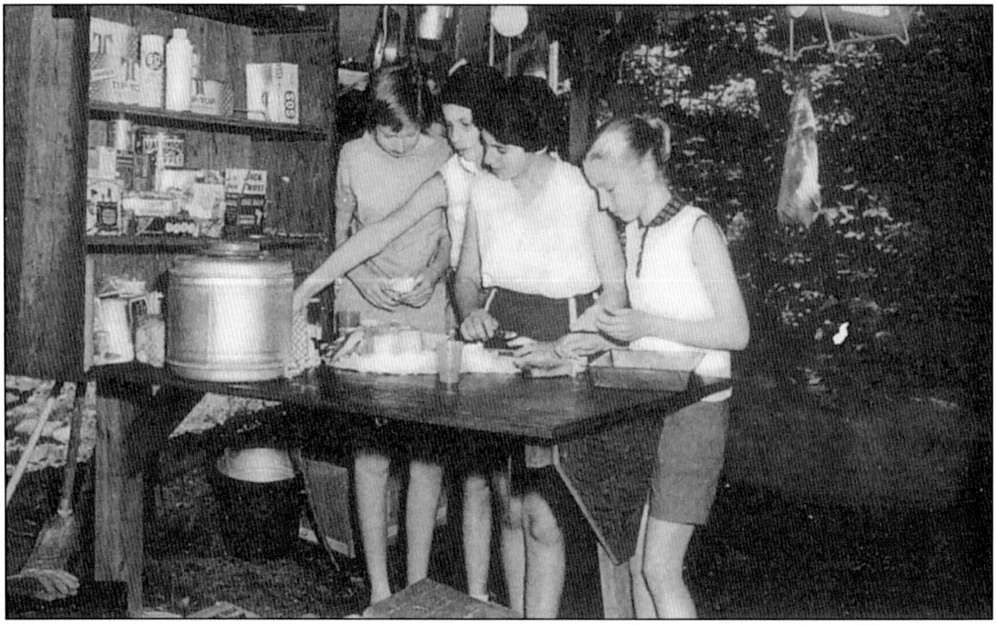

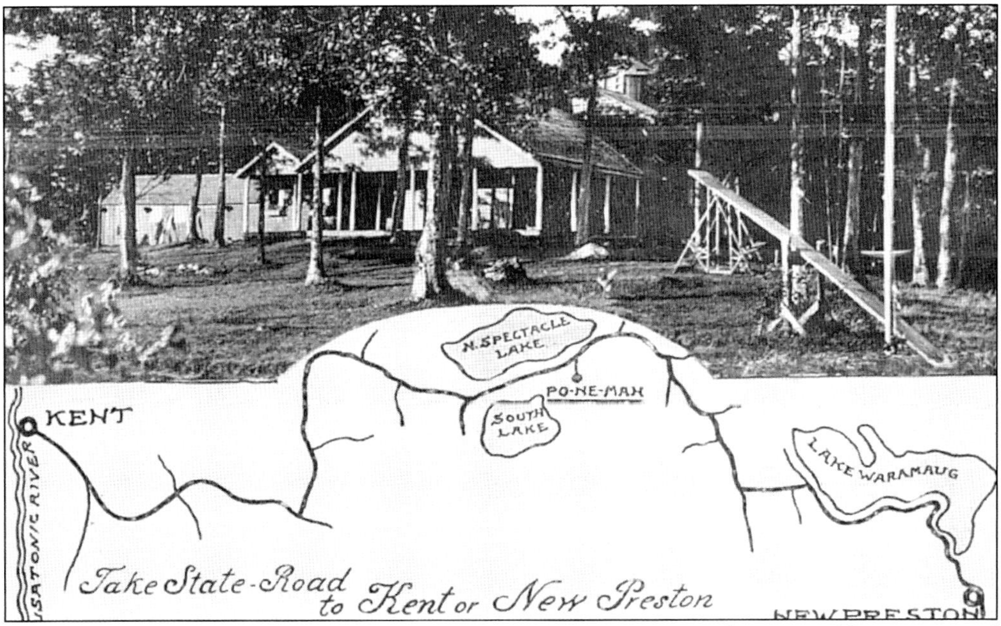

In this 1919 card from Camp Ponema in Kent, a camper writes, "All O.K. and having a good time. Have had two good feeds of fish." The camp was established in 1914.

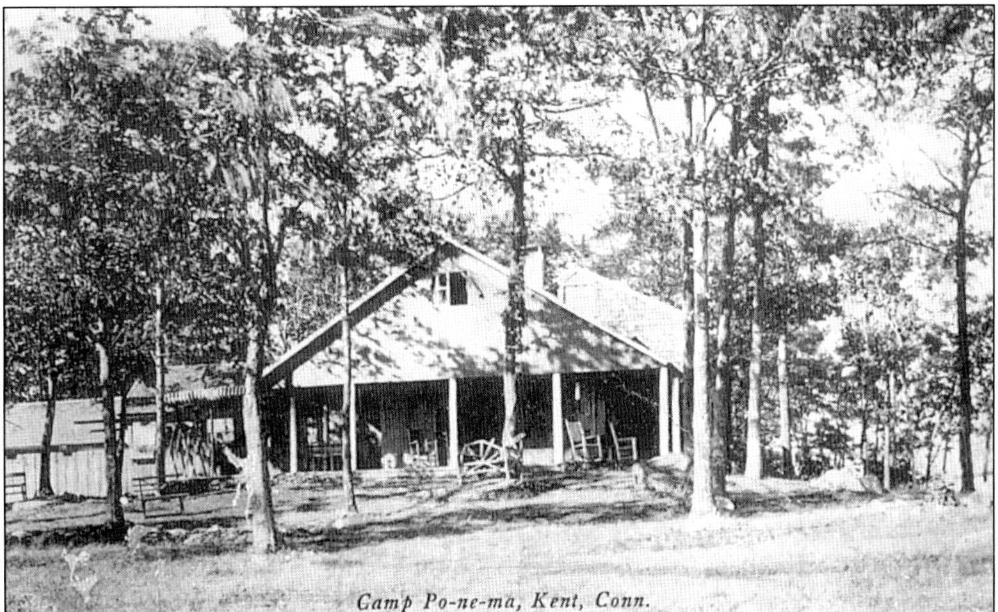

Uncle Leonard Bradley worked laying out trails and putting up signs for "Doc Allen" of Camp Ponema. Years later, the heirs of Mr. Allen continued the camp, and Mr. Bradley went on to a career as a naturalist and botanist.

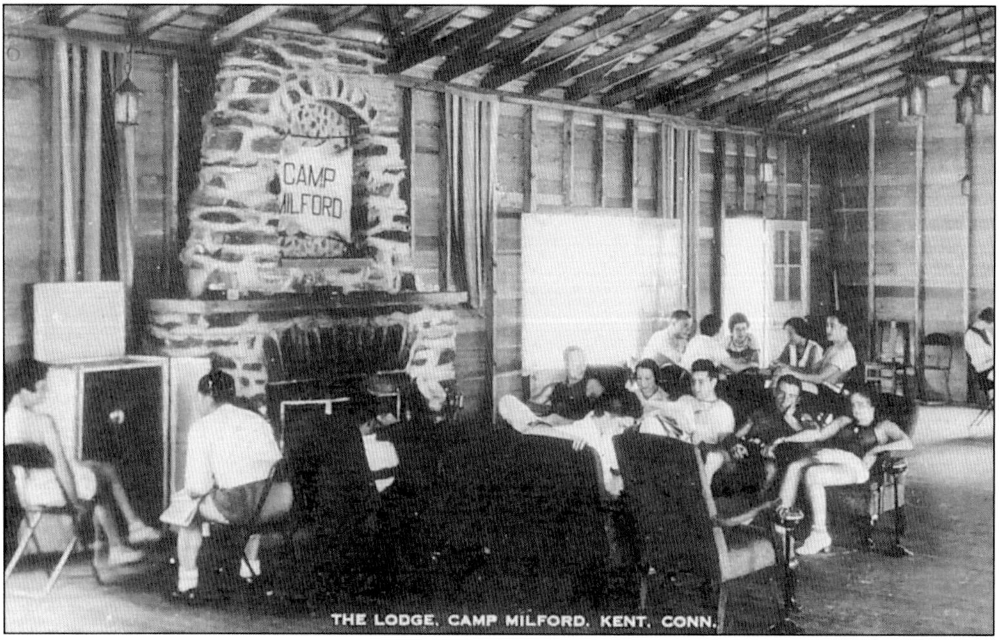

In 1936, a camper described Camp Milford as "very fine country and rustic cabins."

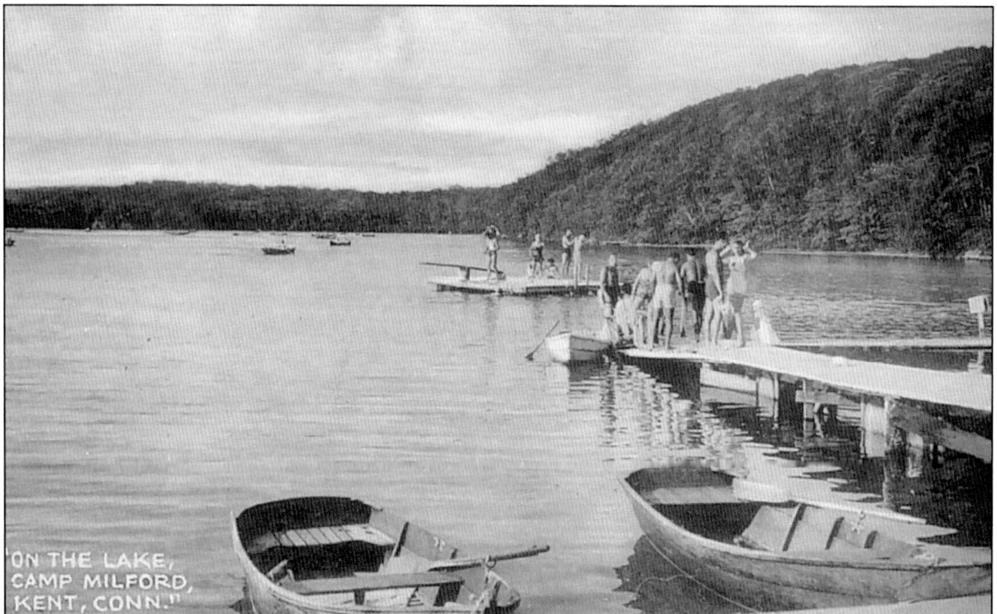

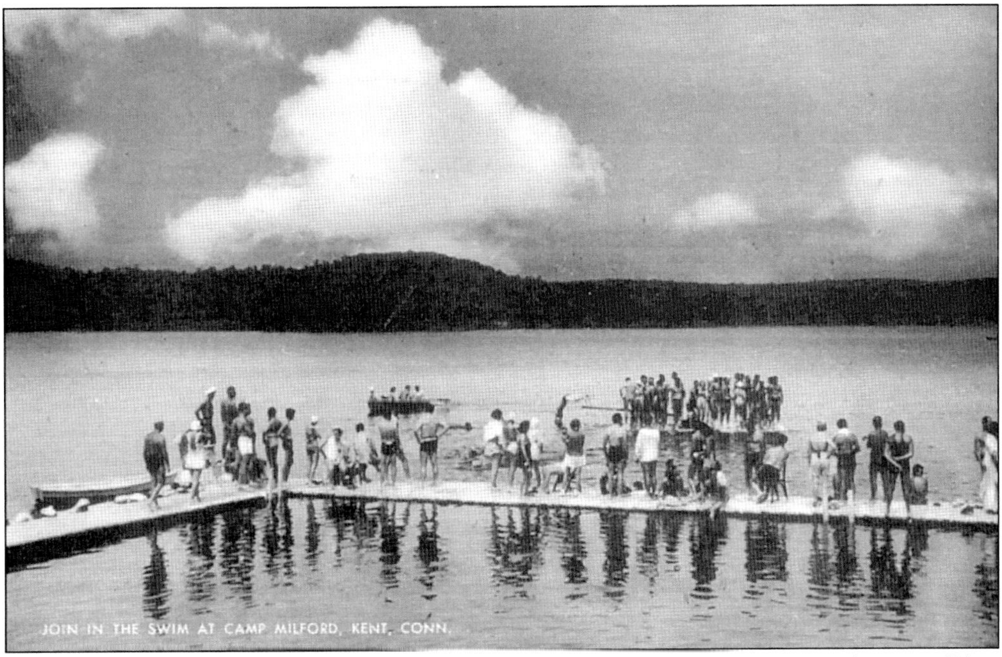

"Join in the Swim" was sent in 1940. "This is really a lovely vacation place. Nothing swell but just for good wholesome fun and relaxation."

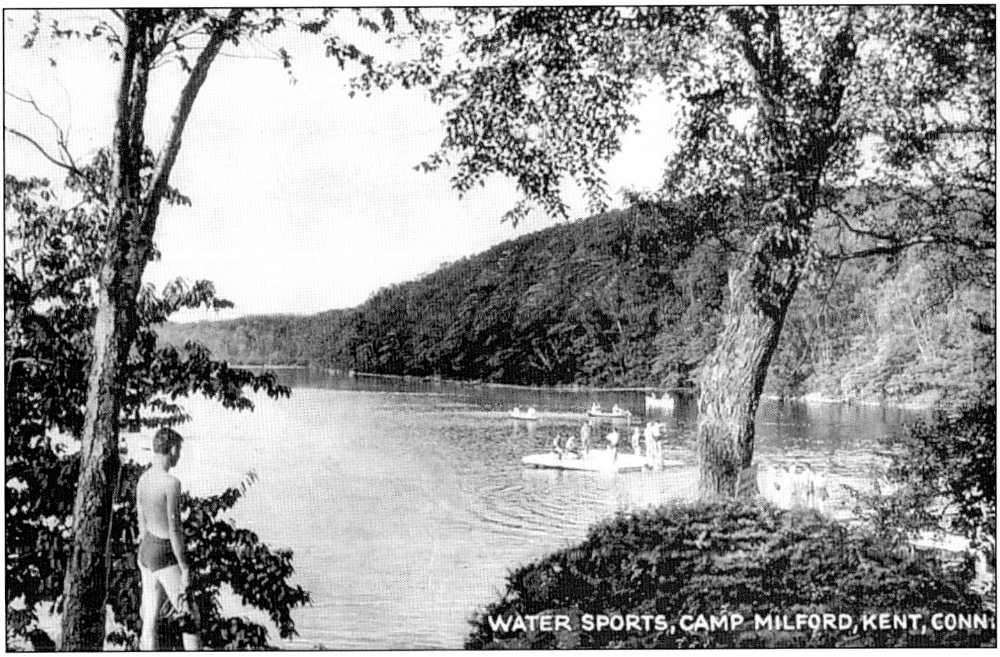

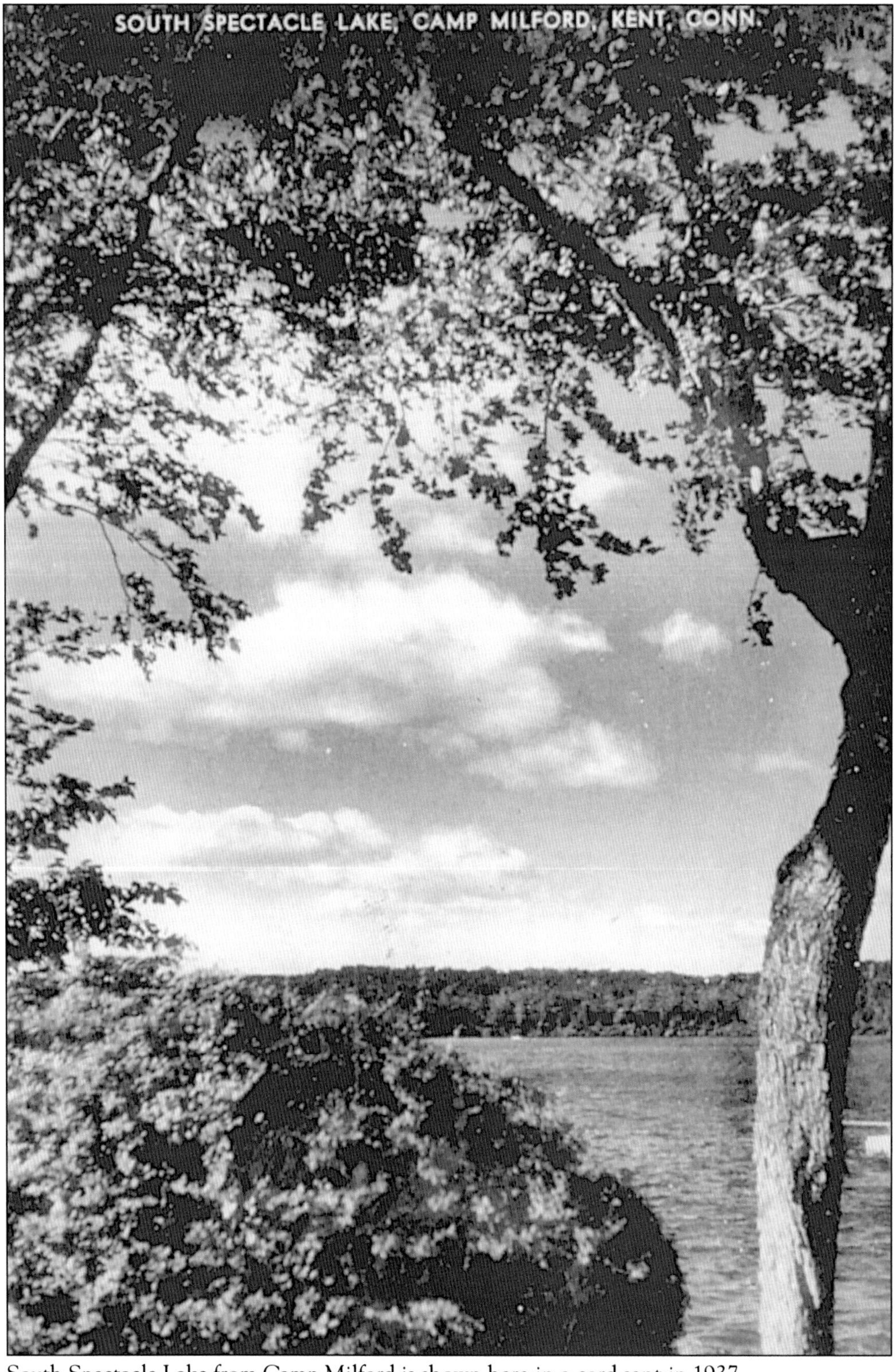

South Spectacle Lake from Camp Milford is shown here in a card sent in 1937.

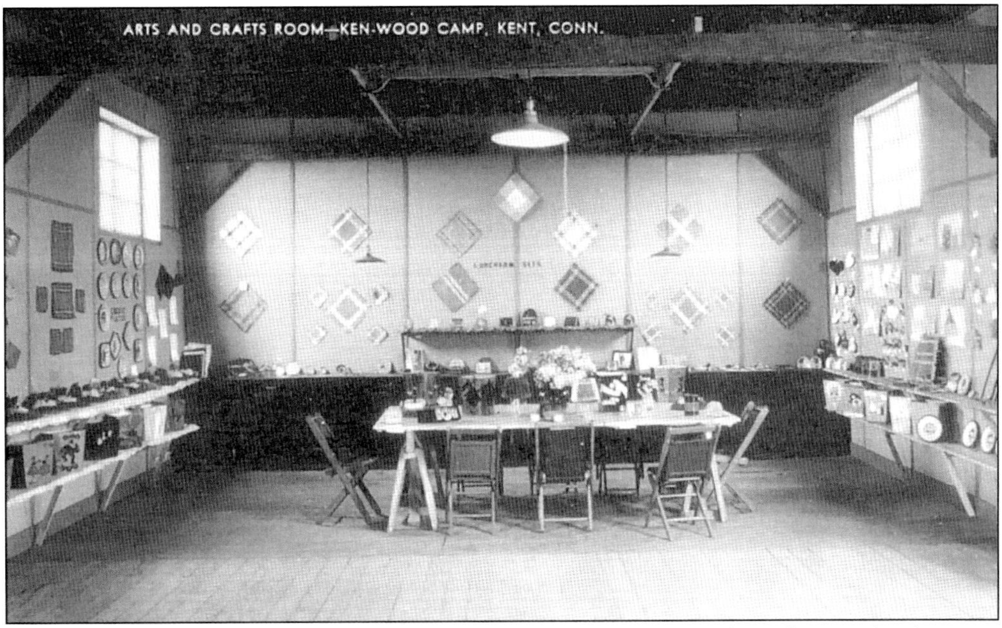

Camp Ken-wood/Ken-mont still operates in Kent off Kenmont Road as a boys and girls camp. It is located on a 500-acre site along North Spectacle Lake.

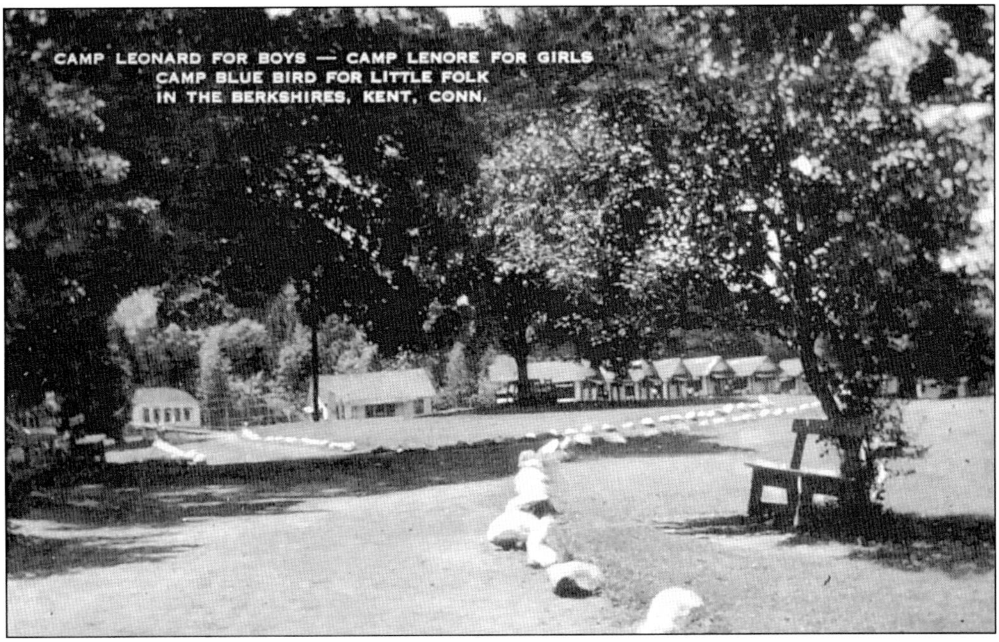

Camp Leonard/Lenore, located on Leonard Pond in Kent, has now been reincarnated as Camp Getaway. It has been run by the Fink family since 1946, first as a children's camp and now as a sports resort.

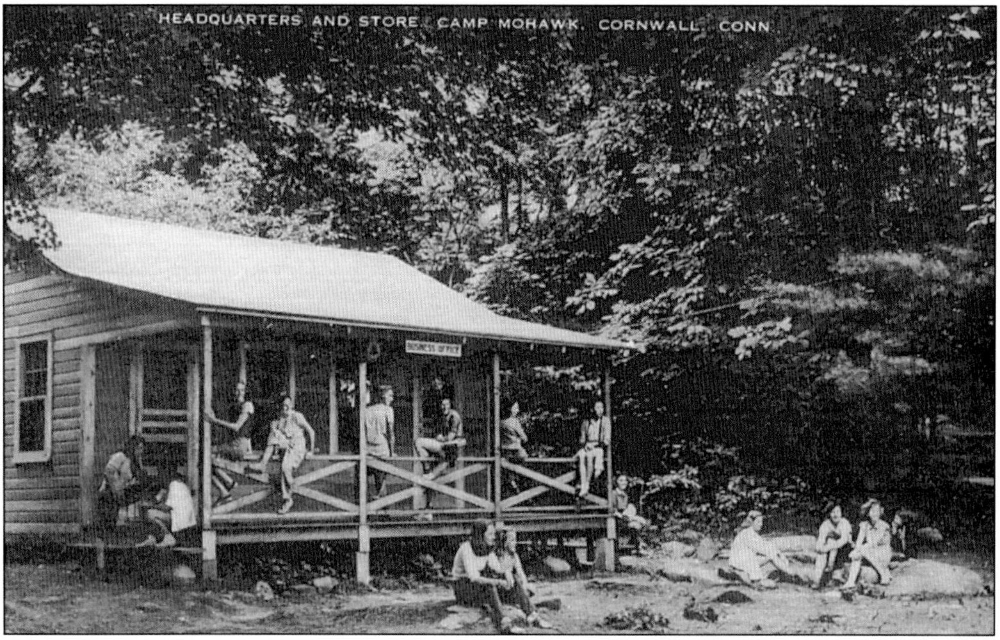

Camp Mohawk is located in Cornwall on the side of Cornwall Mountain. Virginia remembers the camp store from when she attended in the early 1930s.

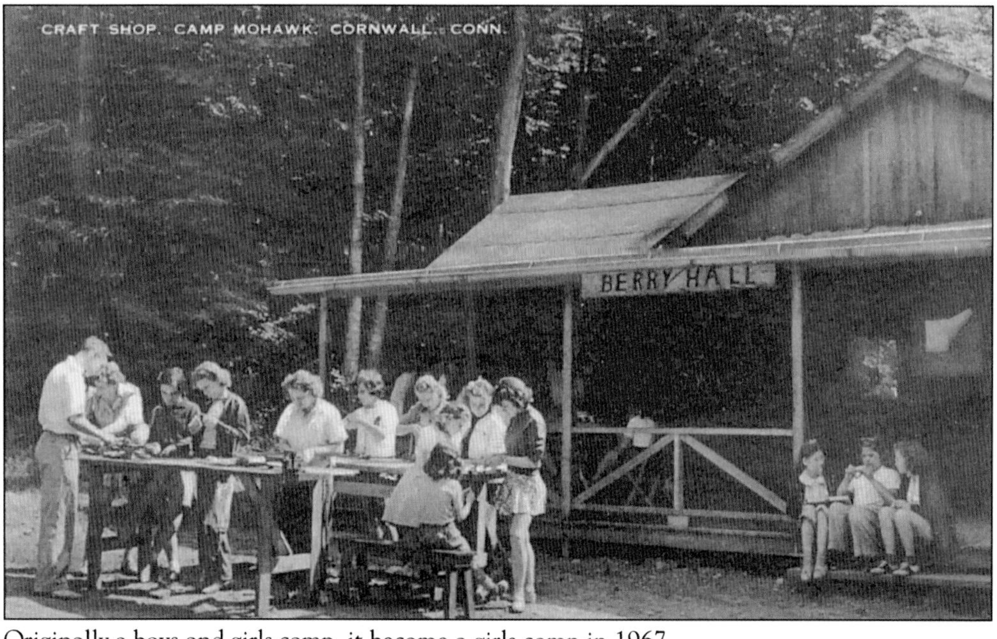

Originally a boys and girls camp, it became a girls camp in 1967.

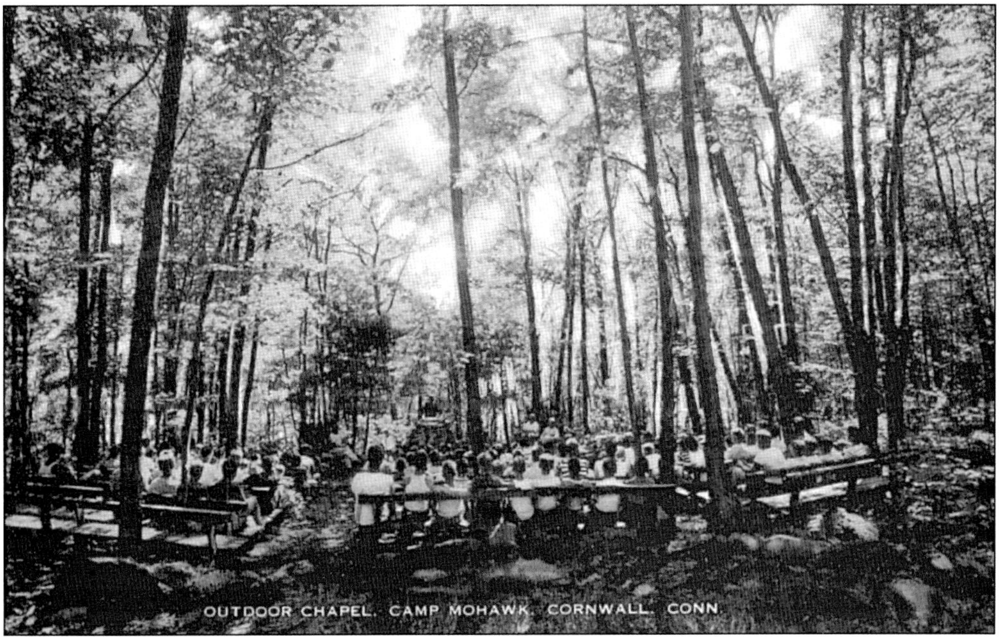

The Camp Mohawk chapel is shown here in 1949. The camp was established in 1919 by the directors of the YMCAs of New Haven, Litchfield, and Fairfield Counties.

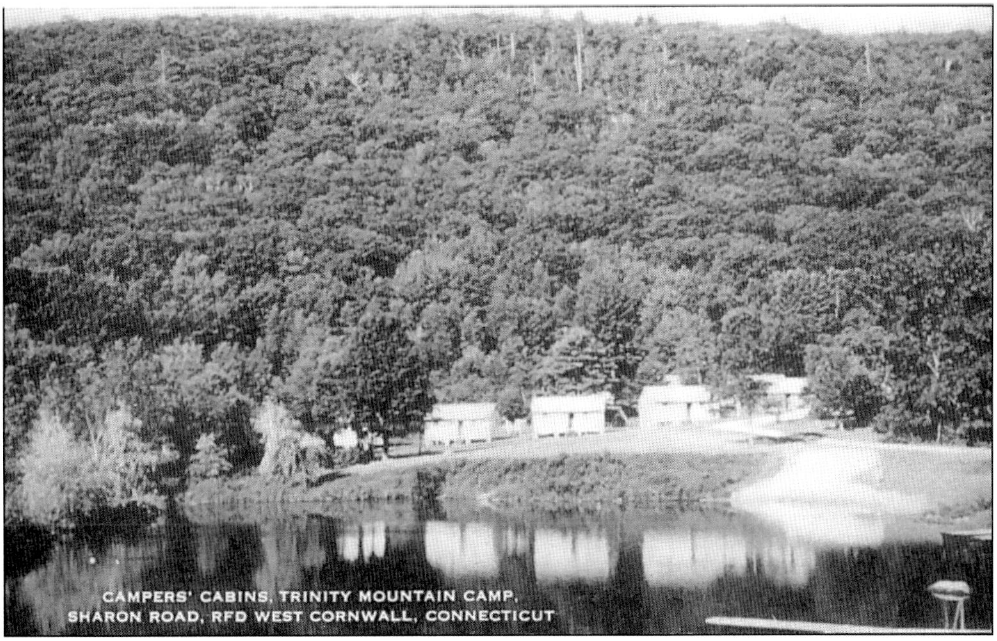

Sharon Road, where this camp was located, bears left from Route 7 after you cross over the river at Cornwall Bridge.

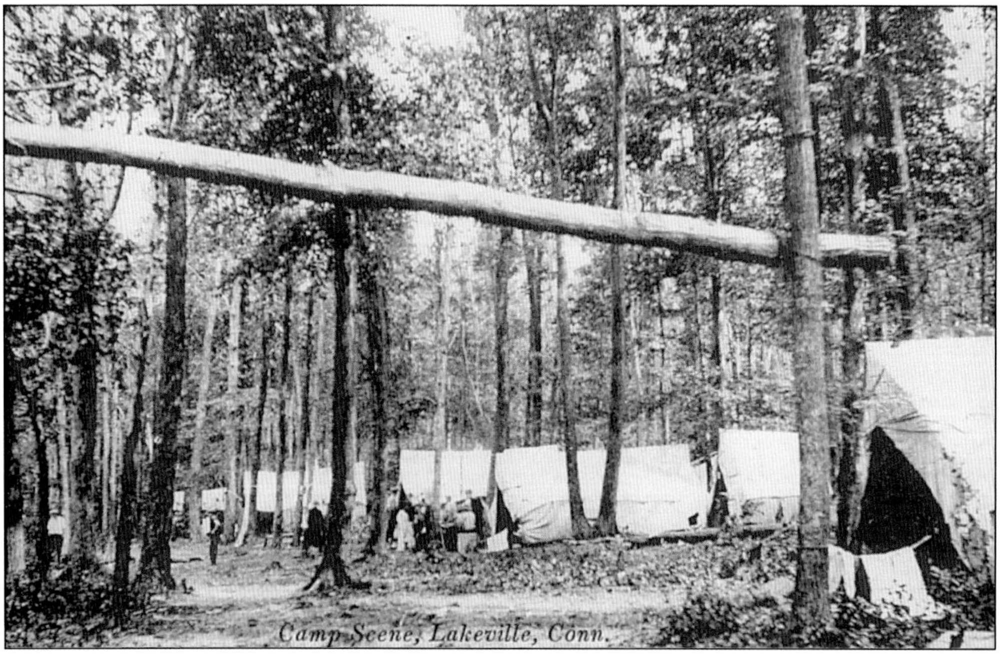

Lakeville and Lake Wononscopomac were also popular destinations for camping, boating, and swimming.

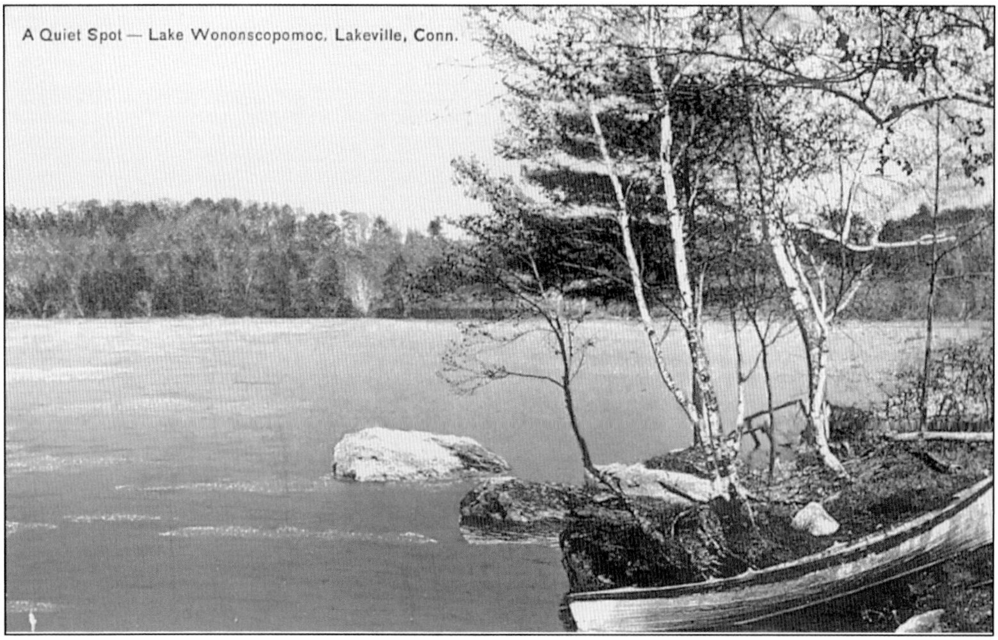

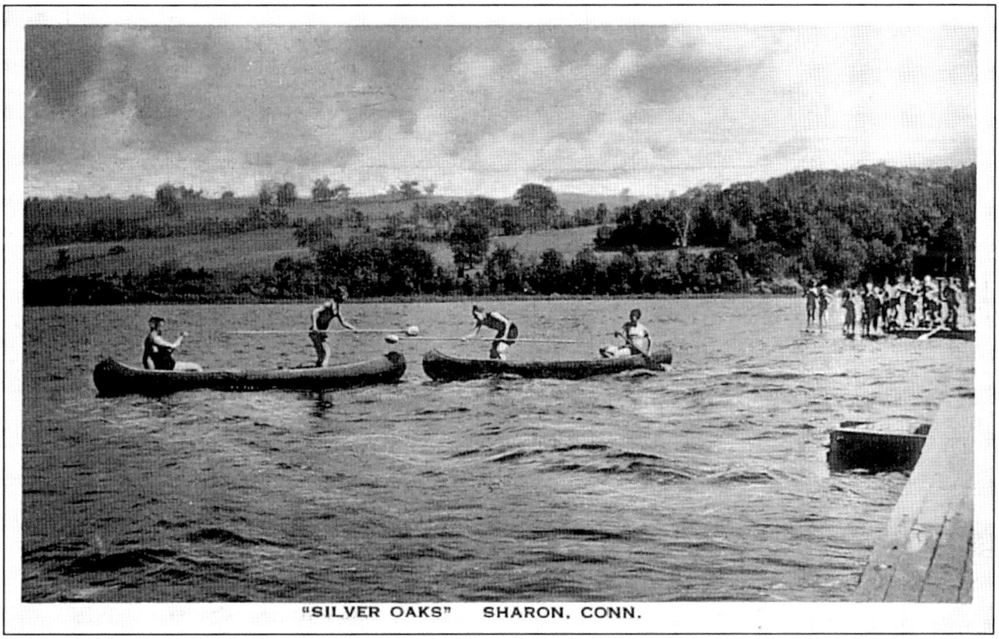

These boys appear to be water jousting at Silver Oaks in Sharon.

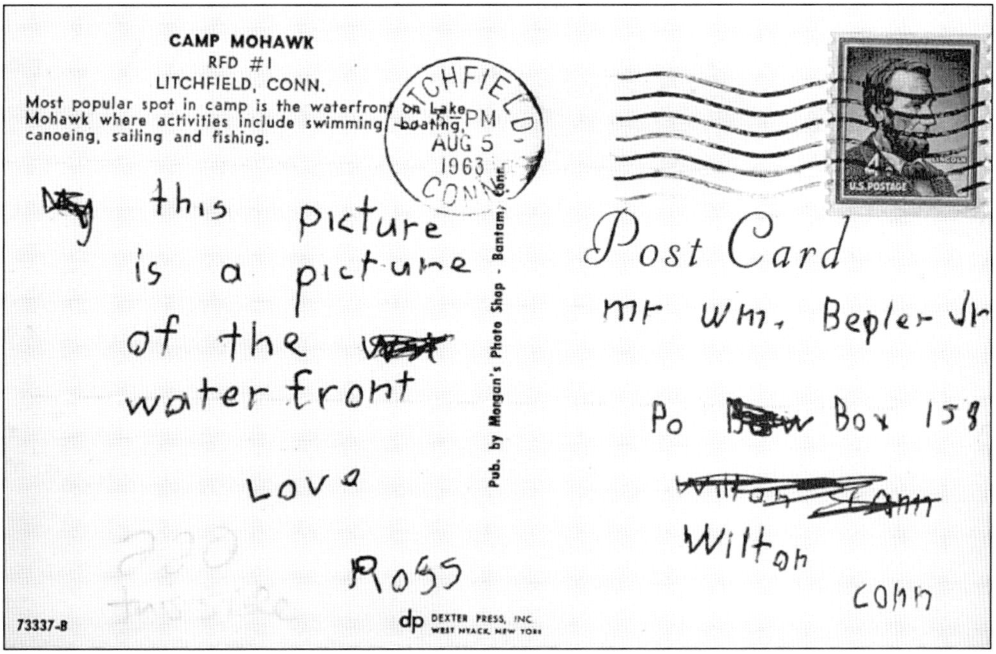

Ross Bepler was the second generation of the family to attend Camp Mohawk.

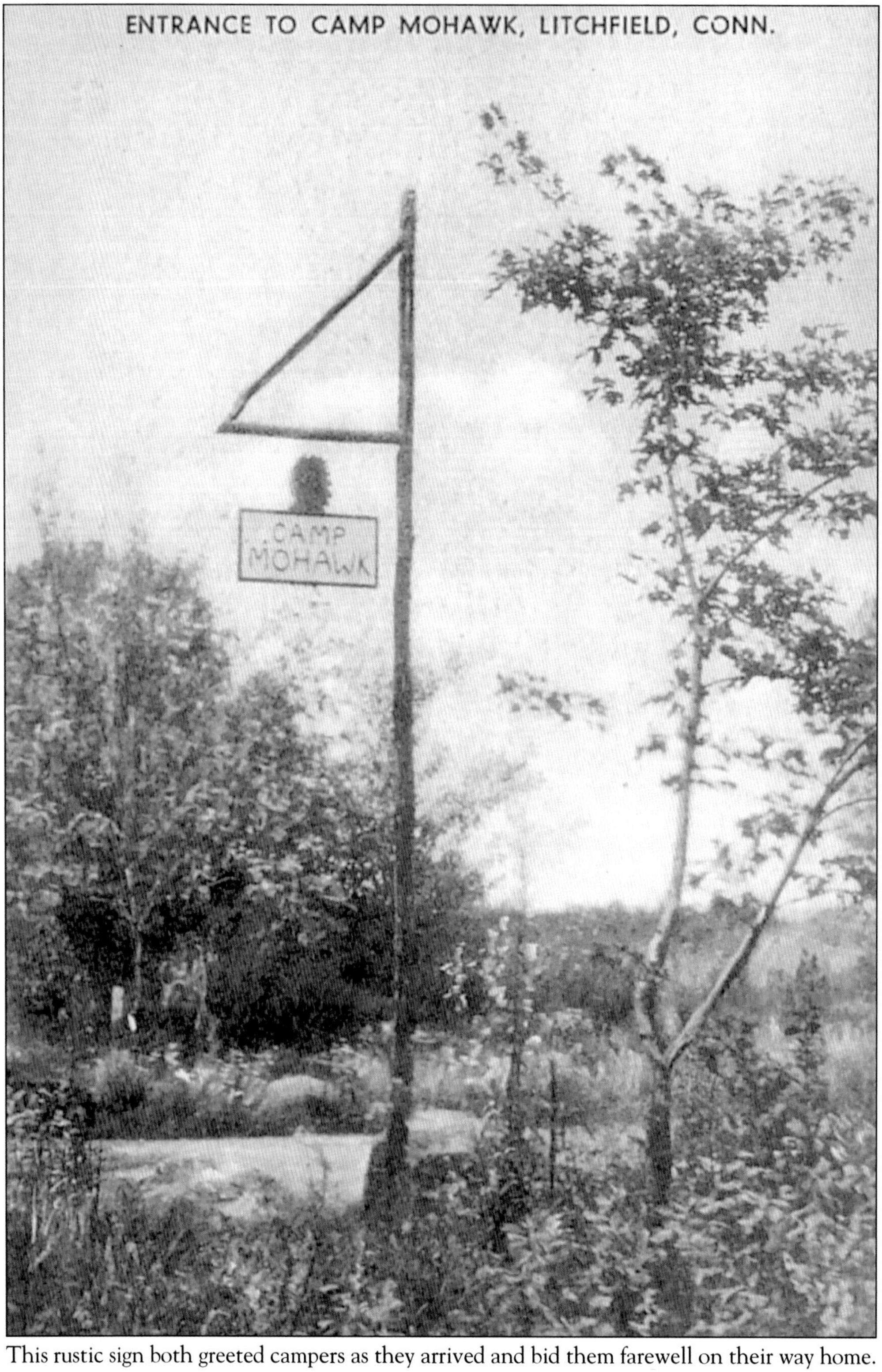

This rustic sign both greeted campers as they arrived and bid them farewell on their way home.